Vanishing Republic

How Can We Save The American Dream?

written by

Mark Anthony

Encore Publishing
P.O. Box 151003
Altamonte Springs, FL 32715-1003

Copyright 1995 by Mark Anthony

Second Printing

ISBN: 0-9646138-0-8

Printed in the United States of America

Cover Design by Gabriel H. Vaughn

Anthony, Mark
Vanishing Republic,
  How Can We Save The American Dream?

Mark Anthony can be contacted via Email at the following
addresses:

America On Line:	**manthony1**
Internet:	**manthony1@aol.com**

Visit Mark Anthony's Conservative MegaCenter
on the Internet:
http://www.conservativemegacenter.com

CONTENTS

Part III
Reforming The System

Chapter 8
Government Waste

Chapter 9
The Collapse Of American Freedom...

Chapter 10
The Ways Of Washington:
Complicated, Inefficient,
Bureaucratic, Wasteful And Myopic...

*"Government is not reason, it is not eloquence — **it is force.**
Like fire, it is a dangerous servant and a fearful master;
never for a moment, should it be left to irresponsible action."*
George Washington

*"Governments are instituted among men, **deriving their
just powers from the consent of the governed."***
The Declaration Of Independence

*"I know of no safe depository of the ultimate powers
of the society but the people themselves; and if we
think them not enlightened enough to exercise their
control with a wholesome discretion, the remedy is
not to take it from them, but to inform their discretion."*
Thomas Jefferson

*"The Founding Fathers looked at the liberties they were losing,
while modern Americans focus myopically on the freedoms they
still retain."*
James Bovard

*"Trust in the Lord with all your heart, and do not lean on your
own understanding. In all your ways acknowledge Him, and
He will make your paths straight."*
Proverbs 3:5-6

1

This Book Is Dedicated To

My Wife Donna

Who Inspires Me To Think About Such

Things...

...And To My Family

Who Raised Me To Believe In Them.

Republic: a state in which the supreme power rests in the body of citizens entitled to vote and is exercised by representatives chosen directly or indirectly by them.

— American College Dictionary

Vanish: to pass out of sight, especially quickly.
Vanishing point: a point at which a thing disappears or ceases to exist.

— American Heritage Dictionary

*"Are these the shadows of the things that will be,
or are they the shadows of the things that may be only?...
Men's courses will foreshadow certain ends to which,
if persevered in, they must lead...
But if the courses be departed from,
the ends will change.
Say it is thus with what you show me!"*

Charles Dickens' *A Christmas Carol*

*"Never doubt that a small group of
thoughtful, committed people can change the world.
Indeed, it is the only thing that ever has."*

Margaret Mead

INTRODUCTION

*"Enlighten the people generally, and tyranny
and oppressions of body and mind will vanish
like evil spirits at the dawn of day."*
— Thomas Jefferson

*"The political crisis of our times has been caused by
the fact that people have been grotesquely misinformed
about the nature and character of government. They
have not had clearly in mind the inherent limits of
government as a beneficent instrument for the
concentration and exercise of power... The political crisis
of our times is the result of governments becoming
gorged with power and running amok with the
undisciplined exercise of power."*
— Clarence B. Carson,
Basic American Government

As children, our parents try to instill in us a sense of character, morals and values. As I grew older and matured, I began to realize what these values meant in regard to our society and our country. More specifically I began to realize what these values meant in regard to the people of influence in our society — our elected officials and the media.

America is faced with a national debt approaching five trillion dollars. Yet, America's eroding fiscal infrastructure is just one aspect of the *"Vanishing Republic."* Our societal infrastructure is quickly eroding as well. Since 1960, violent crime has increased by 550 percent. Illegitimacy has increased over 400 percent. The divorce rate has doubled. Families headed by a single parent have more than tripled. Scholastic Aptitude Test (SAT) averages have fallen by 73 points. In 1988, U.S. children finished lower in science scores than any other country tested. At the same time, education spending rose by 200 percent.

We live in a society where reality is transmitted via ether, filtered though vacuum tubes encased in 25 inch boxes that serve as the centerpiece of our *"living"* room. But, are we as a nation truly living, or are we simply drifting in the breeze, surreptitiously tossed about at the whim of an activist media culture.

We live in a society that ridicules conservative family values. Personal responsibility and the quest for the outer limits of human achievement have been replaced by the notion that government is the solution to all our problems; and that social engineering will lead us to utopia. Ray Kerrison wrote in the *New York Post:*

> "When the city mandated government workers to submit to brainwashing sessions on sexual harassment, Enrique Oppenheimer, an accountant at the Department of Housing Preservation and Development, balked.
>
> 'Not for me,' Enrique said to himself. He had been working in government for 18 years and he had never sexually harassed anyone in his life. As a Bible-reading Pentecostal Christian, he would not dream of it. So he refused to participate.
>
> The upshot is mind-boggling. Today, Enrique Oppenheimer is facing departmental trial for insubordination, with a threat of dismissal if he doesn't cave in. The department has charged him with misconduct in office, claiming he brought 'shame, discredit and disrespect to the City of New York.'"

6

Introduction

So, what has become of the "American dream?" Were we so passive in our consent as to validate the continual abuses of American governance? Did we dishonor our Forefathers by failing to vigilantly enforce the freedoms they *died* to bestow? How could we have allowed the most brilliant concept of government ever devised to digress to a system of policy by lobbyist. These are strong words to be sure. But America is at a crossroads. And although I do not want to be labeled as alarmist, we have reached a point in time in which the decisions that we make today — will determine if there is anything left for our children and grandchildren, tomorrow.

The book you now hold is not about money. It is not about the pursuit of fame. Rather, I wrote this book because I dearly love this country and what it once stood for.

To be fair to you, I must inform you that I am unmistakably a conservative — in both fiscal *and* social policy. I do not conceal that sentiment.

Throughout this book I will provide repeated evidence to support the contention that liberalism is wrong. It is morally wrong. It is socially wrong. It is spiritually wrong. It is fiscally wrong.

Yet, I emphatically state that the purpose of this book is *not* to bash the Democratic party. Nor, is it designed to defend the Republican party. I have taken great pains to eliminate any vestiges of partisan politics. I am a patriotic American first. I am a conservative second, and I am a Republican third. Yet, you will find that I have the courage and conviction to make assessments and criticisms that few other Republicans would dare.

The government actions that have crippled America are not the proprietary domain of either party. Responsibility for our current situation lies with both parties — and attempting to assign percentages of blame would not be a productive exercise given the immediacy of the problem.

There exists, without a doubt, a considerable number of liberals who happen to call themselves Republicans, just as there are many conservatives who claim Democratic affiliation. So, I choose not to delineate by party affiliation, but by the term conservative or liberal — not meaning right or left — *but right or wrong.*

> *Most importantly, this is a book about hope.*
> *It is about the quest for positive change.*

Dr. Wayne Dyer, world renowned human development pioneer, once said, "There are no accidents...the Universe is on purpose."

And so, I submit to you, that our state of affairs did not get this way by accident.

There is an order to the Universe, substantiated by many self-evident truths. I would like to share two of them with you.

> *The strong devour the weak in order to survive.*

When the federal government was given birth by the ratification of The Constitution Of The United States in 1788, its purpose was to protect the people militarily. It had little power other than that, so that the citizens would not be unfairly treated.

Introduction

The federal government was the servant, and the states and their people, its master.

But in the succeeding years, another Universal law would exemplify itself:

For every action there is an equal and opposite reaction.

In order for the federal government to grow, it had to consume the rights and the freedoms of the very people who created it. The government has evolved into a self-feeding imperial monolith because *we let it.* Utopian longing and wishful thinking will not change that.

What we now need are simple steps designed to re-balance the equation.

And so, I give you the blueprint. A simple book which contains simple solutions to complex problems. There will surely be those who deride these suggestions as unworkable, the similarity to the Republican's *Contract With America* not withstanding.

I disagree.

For I composed the bulk of the reforms contained within, months before the Republican's pledge saw the light of day. Coincidence? Hardly. All one needs is a legitimate understanding of American history, the Judeo-Christian values that formed the foundation of our Republic and the Founding Father's noble intentions — and with these tools government reform is simply a matter of common sense.

How much of a difference can we make? Only time will tell. We owe it to our children to try. But, to view my vision as simply a debt to our future progeny misses the point. My vision is one of inclusion; that young and old, with or without children, will fulfill the basic debt of honor of the human race — to leave the wood-pile just a little bit higher than we found it.

Some of us believe The Constitution Of The United States is still worth fighting for.

THE BILL OF RIGHTS OF
THE UNITED STATES OF AMERICA

Amendment I

Congress shall make no law respecting an establishment of religion, or prohibiting the free exercise thereof; or abridging the freedom of speech, or of the press; or the right of the people peaceably to assemble, and to petition the Government for a redress of grievances.

Amendment II

A well regulated Militia, being necessary to the security of a free State, the right of the people to keep and bear Arms, shall not be infringed.

Amendment III

No Soldier shall, in time of peace be quartered in any house, without the consent of the Owner, nor in time of war, but in a manner to be prescribed by law.

Amendment IV

The right of the people to be secure in their persons, houses, papers, and effects, against unreasonable searches and seizures, shall not be violated, and no Warrants shall issue, but upon probable cause, supported by Oath or affirmation, and particularly describing the place to be searched, and the persons or things to be seized.

Amendment V

No person shall be held to answer for a capital, or otherwise infamous crime, unless on a presentment or indictment of a Grand Jury, except in cases arising in the land or naval forces, or in the Militia, when in actual service in time of War or public danger; nor shall any person be subject for the same offense to be twice put in jeopardy of life or limb; nor shall be compelled in any criminal case to be a witness against himself, nor be deprived of life, liberty, or property, without due process of law; nor shall private property be taken for public use, without just compensation.

Amendment VI

In all criminal prosecutions, the accused shall enjoy the right to a speedy and public trial, by an impartial jury of the State and district wherein the crime shall have been committed, which district shall have been previously ascertained by law, and to be informed of the nature and cause of the accusation; to be confronted with the witnesses against him; to have compulsory process for obtaining witnesses in his favor, and to have the Assistance of Counsel for his defense.

Amendment VII

In Suits at common law, where the value in controversy shall exceed twenty dollars, the right of trial by jury shall be preserved, and no fact tried by a jury, shall be otherwise re-examined in any Court of the United States, than according to the rules of the common law.

Amendment VIII

Excessive bail shall not be required, nor excessive fines imposed, nor cruel and unusual punishments inflicted.

Introduction

Amendment IX

The enumeration in the Constitution, of certain rights, shall not be construed to deny or disparage others retained by the people.

Amendment X

The powers not delegated to the United States by the Constitution, nor prohibited by it to the States, are reserved to the States respectively, or to the people.

Allow me to quote Earl Browder, former head of the Communist Party of the United States. His words would be chilling if they were spoken last week, or last month or last year...but they were spoken nearly thirty years ago...

> "America is getting socialism on the installment plan through the programs of the welfare state...
>
> Americans may not be willing to vote for a program under the name of "socialism," but put it under another party label — whether liberal Republican or Democrat — and they're by and large in favor of the idea...
>
> We have no real socialist party, no socialist ideology, but we have a large — and growing — degree of what 50 years ago would have been recognized as socialism."[1]

Our Constitutionally granted freedoms have been eroded for almost one hundred years.

Why did we wait so long?

At the dawn of the new millenium, we find ourselves amidst an unprecedented culture war, and although it will not be a violent battle, it will be no less devastating in its implications. Our very future is at stake. The aforementioned freedoms enumerated in the Bill of Rights have already been deeply eroded. Personal property rights, the defining element which differentiates democracy from socialism, is virtually non-existent. A variety of demented acronyms from EPA to EEOC to OSHA; from the IRS to the DEA, the ATF to the NLRB, all needing little more than hearsay and one of their own administrative law judges to shatter the freedoms that far greater men died to bestow. I have found no Constitutional basis for much of what our government has seen fit

Introduction

to add to its ever-expanding realm of dominion. The Tenth Amendment clearly states:

> **The powers not delegated to the United States by the Constitution, nor prohibited by it to the States, are reserved to the States respectively, <u>*or to the people.*</u>**

We now find our system of governance 180 degrees out of phase. It has become eminently clear that those freedoms not expressly granted by the Bill of Rights, or permissible by the changing whims of multitudinal government bureaucrats, are strictly prohibited.

You have the right to freely enter into contracts — unless the National Labor Regulatory Board finds it inequitable. You have the right to engage in business activity — unless the EPA declares your property a wetland. You have the right to discipline your children — unless your neighbor informs Health and Rehabilitative Services. You have the right to free speech, or to hire whom you wish, or freedom to display your faith — unless the Equal Employment Opportunity Commission intervenes; and to extricate yourself the burden of truth is increasingly **your** *obligation. We have become a nation of fearful citizens, terrorized by a federal bureaucracy whose modus operandi is quite simply:* **"Search and Destroy."**

How could we have let this happen?

Such statements will not garner many supporters from those who reside in the belly of the sow; and their toadies in the media will surely criticize this work — to them I say...

I truly feel for the bureaucrats, sycophants, deadbeats, special interests, lobbyists, food stamp cheats, and perennial welfare parasites — sucklings at the public teat, enjoying the nourishment of government handouts appropriated from the public trough — a wellspring of bastardized good intentions, fed by the negligent benevolence of those who **earn** *their pay.*

Mark Anthony

Reading these words, you may opine that I disdain our government. Nothing could be further from the truth. I love the American system of government; a Constitutional Federated Republic, a mixed government inspired by the English heritage of Richard Hooker and Thomas Hobbes, John Milton and John Locke, Adam Smith, Sir William Blackstone, John Trenchard and Thomas Gordon. A glorious symmetry of checks and balances which arose from the minds of Jefferson and Washington, Pain and Jackson, Franklin and Adams, Monroe and Madison.

What has our government become...and what is it destined to be forevermore?

In the early days of the Republic, when one talked of the central government, they spoke of freedom of opportunity, limited government intervention, natural law, self responsibility, and personal property rights. Now, when talk of government arises, eruptions of dire consequence ensue. The "new" republic dubiously boasts debt by the trillions, regulation by the millions, and subsidies by the thousands. We have entered the age of the "Permanent Congress," a privileged ruling class of 535 men and women each with his or her own personal fiefdom; all but a handful of whom frolic in the waters of progressive, activist interventionism; governed by their good intentions and guided by democratic socialism; coming up for air only briefly to piddle on the Constitution.

*Washington, D.C., has digressed to nothing more than a vast "honeypot" where the once CO-sovereign American people send their tax dollars only to be deposited into the bottomless trough called the United States Treasury, so that politicians and lawyers and lobbyists; special interests and minority "leaders" and the dependent masses may all dive into the money pile, gleefully rubbing their faces in the purloined wealth of a nation — all fighting for the privilege of spending the largest chunk of money that was **never** theirs.*

16

Introduction

This war will be fought with our heart, our mind and the sweat of our brow. It will eventually be won by the truth...that is, if truth matters anymore...

Has a new day dawned? Did the grassroots conservative landslide in November of 1994 signify the end of Leviathan? The future actions of the newly elected — not their words or rhetoric — will tell the tale. We should not be so naive as to believe freedom and Constitutional government will mystically morph out of the moral vacuum of Washington, D.C., based on one election. We should view the electoral victory as a wonderful chance to rebuild our collective dream — an opportunity infrequently bestowed upon cultural dynasties.

In the age of global cyberspace and twenty-four hour news networks, we our blessed with almost instantaneous access to information. But, as Josh Billings observed, "The trouble with most folks isn't so much their ignorance, as knowing so many things that ain't so." My aim is to provide you with the tools to monitor the socio-political landscape, so that we may build on the foundation laid on November 8, 1994.

In Parts I and II, we'll discuss some of the mysteries of our government and political system. The goal of this book, from an educational perspective, is to provide you with information to illustrate how and why the system broke down, as well as provide a "scorecard," if you will, to better monitor the changes brought on by the 1994 election. To enhance readability I have attempted to place the bulk of my reform suggestions in Part III. If nothing else, you'll certainly walk away with a better appreciation of just how much work we have to do.

Washington now knows that America is watching and listening. However, you would be wise to maintain a healthy skepticism over the next few years.

The Second American Revolution

As a child, my favorite subject had always been history. It was a much simpler time. The words multiculturalism and diversity were yet to pollute discussions heretofore based on logic and reason. Young minds were unencumbered by the shadow of political correctness. Right was right, and wrong was wrong. The punishment suited the crime, as we resolutely accepted the castigation we earned for our juvenile transgressions.

We were free to envision the genius of men whose foresight could bear such lasting scrutiny. Our Forefathers were admired as though they were our own — and so they were. Fifteen words inscribed indelibly upon my memory...of what was once, and what should always be...

Governments are instituted among men, deriving their just powers from the consent of the governed.

...I would hold these words dear. I would honor and obey the self-reliance that these words endowed.

Yet, I wondered how such cretins and fools, pimps at the public trough, proselytizing over sycophants, empowered themselves, disregarding the traditions they swore to uphold...

18

Introduction

*Were we so passive in our consent as to validate their treachery? Did we dishonor our Forefathers by failing to vigilantly enforce the freedoms they **died** to bestow?*

*Is tyranny not again before us? For what other definition would you give a land that fears its own Government? Are **we** the* problem? *The fringe — the "right-wing" danger? It seems that we were called that once before...*

> *When they took our money, as our voice fell on deaf ears,*
> *They took our land without remorse;*
> *When they scoffed, and ruled*
> *as the monolith strengthened —*
> *The frightening thing is...*
> ***It's happening again.***

And so the imperial government sought to enslave the last great nation on earth...

> *Itself.*

> *— Mark Anthony*
> ***August 12, 1994***

19

Chapter 1
The Basic Philosophy Is The Problem

"What is conservatism. Is it not adherence to the old and tried, against the new and untried?"
— Abraham Lincoln

"The private economy has become an agent of the federal government...At least 50 percent of the total productive resources of our nation are now being organized through the political market. In that very important sense, we are more than half socialist."
— Milton Friedman,
Nobel Prize winning economist

"The average American works from January 1 until May 8 just to pay federal, state and local taxes. In other words, we are working for five months and we do not have the right to decide how those fruits of our labor are used. Somebody else makes that decision. Keep in mind that slavery is defined as working twelve months a year and having somebody else make the decision on how the fruits of that labor will be used...If we are going to be a moral people, we have to ask: Is it right to take what belongs to one person and give it to another to whom it does not belong?"
— Dr. Walter E. Williams,
John M. Olin Distinguished Professor of
Economics, George Mason University

"The fundamental error of socialism is anthropological in nature. Socialism considers the individual person simply as an element, a molecule within the social organism, so that the good of the individual is completely

20

subordinated to the functioning of the socio-economic mechanism. Socialism likewise maintains that the good of the individual can be realized without reference to his free choice, to the unique and exclusive responsibility which he exercises in the face of good or evil. Man is reduced to a series of social relationships, and the concept of the person as the autonomous subject of moral decisions disappears."
— Pope John Paul II

I've often wondered how someone becomes a liberal, and I've come to the conclusion that *liberals are made, not born.* Stop for a moment and envision a newborn baby. That child comes into the world a "clean slate," if you will. As such, I believe it is safe to assume that there is a basic goodness and virtue and innocence inherent in that child. In other words, if that child were to grow up in a vacuum, with no outside influence either positive or negative, the child would maintain its God given makeup and live a life of certain fulfillment. The child's virtues would multiply, and, in turn, enrich those around him. If you look at what conservatism truly is, we are all born with conservative values — love of our parents, love of our country, honesty, integrity, a work ethic, to strive for personal excellence in improving ourselves and to further fulfill those around us.

Now, imagine what happens when that child grows up in a society in which the media paradigm is overwhelmingly liberal. This is not to say that a child's development is effected solely by media forces devoid of parental influence. But let's face it, no matter how exceptional a child's parents are at preserving his inherent values, the constant bombardment by the activist, liberal media culture will eventually take its toll. Our children can't even watch cartoons without being brainwashed by inane, utopian, communal drivel.

The truths of limited constitutional government, borne of the Founding Fathers, have been replaced by *this?*

So how do liberals perpetuate their omnipotence? Take for example the ever-expanding welfare state, designed to discourage productivity, destroy morale and self-esteem and force dependence on big government. We constantly hear "compassionate" leaders say that the poor deserve to get *their fair share.* This filters down to entitlement beneficiaries who insist that they *"just want to get theirs."* Is money dropping from the sky? Do we all have a divine birthright to *"x"* number of dollars, milked from the benevolent public trough?

This is certainly not consistent with a free-market society. In such a society, the reward is equal to the effort. Think for a moment what the word "reward" means. Each payday, the check inside the envelope is given as a reward for the quality and the quantity of the work the employee **PRODUCED.** In a free market society, the quality of the work a person produces, and what that person's performance **GIVES** to his or her company — and to society — is what determines the **LEVEL OF THE REWARD.**

What a unique concept.

Wouldn't it be great if every job in America were tied to performance! But, of course we can't have that. What we need are $16 billion Emergency Economic Stimulus Packages. We need more make-work jobs that produce nothing. We need pork-corrupted politicians to mandate federal government provided jobs — jobs that perform useless tasks that no one in a free-market economy would pay someone to do.

Liberals have perennially made martyrs out of derelicts and criminals and brainwashed the public (with the help of the media) into believing that poverty is a virtue. At the same time they have portrayed achievers and job creators as evil, self centered parasites on society.

Yet, from my upbringing, if I want a raise I've got to work harder. I've got to produce more. I've got to achieve more. I know I won't receive a reward *until I produce something first.* To paraphrase Dr. Walter Williams: If these people truly want to "get theirs," *they* should be the ones to give something back to society.

I am not implying there are not those who do require assistance.

But there is a conceptual difference between liberals and conservatives in regard to assistance. *Liberals* **give** *a hand-out. Conservatives* **offer** *a hand-up.* Think about that for a minute. If you truly wanted to help your fellow man, you would take a course of action that would allow him to *help himself.* Such self-reliance does not sit well with liberalism. The priests and prophets of utopianism would rather redistribute a nation's wealth — to give the downtrodden a hand-out — which suppresses the poor, restrains them at their current level and breeds dependence.

So why would a government take a course of action that cultivates a growing dependency class? What is the motivation for such a course of action?

Empowerment.

By keeping people dependent upon big government, it ensures the votes of the growing number of poor, and thus guarantees the liberal legislature's re-election It cements in the minds of those in power the elitist notion that government is better equipped to guide your path through life than you are. It also entrenches big government by lining the pockets of millions of Americans with ill-gotten rewards. Lobbyists, consultants, people of all socio-economic groups receiving one form of subsidy or another has locked in corruption, making any efforts to dismantle Leviathan nearly impossible — for to do so would cut off the lifeline to those who profit from it.

America has become a quasi-socialist republic; a pathetic hybrid of government bureaucrats scheming and conniving, regulating and pursuing, seeking and destroying the private sector whose taxes pay their salaries. God help the courageous entrepreneur who desires to start a business; profit and loss are the least of his worries...The Equal Employment Opportunity Commission will tell him who he may hire. The Labor Department will mandate the minimum wage he can pay. They will require he allow the right to family or medical leave, pay time-and-a-half for overtime, and eventually require a contribution to the company health care plan. Around the corner lurks the Environmental Protection Agency to make sure he doesn't improperly dispose of "hazardous" waste like children's baby teeth, or conduct the most minute activity with a chemical company, lest he be obligated to pay for future Superfund cleanup costs.

They'll also be scouring the grounds for any moist areas that could be perceived as "wetlands" — never mind that his business operates in Nevada. He must be careful not to call his secretary "dear" or risk a sexual harassment suit.

And if he should profit — hell hath no fury as that of the government on a successful businessman — the 1993 tax increase will designate his Subchapter S Corporation as "one of those who profited the most from the 80's." He must "pay his fair share" as he is forced into the highest tax bracket.

Would any sane person start a business under these circumstances?

Unfortunately, he doesn't have the benefits of a "government job."

If so, he would have job security regardless of incompetence. He would have high pay, pitifully low work requirements, lavish health, vacation, and sick-day benefits, and a generous federal pension. He would have insanely generous travel allowances, with expenses rounded off to the nearest hundred. He would have incredible power to make his own rules, governing by memo and prosecuting by innuendo. He would be the envy of his friends and the worst nightmare of his enemies. He would contribute little if anything to society, as he produces nothing. He could live a long, happy and stress-free life, unencumbered by the harsh realities of a free-market economy.

He will have made it.

And you and I will have paid for it.

In spring of 1993, liberals in Congress were abuzz with rhetoric citing "the opportunities presented by President Clinton's Economic Stimulus Package." The package contained over $16 billion dollars of pork projects and make-work jobs. Liberals call these *"Investments."*

A bit of clarification is in order. *The American Heritage Dictionary* defines *"investment"* as: "Property or another possession acquired for future financial return or benefit."

In other words, you hope and expect to get back *more* than you materially gave.

I feel compelled to ask this question: Just what exactly do I get for my investment when the government takes a dollar out of my pocket and transfers it into the pocket of someone else?

Therein lies a foundational liberal philosophy. An opportunity is any government program that puts money into someone's pocket for no particular reason. In this case, in the form of "make-work" jobs. Conservatives, on the other hand, see opportunity as the situation that arises when free market forces present an entrepreneurial opportunity in which people risk their time and their capital in order to achieve a reward.

The key phrase being *"Achieve a Reward."*

They're My Kids, Remember?

"What we do to our children, they will do to society."
 — Roman Scholar, Pliny the Elder

"I strive to be the person that I want my children to become. I am not there yet. Therefore, every day I must consciously undertake the task of improving myself. For, I cannot give to my children, that which I do not have."
 — Mark Anthony

"Many of the elite correctly understood that civilization's major task is the upbringing of children; if they could alter the ways we raised children by altering the way we teach them, they could then alter American society to suit their view of the world.

Vanishing Republic

Academics provided much of the intellectual heavy artillery —
citing how endemically corrupt and sick America is. Once
the traditional teachings were discredited and then removed, the
vacuum was filled by faddish nonsense, and the kids lost."
— William J. Bennett,
former Secretary of Education

There can be no doubt that it is as critically important to feed the minds of our children as it is to feed their bodies.

> *But it is essential that we feed them truth. As detrimental*
> *to their body and soul as it would be to feed them a daily*
> *diet of potato chips and call it vitamins —*
> *so to, it would be if we fed them undiluted liberalism*
> *and called it truth.*

I do not wish for my children to grow up in a society that wants to teach them sex education in kindergarten. I do not wish for my children to grow up in a society in which nearly every form of sexual deviancy is accepted as normal. I do not want my children to grow up in a society where moral strength, love of God, character and the quest for excellence, are subordinated to multicultural drivel and the rhetoric of socialistic Shangri-La. I do not wish for my children to grow up in a society where the elected officials and the judicial system think that they know what's best for my children, better than I do. I do not wish for my children to grow up in a society where poverty is a virtue and criminals and derelicts are lionized, as we vilify entrepreneurial job creators.

Yet, the American educational system and the dominant media culture indoctrinates our youth with shame, as well as the

27

fallacious assumption that productive members of the community are the ones who must "give something back to society."

I have nothing against the poor. Just don't ingrain in my children that poverty is a virtue. I have nothing against sex education — just don't say one single word to my child about sex. I can take care of that myself, thank you. My child has no business knowing *your* version of sexual morality.

He's not your child.

Part I

The Making Of Leviathan
Historical Perspectives

Absent from most books dealing with America's socio-political landscape is a substantive discussion of twentieth century history. In Part II we'll examine the deficit, the national debt and the welfare state.

In Part III we'll discuss reforming the system — Congress, lobbyists, the budget and our once exquisite government run amok — and why Washington cannot be counted on to reform itself.

In Part IV we'll debunk the economic myths that fuel oppressive governance and strangle the free-enterprise system, and we'll examine ways to return our great nation to abundant prosperity by allowing welfare beneficiaries to join the party.

But first, let's examine some of the key elements that occurred this century — elements that have become the bedrock of the"Vanishing Republic" — the creation of the Federal Reserve, the implementation of an income tax, the seventeenth amendment, the welfare state and our gradual move to Democratic Socialism, the loss of private property rights and the erosion of natural law and individual responsibility.

Author's Note

The topics discussed in this chapter are based on historical fact, although much of this material is rarely, if ever, taught in textbooks. The purpose of this book is **_not_** to perpetuate conspiratorial *"New World Order"* theories. I simply aim to add a historical perspective to the issues at the core of our *"Vanishing Republic."*

The international bankers referenced in this chapter did what bankers do; they set up banking institutions to lend money. Civilized societies must have a banking system in order to partake of commerce. But fractional banking systems and the creation of fiat — play-like money — are matters of intense opinions and personal prejudices.

I seek not to create villains in the context of conspiracy theories, but to illustrate the actions of the international banking community within the framework of the Founding Fathers' conception of limited Constitutional government, national sovereignty, the national debt, world peace, prosperity, the wealth of nations and the future of our society.

I hope this information will be consumed in the manner in which it is intended. I am only concerned with restoring our country to greatness. My conflict with the Federal Reserve System and the creation of valueless currency is that it is a blatant violation of the Constitution. The underground speculation of the Federal Reserve as a building block of a centuries old conspiracy theory is fodder for cocktail parties, but it has no place here. Peeking around every corner for CFR members or debating the legitimacy of shadow governments, is lunacy. Any such conclusions derived from this information are at the sole discretion of the reader.

Chapter 2
The Destruction Begins...
(Create The Money)

*"The most unconstitutional feature of [the Federal
Reserve System] was that Federal Reserve notes were
made legal tender. The only power over the money
granted to the government of the United States was to
coin money. It has no authority to make tender laws
nor to print paper money. Even the authority to
incorporate national banks was assumed...surely, no
power was granted in the Constitution to any
government to inflate the currency and take away the
value of the money in the hands of the people...the means
was in place after 1913 for the Federal government to
exercise both overt and covert control over the liquid
wealth of the country."*
> — Clarence B. Carson,
> *Basic American Government*

*"Permit me to issue and control the money of a nation,
and I care not who makes its laws."*
> — Mayer Anselm Rothschild

*"We will charge interest on money which we create out of
nothing."*
> — John Houblon,
> First Governor of the Bank of England

In his farewell address, George Washington exhorted the union
to keep the principles of the Constitution intact; to preserve
national independence; to buttress policy and behavior with

religion and morality; and cherish the public credit. All of these areas were compromised or totally destroyed by the federal actions (and the undercurrents which caused them) that took place during the early part of the 20th century.

The core issues that launched America down the slippery slope of Democratic Socialism are these:

♦ The creation of independent agencies with their own legislative, executive, and judicial power, and the elevation to cabinet level status of government entities that had no Constitutional authority.

♦ The genesis of the "activist" president. The Chief Executive became the *"Legislator in Chief,"* proposing a utopian, thematic, social welfare agenda.

♦ The use of imagined or perceived *"National Emergencies"* to validate blatantly unconstitutional, socialistic, big government legislative actions.

♦ The creation of the Federal Reserve and the ability to create money; and thus inflate or deflate the currency.

♦ The 16th Amendment which allowed the government to levy an income tax, and the creation of the Internal Revenue Service to collect it.

♦ The 17th Amendment which consolidated enormous power in the Federal government by removing one of the main checks on that power by the states.

♦ The rise of judicial activism. Case after case was decided based on legal precedent before it that *itself* had no Constitutional authority; thereby giving the judiciary the power to legislate, execute and adjudicate.

◆ The creation of the welfare state; massive government subsidies and the proliferation of unfunded mandates on state governments.

◆ The creation of Social Security.

◆ The practice of giving enormous amounts of paper money in foreign aid, created by the Federal Reserve and "Backed By The Full Faith and Credit of The United States." (Meaning an I.O.U. in the name of the American taxpayers.)

If a country sought to destroy itself, to purposely embark on a path which leads to certain implosion, one could not draw a better blueprint than this. In order to embark on such massive social change first required the creation of a central bank, the ability to print fiat money, a tax system to fund the credit expansion it would create and an incredible shift in governing authority to fully exploit its power.

But why were the Founding Fathers so vehemently opposed to a Central Bank? Why were they disdainful of any tax, lest it be of great importance to national defense? What is the relationship between international banking and military conflict? Is it merely coincidence that Thomas Jefferson failed to renew the charter of the first National Bank in 1811, and war broke out in 1812? Is it coincidence that the Federal Reserve, the 16th Amendment authorizing an income tax, the Internal Revenue Service to enforce it, and the 17th Amendment all occurred in 1913; and the incident that ignited World War I occurred just one year later? Does anyone *really* know for what reason that war was fought?

Mark Anthony

Why aren't the inner workings of the Federal Reserve System taught vigorously and truthfully in our schools? Can any honest historian deny that the creation of a central bank was the turning point in America, and therefore, world history? I would think that the occurrence of such landmark legislation which (coincidentally?) greased through Congress under the most unusual and dubious terms — *legislation that was as blatantly unconstitutional as any act before or since* — would warrant some explanation.

Why is it that the Jeffersonian and the Jacksonian presidents — the standard bearers for limited Constitutional government — looked upon the international bankers (and the fiat money they printed) as if they had risen from the very depths of hell? How many Americans really know what a *fractional reserve banking* system is? What did President Jackson's revocation of the charter of the Second National Bank in 1836 have to do with the depression of 1837; also known as the *"Bankers Panic"* of 1837? What role did the international bankers and the Federal Reserve (two heads of the same coin) have to do with the liquidity crises that caused the stock market crash of 1929 and the subsequent Great Depression; as well as the recessions of 1969, 1973, 1982 and 1990 — not to mention the unprecedented ratcheting up of interest rates in 1994 and 1995?

The pieces fall into place upon inspection of the role central banks play in the fortunes of the world's economic dynasties — and the overwhelming control that they assert.

How The Central Bank Operates

Pull a dollar bill from your pocket. You'll notice the phrase,
> **"THIS NOTE IS LEGAL TENDER FOR**
> **ALL DEBTS, PUBLIC AND PRIVATE."**

This phrase changed the world forevermore. It should be made emphatically clear that the United States government has absolutely no Constitutional authority to print paper money, nor make it legal tender. Article I Section VIII of the Constitution only provides the government the "power to *coin* money and regulate the value thereof." Therefore, to ensure the integrity of the currency, the states were required to use gold or silver in payment of debts.

You see, the Federal Reserve is a *"Banker's Bank"* and our banking system a *fractional reserve system.* Curiously, I searched Grolier's *Academic American Encyclopedia* concerning the Federal Reserve, and I found no reference to "fractional banking" or to "Paul Warburg," *the key architect of it.* You would have similar luck if you conducted the same search of any high school or college textbook.

Interesting.

The Federal Reserve is a *bank of issue* and also a *discount bank.* It issues the currency that is used as money and as such, wields enormous power and ultimate control over the destiny of the United States government.

This is because the Federal Reserve has the power to
inflate or deflate the currency.

35

Make no mistake about it, the ability to inflate or deflate the currency and to control the issuance of paper money is the ability to control governments, to regulate economic activity, to build fortunes and to destroy lives. If the money supply is *inflated,* more money is put into circulation. The classic definition of inflation is *too much currency chasing too few goods* — prices rise, and the value of fixed assets (like those on Social Security or pension plans) declines. The Founding Fathers were vigilantly opposed to printing paper money because it places into the hands of a small group of elite citizens the power of devaluing the people's currency. Therefore, such manipulations were prohibited by the Constitution.

It should also be noted that it takes only a taste of inflation to send entire economies spinning out of control.

At 18% Inflation, Prices Double Every Four Years.

Knowing that the purchasing power of the currency that you currently hold will be cut in half in only four years has the effect of forcing consumers to make buying decisions they would not normally make.

Let me explain.

Assume that you intend to buy a new automobile in a few years, and that automobile is currently priced at $20,000. Now, consider that inflation is running at 18% annually. That means the same vehicle will cost $40,000 four years from now. The price of the car will double, yet your salary will certainly not. Day after day, the paper money you hold has less *real* purchasing power. Would you still wait a few years to purchase that automobile? Of course not; you would buy it as soon as possible. As such, inflation creates an artificial demand for goods and services which breeds ever more rampant inflation; by feeding on itself it accelerates in intensity the longer it is allowed to occur.

Conversely, when the currency is *deflated,* the money supply shrinks and available credit dries up. A severe deflationary environment is also known as a depression. New business loans are not possible, companies cannot purchase new plants and equipment, less profitable companies have cash-flow problems and lose access to credit lines that would have helped them meet payroll and other obligations. Shifts are canceled, production lines are closed and factories are mothballed; jobs are lost as the financial infrastructure begins to crumble. As people begin to lose faith in the economy they remove their assets from financial institutions. Their concern quickly turns into panic as banks close, not having enough currency to meet the sudden demand for dollars.

This is known as a *liquidity crises* — it is more commonly referred to as a *run on the bank.*

The first severe monetary deflation resulted in the "Bankers Panic" of 1837; America's first depressionary economy. Nicholas Bittle, an agent of the Rothschild's of Paris (who play an integral role in Europe's central banks) chartered the Second Bank of The United States which had a twenty year charter beginning in 1816. In 1836, President Andrew Jackson revoked the bank's charter and removed all government funds, forcing the bank to close. This provoked the ire of the Bank of England, which suspended all American *paper* (the loans currently in force at the time). Those loans were called in and the funds quickly removed from the burgeoning American economy. The result was a grim liquidity crisis that resulted in the first depression.

There can also be no doubt that the great depression was caused by fractional reserve banking and the manipulation of the currency. First, the money supply was artificially inflated. This is often called "easy monetary policy." The economy boomed as banks freely lent to virtually everyone. Business loans abounded, production lines increased, goods and services were plentiful.

The average American family found a little taste of prosperity is quite an intoxicant.

As the stock market began its meteoric rise, the banks' easy credit policies continued to fuel the speculators' audacity. The market exploded as Americans shook off their conservative roots to buy stock on ten percent margin.

But inflation can only continue as long as the average citizen has faith and confidence in the integrity of the currency — the slightest hint of bad economic news brings the entire house of cards to a ruinous implosion.

And so it did.

In 1929, the Credit-Anstalt Bank in Austria collapsed. When word reached America, a wave of panic selling erupted as the stock market crashed. Lives were ruined, futures destroyed and billions were lost in a matter of days. In the blink of an eye upwards of 25 percent of working Americans no longer had jobs. Even an economic powerhouse like Ford Motor Company was forced to eliminate 75,000 jobs.

Alas, there were those willing to move in and pick up the pieces, purchasing the devalued assets at pennies on the dollar — *the same people who set up the Federal Reserve System.*

Were the elite families simply taking advantage of an economic opportunity; a matter of *"buy low and sell high,"* or was the entire crisis a matter of manipulating the country's currency; and a surreptitious excuse to create the Leviathan ushered in by the Roosevelt Presidency?

Let's take a look at how the Federal Reserve wields control. First of all, the Federal Reserve regulates the reserve requirements of member banks, and thus regulates the availability of credit. Under the guidelines set forth by the Federal Reserve Act of 1913, member banks were only required to back their currency with a 40% reserve of gold. However, this was radically changed in 1933 and 1934. Americans were *prohibited* from owning gold, with the exception of jewelry and fillings in teeth.

> "Gold contracts were invalidated, bank notes redeemable in gold were called in and paid for by Federal Reserve notes...the government proceeded on a course of credit expansion by inflating the currency. The price of gold was increased from $20 to $35 an ounce...By the early 1970s, the United States had full fledged fiat money — money by government decree — or in short, play-like money."[2]

Eustace Mullins, one of the few "outsiders" to truly understand the Federal Reserve system, has spent 50 years collecting data from Congressional records at the Library of Congress. Mullins dubbed the Federal Reserve *"The Magical Money Machine"* in which a piece of paper is inserted in one end and a $100 bill comes out the other. By its own admission, the Federal Reserve has the ability to simply "create" money out of nothing! Under the terms of the Federal Reserve Act, as soon as that $100 bill comes off the press, it immediately becomes a debt of the United States government — which is really a debt of the United States taxpayers — *and interest begins to accrue at that point.*

And so began an unparalleled proliferation of credit expansion.

> *Since 1913, "The Magical Money Machine" has helped create a $4.7 trillion national debt; a debt that increases at the rate of more than $20,000 a second — money that was created out of nothing — and all of it with your name on it.*

The measure of control levied by Federal Reserve requirements is relatively easy to comprehend. You see, there is generally only enough currency on hand at member banks to meet current cash needs. This is what fractional reserve banking is all about. The Federal Reserve may increase or decrease the money supply by the following means. It can raise or lower the reserve requirements of member banks. *Lowering reserve requirements* increases available credit; leaving more money in circulation for the banks to lend to businesses, for home mortgages, car loans and the like. On the other hand, by *increasing reserve requirements,* credit is tightened; less money is available for the banks to use and economic activity is stifled.

The second form of manipulating monetary policy is by raising or lowering the *discount rate* the Federal Reserve charges its member banks. When your bank lends you money or finances your credit card debt, it makes money on the difference between the *discount rate* and the interest rate it in turn charges you. By raising or lowering the discount rate, the Federal Reserve indirectly controls the interest rates the banks charge to everyone else. Remembering that interest rates are the *cost of money,* it is easy to see the effect higher interest rates have in slowing economic activity. It is more expensive for new businesses to open their doors. It is more expensive for existing businesses to expand and become more efficient as the cost of financing new research and development rises as well.

Lowering the discount rate has the opposite effect of *stimulating* the economy.

The irony is that we have been conditioned to praise the unconstitutional manipulations of the Federal Reserve. "Keep inflation in check," each incoming President demands of the Chairman of the Federal Reserve. And so, at the slightest hint of inflation, the Federal Reserve Chairman incrementally raises the discount rate charged to member banks; and the banks in turn raise the interest rate they charge to their customers; and by morning everything in America costs a little bit more.

On what Constitutional authority?

The third means of control is the Federal Reserve has the ability to finance the debt of the United States. The Treasury has two means in which to finance our continual deficits. It can sell Treasury instruments, like T-Bills and Bonds through its regular auctions, or it can enlist the help of the Federal Reserve's printing press.

Exercising the latter is a simple matter. The Treasury notifies the Federal Reserve of its cash needs. The Federal Reserve then, in effect, writes the Treasury a check. (Why not? It's your money.)

The Treasury then cashes the Federal Reserve's check at a member bank.

But where does the money come from?

> *The Federal Reserve prints it. This is called Monetizing the Debt; the fiat money the Federal Reserve prints immediately becomes the debt of the taxpayers of the United States — payable to the Federal Reserve Banks which print the money — banks whose stock is privately held.*

Imagine this scenario: A truck from the local paper mill pulls up to the Federal Reserve and unloads reams of blank paper. The Federal Reserve then inserts the paper into *"The Magical Money Machine"* and extracts $100 bills from the other end. Then you take your paycheck to a member bank and you exchange your *real assets* — the fruits of your labor — for pieces of paper money the Federal Reserve created out of thin air. But, before you ever receive your paycheck, the United States government (which is indebted to the Federal Reserve) withholds income taxes to pay for the credit expansion financed by the Federal Reserve.

> *Let me be clear. The very term "Income Tax" is a misnomer. There is no such thing as a tax on your "income." All taxes are actually <u>property</u> taxes; or taxes on your real personal property. In this case,*

the tax that is withheld from your paycheck is most certainly a tax on your personal property — it is a tax on your labor.

The ability to print paper money and to inflate or deflate the value thereof is unfathomable power for unelected, unaccountable, private interests to wield over the citizens of the United States. There can be no doubt that in 1913 the United States government gave away our very sovereignty to those who control the currency. All while the Founding Fathers — and the Constitution they drafted — explicitly prohibited them from doing so.

The Year 1913 — Curious Circumstances

On November 22, 1910, a group of seven men met in Hoboken, New Jersey, and rode on a private train to Jekyll Island, Georgia. Among them were Frank Vanderlip, president of Rockefeller National City Bank of New York; Henry P. Davison, senior partner of J. P. Morgan Company; Charles D. Norton, president of National Bank of New York, (in which Morgan held a considerable interest); Benjamin Strong, president of the Morgan Bank; Senator Nelson Aldrich of Rhode Island; A. Piatt Andrews, assistant secretary of the treasury; and German Banker Paul Warburg. Historical record shows close interrelationships existed among those present and the international banking community, as well as those known as the "Money Trust" in the United States. Senator Aldrich, for his part, was a close personal friend of the Rockefeller family. His daughter married John D. Rockefeller II and one of their children was named Nelson Aldrich Rockefeller. Warburg was a close associate and agent of the Rothschild family and a well known expert on European central banking. He came to America in 1902 and married the daughter of Solomon Loeb, one of the founders of the immensely powerful Kuhn, Loeb and Company.

Whether these interrelationships have relevance is yours to decide. I will offer this quote from Frank Vanderlip in 1935. It appeared in *The Saturday Evening Post:*

> "There was an occasion near the close of 1910, when I was secretive, indeed as furtive as any conspirator...since it would have been fatal to Senator Aldrich's plan to have it known that he was calling on anybody from Wall Street to help in preparing his bill...I do not feel it is any exaggeration to speak of our secret expedition to Jekyll Island as the occasion of the actual conception of what eventually became the Federal Reserve System."

There are several vexing questions. What was the great need for a central bank in the United States, as America had virtually no debt at the time and was not involved in war?

> *For what purpose would such a prosperous nation need a fractional reserve banking system? Why did the men who concocted the foundations of the Federal Reserve Act meet in secret? Why was the architect of what would become the Central Bank of The United States — The Federal Reserve — a German Banker named Paul Warburg? Is there any significance that he had close ties to Europe's Central Bankers?*

44

Was the existing Constitutional system of coining genuine money and requiring banks to have enough reserves on hand to meet deposits at all times so dangerously flawed that it needed to be scrapped? It should be noted that this "flawed" system allowed America to usher in the industrial revolution and be virtually free of debt in 1913.

Now, after 81 years of fractional banking and fiat money, we find our once proud nation $4.7 trillion dollars in debt; the world's premier debtor nation, begging money from foreign entities that used to call us "Sir."

We traded our sovereignty for *this?*

And more importantly: Why are so many tax-paying citizens asking themselves these questions for the very first time? Shouldn't such important topics have been judiciously discussed at the university level, if not in high school?

The Federal Reserve System

The Federal Reserve Act of 1913 authorized up to 12 regional banks. They are: New York, Boston, Philadelphia, Richmond, Atlanta, Dallas, Kansas City, St. Louis, Chicago, Cleveland, Minneapolis and San Francisco. The name "Federal" is illusory in that the stock of the Federal Reserve is held by the member banks. But who owns the stock of the member banks?

The stock is divvied up among 100 families.

For example, the Federal Reserve Bank of New York had a reported 203,053 shares. Among the owners are the Rockefeller family's National City Bank (now Citicorp) which took 30,000 shares, the National Bank of Commerce (also known as Morgan Guaranty Trust) which took 21,000 shares, Morgan's First National Bank had 15,000 shares and Chase National, 6,000 shares. The most important fact is this:

The United States does not own, and has never owned, one share of the stock of any of the Federal Reserve Regional Banks.

Conducting the affairs of the Federal Reserve is the Federal Reserve Board, or Board of Governors. Once again, the governing body provides the illusion of direct Federal control in that the President of the United States appoints the seven members of the Board, as well as the Secretary of the Treasury and the Comptroller General. But the appointees of the Board of Governors serve a term of 14 years, which effectively "put[s] them out of the power of the president," as Colonel Edward House, the most powerful advisor to Woodrow Wilson, duly noted.

And what about the governing boards of the regional reserve banks? These boards are made up of nine individuals, six of whom are appointed by the member banks. But upon closer inspection, one finds that "only three of these may be bankers; the other three must be from business or agriculture. Furthermore, the remaining three members that make up the nine are appointed by the central Federal Reserve Board, and executive officers come from these."[3] However, perception is not reality. Appointments, and therefore control, have become increasingly centralized as banking interests and political leaders became intertwined.

Vanishing Republic

Historical fact shows that Woodrow Wilson, a man of dignity and principle, was hand picked by the "Money Trust" to run for President in 1912. There are some who have surmised that Wilson's victory was the fluke of a four horse race, as the Republican party was fractionalized by the choice between Teddy Roosevelt, who ran on the Bull Moose ticket and Wilson, who was the governor of New Jersey (William Howard Taft and Eugene Debs, a Socialist, were the other two). The record shows that Wilson was strongly supported by some members of the "Money Trust": the Rockefellers, Bernard Baruch, Thomas Fortune Ryan, Jacob Schiff and Adolf Ochs; while Roosevelt was supported by the agents of J. P. Morgan: George Perkins and Frank Munsey.

Was the Republican vote split by design?

Also hand picked was Wilson's chief aid, Colonel Edward Mandell House, son of a wealthy Texas financier. Of House, Scribner's *Concise Dictionary of Biography* says: "No other American of his time was on such close terms with so many men of international fame."

The first governor of the Federal Reserve was Benjamin Strong, president of the Morgan Bank; and one of the seven in attendance at Jekyll Island. More recently, Paul Volcker served as Fed chairman from 1979 to 1987. Volcker was vice-president of Rockefeller's Chase Manhattan Bank from 1965 to 1968, and president of the New York Federal Reserve Bank from 1975 to 1979. Is it a conflict of interest that men who were employees of the moneyed elite, would then serve as chairmen of the Federal

Reserve system in which those same families have major shareholdings?

It should not surprise anyone that the destiny of America is controlled by those wealthiest of all Americans. It has always been that way in every country the world has known.

> *And although those of us of more modest means will never wield such power, at least we should have the sovereignty the Founding Fathers guaranteed by the Constitution —* ***that our money should be whole.***

By the 1970's what was left of the gold standard was removed. Our currency is now 100% fiat money. The question we must be asking ourselves is what are the true intentions of a small group of people who designed a system which places the power to control the currency, and the ultimate use of the credit of the United States government (and its people) into their own hands, by way of a privately held bank?

In contrast, the Founding Fathers were also the landed gentry; the wealthy elite. *But they were governed by natural law, handed down from God to man.* They knew of man's sinful nature and set out to construct a government that implemented a unique system of checks and balances in order to avoid such a consolidation of power. This system was designed so that the elected officials would serve at the pleasure of the co-sovereign citizens of the United States of America.

> *Why are we running continual deficits that benefit no one except the owners of the Central Banks? Why have our*

leaders continually sent Federal Reserve Notes to every foreign government imaginable — then forced the middle class to pay for such lavish foreign aid — as well as paying for the proliferation of social welfare programs doled out in this country? And why doesn't anyone want you to ask these questions?

We are left to further ask ourselves: *what are the true intentions of those who have defiled and destroyed our Constitution, eroded the balance of power it dictates, devalued our money and sold our sovereignty to those who print the government currency?*

The answer to these questions will be of monumental importance if we are to rescue our *Vanishing Republic.*

The echoes of our ancestors ring loud and true...

"The bold efforts the present bank has made to control the government, the distress it has wantonly caused are but a premonition of the fate which awaits the American people should they be deluded into the perpetuation of this institution or an establishment of another like it."
— President Andrew Jackson,
upon revoking the charter of the
Second Bank of The United States, 1836

"You are a den of vipers, I intend to rout you out by the eternal God, I will rout you out. If the American people only knew the rank injustice of our money and banking system, there would be a revolution by morning."
— President Jackson,
addressing the international money interests

49

"I believe that banking institutions are more dangerous to our liberties than standing armies. Already they have raised up a moneyed aristocracy that has set the government at defiance. The issue power should be taken from banks restored to the people to whom it properly belongs."
— Thomas Jefferson

"Whoever controls the volume of money in any country is absolute master of all industry and commerce."
— President James Garfield

"The Federal Reserve (privately owned banks) is one of the most corrupt institutions the world has ever seen."
— Congressman Louis T. McFadden,
Chairman of the U.S. Banking
& Currency Commission for 22 years

"The only honest dollar is a dollar of stable, debt-paying purchasing power. The only honest dollar is a dollar which repays the creditor the value he lent and no more, and requires the debtor to pay the value borrowed and no more."
— Senator Robert L. Owens, 1913

"The youth who can solve the money question will do more for the world than all the professional soldiers in history."
— Henry Ford, Sr.

Chapter 3
The Destruction Continues...
Spend (Give Away) The Money

On February 25, 1913, the 16th Amendment was ratified and the floodgates of government expansionism were blown open. The 16th Amendment was a single, simple sentence that allowed the federal government to tax the property of the American people in order to finance the debt that the Federal Reserve System would create. It reads:

> **"The Congress shall have power to lay and collect taxes on incomes, from whatever source derived, *without apportionment among the several States, and without regard to any census or enumeration."*** (My emphasis)

Quite simply, the purpose of the 16th Amendment was to undue Section 9, Article I of the Constitution, and in doing so, permitted the Federal Government to redistribute the wealth. This section of the Constitution reads:

> **"No Capitation, or other direct, Tax shall be laid, *unless in <u>Proportion to the Census or Enumeration</u> herein before directed to be taken."*** (My emphasis)

In other words, no tax is Constitutional unless it benefits all American people equally. To tax the people for the purpose of social programs that benefit only some of the citizens is unequivocally unconstitutional. And so, history clearly shows that

51

the ability to *tax* evolved solely to allow government the ability to *spend*. Except in time of war, our government was fiscally sound — in 1900, the government ran a *surplus* — receipts were $567 million and expenses $521 million.

Where was the *need* to tax the American people?

And since that time...

In 1994 the Federal Budget was over $1,500 billion (one and a half trillion dollars) while revenues were several hundred billion dollars less, and the national debt stood at roughly $4.7 trillion. Yet we continue to give billions of American dollars in foreign aid all over the world. In the twenty year period between 1945 and 1965 economic and military aid totaled over $100 billion.

Just how did the Federal Government obtain enough power to rape the wealth of the American people?

The final element in that infamous year was the 17th Amendment which was enacted on May 31, 1913. The 17th Amendment allowed that the election of members of the Senate would be by the people rather than the State Legislature. This was a democratic move which on the surface appears to place more power in the hands of the people, but in actuality removed a foundational principle of the balance of power. The true beauty of the system of government which the Founding Fathers designed is not simply the checks and balances, consisting of separate Executive, Legislative and Judicial Branches; but also that power is to be *shared* among the Federal and State governments, and the people. The House of Representatives is supposed to be just that, and as such, the Representatives are elected by the people. Members of the Senate, on the other hand, were to be elected by the State

Legislature, thus providing to the States a key check on Imperial Government.

Without Senate approval, legislation cannot become law, Presidential appointees cannot be confirmed and treaties cannot become law. The fact that Senators were directly responsible to the State Legislatures that elected them made it possible to stop legislation that violated the defined powers of the Federal Government or impugned on the Constitutionally granted powers of the States. It is in this manner that the balance of power between the Federal Government, and the State Governments which created it, would be upheld.

The 17th Amendment has been largely overlooked in the grand scheme of American government; but clearly, without it, the other two pieces of the puzzle: the creation of the Federal Reserve and the enactment of an income tax could not have been exploited with such impunity.

And there you have the three building blocks on which Leviathan would be built: a Federal Reserve System that had the authority to create money out of nothing; an income tax on the American people to repay the debt the Federal Reserve would perpetuate; and the elimination of the States' single greatest check on runaway Federal power.

Once these Constitutional barriers were removed, American freedom would quickly begin to erode. Consumed by the very government the States created, they became mere Colonies; lackeys under the rule of the unchained beast. Forgotten were the rights of the States — and the people — as well as the 10th Amendment which reads:

"The powers not delegated to the United States by the Constitution, nor prohibited by it to the States, are reserved to the States respectively, or to the people."

The First American King

[The] "New Deal Administration has dishonored American traditions...The powers of Congress have been usurped by the President. The integrity and authority of the Supreme Court have been flouted. The rights and liberties of American citizens have been violated...The New Deal Administration constantly seeks to usurp the rights reserved to the states and to the people. It has insisted on the passage of laws contrary to the Constitution...It has dishonored our country by repudiating its most sacred obligations."
— Excerpted from Republican Party platform, 1936[4]

Throughout history, few Americans have had the courage to view Franklin Delano Roosevelt in a Constitutional light. If one's conception of the role of government is that it should be parent and provider, nurturer and care giver, healer and supplier of food, housing and income, then FDR could be called our greatest President. If one wishes to live free in a land governed by natural law, equality of opportunity, and direct personal responsibility under a God-fearing Constitutionally Federated Republic, then he was surely one of the worst.

The Constitution clearly outlines the President's obligation to uphold the supreme law of the United States Government:

"All presidents, as part of their oath of office, are sworn to uphold the Constitution: Before he enter on the Execution of his Office, he [the President] shall take the following Oath or Affirmation:— 'I do solemnly swear (or affirm) that I will faithfully execute the Office of President of the United States, and will to the best of my ability, preserve, protect and defend the Constitution of the United States.'"

But liberals, like thieves and criminals, are opportunists. They prey on the disadvantaged who have suffered from circumstances that a socialistic government itself has created. This is the tool of the activist President; the needs of the people are perceived as an "emergency" — and so they offer to fight the *"war"* on joblessness, the *"war"* on poverty, the *"war"* on crime; and the answer is always sweeping new government programs ubiquitously called "reform." With such reform inevitably comes more government. The solution is *not* more government.

Rather, the problem is and was big government in the first place. "Urban Renewal," and mismanaged, ill-conceived, public housing programs have decimated our inner cities; and what is the solution?

More government spending.

Able-bodied Americans are jobless due to confiscatory tax rates and draconian regulatory control run amok; and what is the solution? Increased taxes to fund job retraining programs and additional welfare benefits. Our streets are riddled with derelicts and criminals bred by the *"Great Society"* that has refused to punish them; and what is the solution?

Billions spent on social programs to combat the "root causes" of crime.

Unfortunately, morons and fools refuse to learn the repeated lessons of history.

If Government spending on job training is the solution to joblessness; if Government spending on welfare programs is the solution to eliminating poverty; if Government spending to fund social programs is the solution to our crime problem — THEN WE WOULD HAVE NO JOBLESSNESS, WE WOULD HAVE NO POVERTY, AND WE WOULD HAVE NO CRIME.

We have spent trillions of dollars over the last 60 years in order to find out that these programs have the exact opposite effect of that which they intend to accomplish. Yet we continue to throw more money at the problem, further enslaving the very people we wish to help.

There can be no arguing that fractional reserve banking was responsible for the Great Depression; and there can also be no arguing that FDR took advantage of the misery it brought to the American people, in order to advance Leviathan. The wanting public ate up the programs of the New Deal because Roosevelt knew that a hungry man, with an equally hungry family, will accept a piece of bread, caring not what string is attached to the other end.

It has always struck me as odd the extent to which President Roosevelt is deified. If the United States were a Monarchy, and FDR its King, then he certainly would be within his authority to enact such sweeping social change and oppressive government interventionism.

But we are not a Monarchy, and the President is not our King.

The United States is a Constitutionally Federated Republic, and as they assume office, members of Congress are sworn to uphold the Constitution. It is their responsibility to meticulously check each new piece of legislation to ensure that they are not casting an affirmative vote for an unconstitutional bill. Yet, Congress now votes on multi-billion dollar "omnibus" legislation without ever reading it. Above that, it is the President's responsibility to review legislation for its Constitutionality before signed into law.

If one has the courage to view President Roosevelt within the constraints of the Constitution which he swore to uphold, his performance was disgraceful. It is for this reason the foundational principles of *Natural Law* and *Limited Constitutional Government* are integral parts of this work.

> *Today, many Americans see nothing wrong with the monumental change brought on by the New Deal. In today's revisionist society, perception is reality; and the truth be damned. In the new era of "Me First," of the law of man taking precedence over Natural Law, reality has become whatever an individual believes it to be — and that reality is based upon the experiences and ideals that each person is raised upon.*
>
> *But too often those ideals are based on government as Big-Brother...and those realities are as false as a drug-addled euphoria.*

Now, after generations have been raised on the New Deal and the Great Society, we have built a dependency class for the simple reason that today's hand-out is tomorrow's expectation. Our children are raised on the notion that government will be there to take care of their every need. Once the American people had a taste of Big-Brother's false benevolence, generations forevermore were hopelessly addicted. What many do not understand, or refuse to understand, is that government intervention is self perpetuating. Once the American people in their time of great need allowed the government to break free from the Constitutional mold that constrained it, we forever gave up the right to be a co-sovereign, free people. Now, millions of Americans can not fathom life without the safety net of government programs. This is a perception of reality that will eventually doom us all.

We need to have the courage to realize that if we did not have a fractional reserve banking system, we would never have had the Great Depression. If we did not have the Great Depression, the welfare state could not have been justified. If the welfare state had not been created, government could not have built a dependency class. If the Federal Reserve did not have the ability to create fiat money, then we could not have amassed a $4.7 trillion debt supporting the dependency class.

If government constrained itself to the powers granted it by the Constitution, we would not have a $1.6 trillion annual budget. And if we did not have a $1.6 trillion budget, we would not need confiscatory tax rates to service it. Said President Franklin Pierce, who served from 1853 to 1857, "If the Federal Government will confine itself to the exercise of powers clearly granted by the Constitution, it can hardly happen that its action upon any question should endanger the institutions of the States or interfere with their right to manage matters strictly domestic according to the will of the people."

FDR was elected on November 8, 1932, but in those days the inauguration was not until March of the following year. The duplicity of President Roosevelt was shown even before he took office, as he refused the urging of President Hoover to take steps to stabilize the economy. Of this interim period, historian Arthur S. Link wrote:

> "President Hoover had been trying to win Roosevelt's approval for policies that would stabilize the financial situation and restore public confidence. In private conference and by letter Hoover exhorted the President-elect to announce that he would balance the budget, maintain the dollar at its current value in gold, and cooperate with the European powers in stabilizing currencies and exchange rates. Roosevelt refused...."[5]

By taking such action, a banking "crisis" could have been averted, but it was not; and sweeping new powers were given to the President as well as the Federal Government so that just such a "crisis" would not recur. Link wrote, "The first sign of crisis came on October 31, 1932, when the Governor of Nevada declared a twelve-day holiday...On February 4, 1933, Governor Huey P. Long closed the banks of Louisiana; ten days later the Governor of Michigan declared a banking moratorium for a week. Then during the ensuing three weeks, state after state succumbed, until the climax of the crisis came in the early morning of March 4, when Governor Herbert H. Lehman closed the New York banks for two days. By the hour of Roosevelt's inaugural, banks were either closed or doing business under severe restrictions in forty-seven states."

Where was the Federal Reserve in all of this? Was it not created for the express purpose of eliminating such banking crises? But no, the vast powers granted to the Federal Reserve were not enough to eradicate the banking crisis — and why should they? Those same powers were the cause of the monetary deflation that created the Great Depression.

And what was the answer? Sweeping *"reform"* legislation.

Later on March 4, Roosevelt was inaugurated. The next day he called a special session of Congress, and the day after that mandated a four day banking holiday, though he had no Constitutional authority to do so. Furthermore, gold, silver and currency were not permitted to leave the country. Roosevelt's policy makers drew up legislation to deal with the crisis and presented it to Congress on March 9th. Virtually every rule ordinarily involved in passing legislation was broken. The bill did not make its way through the appropriate committees for examination and consideration, no public hearing took place, and it was never placed on the legislative calendar. The Chairman of the House Banking and Currency Committee rose before the House and read the bill aloud from the *only existing copy* of the proposed legislation. After less than forty minutes of debate, a vote was called for and taken, which passed unanimously. Only hours later it was also passed in the Senate by a 73-7 margin.

The legislation placed heretofore unheard of (and Constitutionally unauthorized) power over banking and financial markets in the hands of the President. In an amazing example of the arrogance of his king-like power, Roosevelt and Henry Morganthau, the Secretary of the Treasury, *set the daily price of gold...Under what Constitutional authority?*

Wrote John T. Flynn:

> "Thereafter each day Morganthau and Roosevelt met, with Jesse Jones, head of the RFC, present, to fix the price of gold. They gathered around Roosevelt's bed in the morning as he ate his eggs. Then [Morganthau] and Roosevelt decided the price of gold for the day. One day they wished to raise the price. Roosevelt settled the point. Make it 21 cents, he ruled. That is a lucky number — three times seven. And so it was done. That night Morganthau wrote in his diary: 'If people knew how we fixed the price of gold they would be frightened.'"[6]

The Hundred Days

"It is hardly a lack of due process for the government to regulate that which it subsidizes."
     — *Wickard v. Filburn,* Supreme Court, 1942

The first hundred days of a modern Presidency are met with considerable fanfare; they are charted and compared against the preceding Chief Executive's achievements. Under President

Roosevelt, the Hundred Days are referred to in upper case in that they made history. Unlike any other time before or since were laid such deep roots of wealth redistribution. The most far reaching legislation of those Hundred Days was the National Industrial Recovery Act which attempted to regulate industry in ways heretofore unimaginable. A sample of the verbiage from that Act reads like a page out of Karl Marx's *Das Kapital:*

> "...to provide for the general welfare by promoting the organization of industry for the purpose of cooperative action among trade groups, to induce and maintain united action of labor and management under adequate governmental sanctions and supervision, to eliminate unfair competitive practices to promote the fullest possible utilization of the present productive capacity of industries... to increase the consumption of industrial and agricultural produces by increasing the purchasing power... employees shall have the right to organize and bargain collectively...employers shall comply with the maximum hours of labor, minimum rates of pay, and other conditions of employment, approved or prescribed by the President. "

The legislation allowed industries such as automobile, beef, poultry and many others to codify various aspects of their business, leaving the President of The United States with final say over the codes if the industries themselves could not come to terms. Minimum wages were set, maximum hours determined and the foundation of a democratic socialist economy was formed, as sweeping new regulatory powers were given to the Federal

Government — with no Constitutional authority to enact the least of it.

The Tennessee Valley Authority placed the government into the electric business using the tax dollars of the people at large to provide the benefit of subsidized electricity to a small percentage of citizens; a blatantly unconstitutional act. TVA was followed by The Farm Credit Act, the Emergency Railroad Transportation Act, The Federal Securities Act, The Employment System Act, as well as providing massive unemployment relief under the auspices of the newly formed Civil Works Administration.

The Civilian Conservation Corps offered the first prodigious make-work jobs program by enlisting a group of young quasi-military tree-huggers. The young men were placed in camps; a small sum was paid to their parents as their progeny were given food, lodging and a meager wage for their ecological efforts. The Civilian Conservation Corps was a liberal coup — it provided thousands of make-work jobs for America's youth, while at the same time planting the seed of Big-Brother as provider — all in an environmental setting.

To widen approval for its social program, the Federal Emergency Relief Act earmarked Federal funds to be allocated to state and municipal governments so that they could sponsor their *own* make-work jobs.

But a fact often overlooked in today's history books is the new social welfare state sought first to break the American spirit by compromising its strongest link — the American Farmer. On May 12, 1933, the Agricultural Adjustment Act passed. The Secretary of Agriculture was given the power to determine how much acreage would be planted, what crops would be grown, and what price would be charged. Among the Secretary's powers are "To provide for reduction in the acreage or reduction in the production for market, or both, of any basic agricultural commodity...To enter into marketing agreements with processors, associations of producers and others engaged in handling...To obtain revenue for extraordinary expenses incurred by reason of the national emergency... [by levying] processing taxes."

The federal controls mandated by the Agricultural Adjustment Act were to be terminated once the President deemed the agricultural "emergency" was over.

Unfortunately the emergency has yet to end. Here's what they don't tell you in the history books: Government price supports *caused* the so-called "emergency" in the first place. During World War I the government guarantees inflated the farmers' wheat prices. This triggered a massive increase in wheat production which resulted in huge surpluses, ultimately driving many wheat farmers out of business. Wheat farmers again went to the government to remedy the debacle it had wrought; and in 1929, under President Herbert Hoover, Congress created the Federal Farm Board.

Immediately bestowed upon the Farm Board was the largest non-defense budgetary authorization to date — $500 million — with which President Hoover exclaimed, "I invest you with responsibilities and resources such as have never before been conferred by our government in assistance to any industry."

Once again, government intervention destroyed free-market forces.

Vanishing Republic

The subsidies priced American wheat and cotton out of the world market, which quickly destabilized. Prices plummeted and the market for two of America's most important crops was decimated.

> *You'll find this pattern repeated over and over throughout the twentieth century; I call it the Subsidy Two-Step. Here's how it works: Step One: Political leaders, bureaucrats and special interests create an "Emergency." Their willing accomplices in the media help substantiate its devastation. The only answer, of course, is more subsidies, taxes or regulations — or a combination thereof (curiously, less government and faith in the free-market system are never mentioned). The government intervention inevitably ruins the industry, community or race that it wished to help...which brings us to Step Two.*
> *Now, a disaster in exponential proportion to the first situation exists; and what is the solution? Even more oppressive government intervention with a pursuant loss of freedom, Constitutional rights, money and property.*

In *Lost Rights, The Destruction of American Liberty*, author James Bovard wrote:

> "The political destruction of agricultural exports is the key to understanding how American farmers became government dependents...government administrators were so concerned about maintaining a stranglehold on the wheat supply that they would seize the title to a farmer's entire wheat harvest if he planted a single acre more than local farm bureaucrats permitted...In 1954, Congress set the U.S. price support for wheat at roughly double the world price

and imposed new mandatory production controls on wheat and corn farmers. In 1955 and 1956, USDA arrested or sued more than 1,500 farmers for growing more wheat than was permitted. Stanley Yankus, a Michigan farmer arrested for illegally growing wheat to feed his chickens, told the House Agriculture Committee in 1959, 'I am not fighting for the right to grow wheat. I am fighting for the right to own property. If I am forbidden the use of my land, then I do not own it. How can you congressmen justify the laws which have destroyed my means of making a living'...By 1960 the United States was spending over a billion dollars a year just to store surplus commodities."[7]

Another factor overlooked by historical revisionists is when the government involves itself in actions that are strictly prohibited by the Constitution, such as the multitude of subsidies and regulation, the effect is to pad the accounts of the rich, make the poor suffer and then ask the middle-class to foot the bill. A case in point is farm subsidies: "It has been estimated that the lowest 56 percent of the farmers received only seven per cent of the subsidies. Most of the aid has gone to the larger commercial farmers, particularly those who produced basic commodities like wheat, corn and cotton. In 1960, 296 cotton growers received more than $30 million in government price supports. The largest amount received by a single producer was $1,236,048 which went to a Mississippi cotton company owned by an English firm."[8]

This is the way it has always been.

Originally, government intervention was ostensibly to help the small family farmer survive, yet many of those farmers have long since been driven out of business. Rather, federal farm subsidies destroyed a special piece of the American dream, as the family farm has been consolidated into today's corporate Agri-Business giants.

In 1981 Congress increased subsidies on many crops. In a little over a year, the inflated prices offered for the subsidized crops produced a huge surplus. The answer? The Payment in Kind program (PIK) enacted by the Reagan administration in 1983 paid farmers to idle "seventy-eight million acres — the equivalent of leaving idle all the cropland in California, Montana, Colorado, Kentucky, Louisiana and Wisconsin."[9]

The problem with this type of Socialistic command economy is that markets have thousands of interrelated components, making it impossible for bureaucrats to effectively utilize resources. A surplus or an inflated price in one commodity adversely affects all related components. The higher feed grain prices caused by the PIK program cost cattle, egg, pork and poultry producers seven billion dollars, and farm related payrolls declined by 250,000.

Every year, billions of taxpayer dollars are wasted through Federal payoffs to set aside millions of acres of farmland — 55 million acres in 1993. And just as agricultural subsidies have destroyed that bit of history that was the family farmer, so too has the government ruined thousands of small rural towns — the last vestiges of those who worked the farms. "Sen. Kent Conrad of North Dakota complained that the [Conservation Reserve Program] has 'absolutely wiped out small town after small town as we took land out of production.' Partly as a result of the government's shutting down the farms, over half of the nation's rural counties lost population between 1980 and 1990. A 1992 USDA study concluded that idling farm acreage in northern Missouri had reduced total economic activity in that region by almost 6 percent.

"Federal farmland shutdowns, by decreasing U.S. harvests, undermine U.S. exports; between 1981 and 1992, the U.S. share of the world wheat market fell from 47 percent to 35 percent...Government first artificially raises the price and then artificially restricts production. The federal government annually shuts down a large part of rural America to 'compensate' for this political mismanagement of farm prices."[10]

In sharp contrast to President Franklin D. Roosevelt, President Martin Van Buren was faced with a similar temptation to sharply expand the reach and scope of the Federal Government in 1837 — under amazingly similar circumstances. Just as Roosevelt capitalized on the downtrodden populace caught in the clutches of the Great Depression, Van Buren presided over a nation reeling from the first depression. Said Van Buren:

> **"All communities are apt to look to government for too much. Even in our own country, where its powers and duties are so strictly limited we are prone to do so, especially at periods of sudden embarrassment and distress. But this ought not to be. The framers of our excellent Constitution and the people who approved with calm and sagacious deliberation acted at the time on a sounder principle. They wisely judged that the less government interferes with private pursuits the better for the general prosperity. It is not its legitimate object to make men rich or to repair by direct grants of money or legislation in favor of particular pursuits losses not incurred in the public service. This would be**

substantially to use the property of some for the benefit of others. But its real duty — that duty the performance of which makes a good government the most precious of human blessings — is to enact and enforce a system of general laws commensurate with, but not exceeding, the objects of its establishment, and to leave every citizen and every interest to reap under the benign protection the rewards of virtue, industry and prudence."

Amen.

Compromising The Courts

Initially, many of FDR's New Deal initiatives met with considerable opposition on Constitutional grounds. In 1935 and 1936 the Supreme Court ruled against New Deal provisions in eight different cases. Only the Tennessee Valley Authority and the 1933 banking reform legislation held up to judicial scrutiny.

The Federal courts reacted in kind. In "1935-36 federal judges issued some sixteen hundred injunctions preventing federal officers from carrying out federal laws."[11]

But the Constitutionality of an unemployed man's meal ticket means little when he has young, hungry mouths to feed.

And so, the nation's resolve to resist the onslaught of New Deal socialism died as the ballots were cast on November 3, 1936. Roosevelt received 27.7 million votes to Alfred M. Landon's 16.6 million — Landon carried only the electoral votes in Maine and

Vermont. FDR's Democratic allies had majorities of 328-107 in the House and 77-19 in the Senate.

Given a clear mandate Roosevelt sought to obliterate his last remaining obstacle, as he threatened to "pack" the courts. FDR sent a judicial reform proposal to Congress that would have increased the Supreme Court from nine to fifteen justices, as well as adding 50 benches to the Federal courts. On May 9, 1937, the President addressed the nation, accusing the courts and his congressional opponents of what we now call "gridlock."

Amazingly, Roosevelt admonished the courts for the very transgression he was guilty of, saying:

> "We have, therefore, reached the point as a Nation where we must take action to save the Constitution from the Court."

The Senate Judiciary Committee, undeterred, rebuked FDR's court reorganization, saying:

> "It points the way to the evasion of the Constitution and establishes the method whereby the people may be deprived of their right to pass upon all amendments of the fundamental law...
> Under the form of the Constitution it seeks to do that which is unconstitutional. Its ultimate operation would be to make this Government one of men rather than one of law, and its practical operation would be to make the Constitution what the executive or legislative branches of the Government choose to say it is — an interpretation to be changed with each change of administration."[12]

That noble rhetoric not withstanding, the courts dutifully caved in to Roosevelt's intimidation.

The law and the court system have never been the same.

Chapter 4
What Have They Done To Our Government?
(What's So Bad About God And Country...And Sovereignty...And Patriotism?)

"The Americans are the first people whom Heaven has favoured with an opportunity of deliberating upon, and choosing the forms of government under which they should live. All other constitutions have derived their existence from violence or from accidental circumstances, and are therefore more distant from their perfection, which, though beyond our reach may nevertheless be approached under the guidance of reason and experience."
— John Jay, 1777

"Socialism has been the dominant concept driving such practices as government control of or regulation of economies, the redistribution of wealth by government, the efforts to remake man and society, the secularization of life, and the intrusion of law into every area of life. Socialism is the main fount of the notion that the public (i.e., society, government, or whatever organizations there may be) is obligated to provide nourishment for the hungry, better working conditions for the employed, opportunity for those lacking it, and all sorts of goodies for those who need, want, or demand them. Socialism is moved by a vision of utopia which can be achieved if people will only forego their self-seeking and join their efforts in the common quest for well-being. This utopianism is often beneath the surface, but it is nonetheless the impelling vision...Socialism, as implied

above, is the main source of the notion that government is supposed to be the Great Provider for the well being of the populace."
— Clarence B. Carson,
Basic American Government

Two internal means exist in which to destroy nations. The first, and quickest way, is by destroying free market forces. This has been shown in many forms: Fascism, Socialism, Communism and **Democratic Socialism;** also known as evolutionary, gradualist or *Creeping* Socialism, which is evidenced by a formerly free, democratic nation slowly consumed by social welfare programs, high taxes and centralized government planning, regulation and subsidization (sound familiar?).

Allow me to further quote Carson who provides an alarmingly accurate definition of what our once glorious Republic has become:

"Evolutionary socialism has been the dominant form of socialism in Western Europe, North America, and much of the rest of the world. Extended and covert evolutionary socialism has wrought Leviathan in the United States. Great increases of government action have everywhere accompanied the passage of socialist measures. The most distinctive feature of evolutionary socialism is that it was a program for working within the existing political, economic, and institutional system to change and reform it from within. In even broader terms, evolutionary socialists are *gradualists, democratic,* and *statist.*

They are gradualists in believing that ends of socialism can be achieved by steps and stages within a country, that violent revolution is not essential. To put it another way,

73

they are ***reformists,*** not revolutionaries. They have
generally professed devotion to popular rule and what are
commonly thought of as democratic procedures. One of
the large myths of socialism is that the bulk of the populace
really wants socialism. If that were true, if the people were
fully enfranchised and faithfully represented, socialism
would be installed...In consequence, *evolutionary*
socialists cling to their profession of democracy with elitist
tactics when it is to their purpose and by defining
democracy to include such ideas as equality, equity, and
the like. Evolutionary socialists are statists in that they
believe in the use of government to achieve their ends. "[13]
(My emphasis)

The destruction of freedom and representative governance when
accomplished by these means is only temporary. It may last a few
years or a few decades, but eventually Socialist regimes will
always fail because the moral fabric rests in the people, and those
people will eventually overthrow the Socialist government and
re-establish democracy in their image. This must, by definition,
take place because government is intended to be controlled by the
people, and as such, the moral center of the people will be reflected
in the governments they form.

However, those who wish to control governments and enslave
people have learned the lessons of history well. It has become
evident that the only way to destroy government with lasting
results is to destroy the moral fabric and religious underpinnings of
society. This is accomplished by negative or condescending or
fear-mongering media practices and intimidating legislative action,
followed by obtuse judicial rulings. To destroy governments with

any permanence, *Natural law* — based on Judeo-Christian truths — must be replaced by the law of man. Natural law, which flows from God to man, must be replaced with law derived from man's sinful nature. If the moral center of the people is compromised and replaced with immoral behavior and baseless values under the guise of tolerance, the formation of an abominable government — one which places the freedom and assets of many, into the hands of a few — is possible. The elite may then parcel out said freedoms and riches as they choose.

In 1992, historian Clyde Wilson wrote these chilling words:

> "It is true that we live in a very different world from our [Founding] Fathers and that our solutions cannot always be the same as theirs. But our problem is the same — the harnessing of power...Consolidation of power is not so much inherent in our current state as it is the product of choices made and institutions constructed in the past that showed a bias in favor of gigantism over humane scale, centralized control over freedom, and elitism over democratic rule...But the restraint of power is a necessary first step for all progress...Leviathan has gotten loose from the harness our forefathers so skillfully fashioned for him. He has knocked over the fence, laid waste our gardens, and waxed fat on our substance. We must begin to look to our husbandry, but first we will have to chain the beast."[14]

And so the destruction of our moral fabric and religious underpinning has begun. Judeo-Christian teachings designed to build principle of character have been removed from public schools. The Ten Commandments are viewed by the National Education Association as subversive brainwashing; yet condoms are freely distributed, birth control is counseled, and alternative lifestyles are deemed virtuous. Evangelical Christians are viewed as right wing extremists while new-age moral relativists are depicted as enlightened intellectuals. The media are less trusting of conservatives in government than those who cheat on their wives. The Boy Scouts are reviled because of their value-set, and ridiculed for not allowing homosexual troop leaders. The Equal Employment Opportunity Commission is champing at the bit to add the arrow of "Religious harassment" to its quiver. The tax dollars of those whose religions oppose eugenics will be used to fund health care reform that includes abortions; and before long, euthanasia. We are bombarded with the spirit of "live for the day" and instant gratification, callously forgetting the Higher power...And it is all being done by design...couched in good-intentioned utopian rhetoric.

Said Lester Frank Ward, a pioneer in American socialist thought: "The individual has reigned long enough. The day has come for society to take its affairs into its own hands and shape its own destinies." (You may want to re-read the quote of Pope John Paul II at the beginning of Chapter 1.)

As such, the destruction of the moral fabric and religious foundation of a nation is not just exemplified in how many Americans attend church on Sunday, but in the actions of those who have had their principles compromised. This is critically important. Look in the classified section in the newspaper of any moderate sized American city, and you'll find literally thousands of minimum wage jobs unfilled. Why? Because the government has provided to the poor of this country of package of income and benefits to the point that accepting those jobs would be a *cut in pay*.

I can hear the liberal elitists already — "How dare you call the poor of America 'well-off?'" That's not what I said. When one considers all the forms of public assistance; from welfare checks to food stamps; from Medicaid to Aid to Families with Dependent Children (AFDC) to job training; the package of benefits is well over $30,000 per person. This is not compassion; this is surreptitiously addicting millions of Americans to government dependency.

Allow me this analogy. You have a sixteen year old son who could make about $125 a week working a summer job. But what if you gave that child a package of income and benefits that far exceeded that which he could earn by working? Let's say you gave him a fifty dollar per week allowance, made his car payment, gave him a credit card to pay for his gas, bought his clothes and food and gave him shelter and money to purchase incidental items, like CD's, magazines and concert tickets. *What incentive would he have to work?* If you added up the package of income and benefits you provided, it would surely be three or four times what he could *earn* given his skill level.

> **More importantly, where would he learn the lessons of personal responsibility, work-ethic, discipline, honor and achievement? More frighteningly, lacking these lessons, what lessons *would* he learn; and *from whom would he learn them?***

Mark Anthony

Survival Of The Fittest...No More

In America's time of great "need," an opportunistic President by the name of Franklin Delano Roosevelt saw fit to change the laws of nature. And to all you who reminisce fondly of the New Deal...consider this: FDR has not been to our inner cities lately. I have.

Some of my dear friends are teachers in the Head Start Program. The Head Start Program is a pre-school/day care atmosphere that places mostly impoverished young children into a loving, nurturing, learning environment for a few hours each day. I see those beautiful, smiling faces — sweet little cherubs, brimming with the innocence of youth; and the wonderful women who teach and care for them; surrogate parents though they are; they freely share a genuine, sincere love that is truly a beauty to behold.

But what lies outside those doors is another world, entirely.

You may consider this a posthumous letter to Mr. Roosevelt, as well as to President Lyndon Johnson, whose Great Society programs added to the legacy of the New Deal.

To them, I respectfully say:

> **You should have known...Liberalism;**
> **like Government itself, can not create —**
> **it can only destroy.**

I've often wondered why that is. Now, I know.

Think back thousands of years. God placed man on this earth and all the animals who share it. Since that time, every species

78

has changed and evolved. That change was self-perpetuating —
only the strong would survive. This, scientists call, *Survival of The
Fittest.*

And it does not simply apply to bio-physical change. Man is a
unique creature in that he has the ability to alter his personal or
collective environment in ways superior to all other species. Faced
with adversity, many of our greatest advances have come. Was
the very creation of the United States — the most brilliant concept
of self-government, the freest nation on earth — not the product of
many brilliant men and women whose efforts were provoked by
extreme adversity?

And so we changed our environment.

Survival of The Fittest.

Man can be very resourceful under the strain of adversity. This
is part of God's plan, and the fiber of existence. We have been
given this wonderful planet along with the gift of life. What we
do with it is up to us. How many times has a plant closed and
some enterprising young man or woman opened his or her own
business to profit and growth. Many others have failed; but that
too is part of the plan. Man has the *opportunity* to fail, so that he
may learn and improve...and try again.

Survival of The Fittest.

People do what they must to provide for their families, that they
would have adequate food and shelter and clothing and education.
It is no sin that a man takes a second job or works overtime if need
be to provide for his family. Hard work (rewarded) is a virtue in
itself. In time of great need one went to church. There, needs

were administered to with the love of the congregation, *with no strings attached — no long lasting ill-effects.*

And so you have the evolution of Man, constantly improving his standard of living: the creation of the United States of America in the 18th century; The Industrial Revolution in the 19th century — then the light bulb, the telephone, the automobile and the airplane — and then...the Great Depression.

And the New Deal.

That was when everything changed.

Let us never forget that all depressions are machinations of Central Banks. The Constitution gave Congress the power to "coin money and determine the value thereof..." It granted absolutely no authority to print monopoly-like paper money. The ability to print money is the ability to inflate or deflate the currency — to devalue the money that the people hold in their hands. It is the power to create and the power to destroy; as well as the power to induce a monetary deflation which causes a depression.

America made it through the first depression, the "Bankers Panic" of 1837, without such sweeping programs. But, not this time.

Survival of The Fittest would be no more.

Democratic Socialists played on the vulnerability of the people. The servant would become the master; the populace subjugated to the unchained beast.

Forevermore, government would be the nurturer, the care-giver, the protector and provider. If a man be hungry...he would be fed. If he needed shelter...he would be given a home. If he needed a job...one would be provided — not from the loving benevolence of his congregation, but by the silent authority of an unseen hand. Not the hand of God, but the hand of Government. But government does not give, without a price.

> *The human spirit had been broken. Man no longer needed to strive...he needed only to ask.*

The family unit began to erode. *It was no longer necessary.* The Church lost its influence. Its role of provider in time of pain was no longer sought by the community as the Church asks only that its gift be used responsibly...the government asks nothing — it cares not how its offering is used; whether it be for drugs or alcohol, cigarettes or sleaze.

When I walk through these communities I see lives destroyed, families torn apart and neighborhoods that resemble battle zones. I see angry faces and misguided youths. I see rot and decay and pain and vice...and I see the faces of little children, who have yet to learn that their future has been stripped away by a government that lost faith in the human spirit...more than 60 years ago.

Let me tell you a story. I grew up in Pennsylvania. It was a beautiful place; a wonderful place to grow up; and a great place to be a kid. In high school I had many friends, and all of us — except one — worked summer jobs. You see, his family was well to do. His father was well known and respected in the community. His job kept him away from home an intolerable amount of time as his services were of great need and demand. His father was a fine and noble man, but he had one flaw: His occupation left him little time to spend with his son.

And instead of the nurturing and guidance the boy needed, he gave him a car, a generous allowance, and virtual carte blanche to purchase whatever he desired. In his freshman and sophomore high school years, he worked a summer job like the rest of us. By his senior year, his father was almost never home; and in his guilt he purchased his son a sports car that was the envy of all.

That was the last summer our friend worked.

From then on, he spent his time driving around, listening to his radio. He smoked marijuana during the day, and had a few beers at night. This went on through college; an exclusive school in the northeast. And although we went to different schools, in the summer we still worked and socialized together. He was an exceptionally bright student, one of the best in our high school. Yet his marijuana use graduated to hashish and speed and cocaine, and his grades were failing, or just barely passing. After the second year of college he stopped socializing with us entirely.

He had other, more *enlightened* friends.

At the age of 21 I moved to Florida. As my college friends scattered, we maintained little contact. Just after my thirty-first birthday, I saw two of my close friends, one of whom lived in Orlando, as well. He was an engineering major with a fine job. The other had received a masters degree in engineering from one of the country's best universities. He now worked for a defense contractor designing missile systems. I asked them about our other friends: one was a police officer, another owned a restaurant — all were doing very well — all but one.

Vanishing Republic

Our wealthy friend who seemed to have it all was last known to be flying back and forth from Florida to Pennsylvania, smuggling heroin in his cowboy boots for a local drug dealer.

That was the last time any of us heard of him.

How will we as a society define compassion?

The answers to the problems before us cannot be found in larger government, they can only be found in more freedom. For big government is the reason we have joblessness. It is the reason we have too little prosperity; too few well paying jobs. It is the reason we have a trade imbalance. It is the reason we have high insurance premiums. It is the reason we have high crime rates and low education levels. No, the answer is not more government, it is less government; government that governs by the people and for the people — not *to* the people. Our government, and those employed by it, must be accountable to us, or else our sovereignty will be sold to the highest bidder, just like the office buildings that are now sold to foreign investors.

In order to understand what we are dealing with, we must understand what our government was, where it came from, what it has become, and what it will eventually be if we don't act smartly and swiftly. Time and again it has been proven that liberty and big government are mutually exclusive entities.

As Attorney Andrew Hamilton eloquently said in 1734,

> "Power may justly be compared to a great river, which, kept within due bounds, is both beautiful and useful; but when it overflows its banks, it is then too impetuous to be

stemmed; it bears down all before it, and brings destruction and desolation wherever it comes.   If then this is the nature of power, let us at least do our duty, and like wise men (who value freedom) use our utmost care to support liberty, the only bulwark against lawless power, which in all ages has sacrificed to its wild lust and boundless ambition, the blood of the best men that ever lived...That, to which nature and the laws of our country have given us a right, — the liberty — both of exposing and opposing arbitrary power...by speaking and writing truth."

Chapter 5
Natural Law
What Our Government Was

"The Deity, from the relations we stand in to himself and to each other, has constituted an eternal and immutable law....Upon this depend the natural rights of mankind"
— Alexander Hamilton

"Sir Ernest Barker put thus the idea of natural law: 'This justice is conceived as being the higher or ultimate law, proceeding from the nature of the universe from the Being of God and the reason of man. It follows that law — in the sense of the law of the last resort — is somehow above lawmaking.'"[15]
— Russell Kirk

"These rights have usually been referred to as 'natural' rights. They are natural because they are understood to arise from the nature of things. The nature of things, further, was generally understood to have been made a part of them by the Creator, hence the rights were God-given. That rights subsist in the nature of things can be illustrated by reference to those rights which the Founders usually alluded to as summarizing them all: the rights to life, liberty, and property."
— Clarence Carson

The Founding Fathers, in forming a Constitutional federated republic, sought the goal of limited constitutional government specifically because of man's inherent sinfulness. Man could not be trusted with such incredible power. They had borne witness to

85

the destructive elitist notion that a small group of men, in their superiority, could use oppressive government force to impose their will on the populace. They felt that man's rights under natural law — the law of God — preceded the law of man, and thus built a government of shared authority between the states, the central government and the people, in order to ensure the preservation of life, liberty and property.

> *It was clear to the Founding Fathers that people have rights and government has powers; and that the rights of the people are conferred onto them by their creator, and the powers of government are in turn, given to it by the people.*

John Trenchard and Thomas Gordon were Englishmen who contributed greatly to the ideals of limited government and individual liberty in the early 1700's. They explain how powers are transferred from the people to the government and the consequence of breaching those powers.

> "All men are born free; Liberty is a Gift which they receive from God; nor can they alienate the same by Consent, though possibly they may forfeit it by crimes..
> The Right [meaning, the power] of the Magistrate arises only from the Right of private Men to defend themselves, to repel Injuries, and to punish those who commit them:
> That Right being conveyed by the Society to their publick Representative, he can execute the same no further than the Benefit and Security of that Society requires that he should. When he exceeds his Commission, his Acts are as

extrajudicial as are those of any private Officer usurping an unlawful Authority, that is, they are void...."[16]

Said Russell Kirk, "natural law, as a term of politics and jurisprudence, may be defined as a loosely knit body of rules of action prescribed by an authority superior to the state. These rules variously...are derived from divine commandment; from the nature of humankind; from abstract Reason; or from long experience of mankind in community. But natural law does not appertain to states and courts merely. For primarily it is a body of ethical perceptions or rules governing the life of the individual person, quite aside from politics and jurisprudence."

The Founding Fathers knew from experience that the ethics of their descendants are not guaranteed. They knew that power has the capability to corrupt. They also knew the danger of reverting away from natural law. "Both John Locke and Thomas Jefferson refused to allow atheists into their governments because atheists would not keep oaths. Oaths have to be sworn before God, and since atheists acknowledged no God, Locke and Jefferson maintained that they could not be trusted."[17]

And so the Bill of Rights was added to the Constitution of The United States — and this is critically important — not to enumerate the rights of the people, for they are bestowed by their Creator, but to limit the powers of the government.

Phrases like *"Congress shall make no law"* in the First Amendment and *"The right of the people to keep and bear Arms, shall not be infringed"* in the Second, make this point eminently clear.

In the Massachusetts Declaration of Rights, John Adams wrote:

> "All men are born free and independent, and have certain natural, essential, and unalienable rights, among which may be reckoned the right of enjoying and defending their lives and liberties; that of acquiring, possessing, and protecting property; in fine, that of seeking and obtaining their safety and happiness."[18]

The danger of subjugating natural law to the ill-intent of elitist governance cannot be understated. Political thinkers have repeatedly forewarned us. Kirk noted, "The most important early treatise on natural law is Cicero's *De Re Publica*. The Ciceronian understanding of natural law, which still exercises strong influence, was well expressed in the nineteenth century by Froude: 'Our human laws are but the copies, more or less imperfect, of the eternal laws so far as we can read them, and either succeed and promote our welfare, or fail and bring confusion and disaster, according as the legislator's insight has detected the true principle, or has been distorted by ignorance or selfishness.' "[19]

The importance of Froude's statement is that Congress and the President are obligated to inspect legislation and see to it that it is not in violation of the Constitution. Clarence Carson wrote, "The Jeffersonians believed very strongly that those in all three branches were bound both to interpret the Constitution and observe its limits. Before passing laws the members of Congress should satisfy themselves as to their constitutionality. Before approving measures passed by Congress, the President should decide for himself about the constitutionality of them, and if they were not, he should veto them on the grounds of their unconstitutionality...This is a far cry, of course, from the present day attitude of many Congressmen which is the highly irresponsible view that they will go ahead and approve the bill before them and leave to the courts the question of constitutionality."

Remember, the Bill of Rights was added to the Constitution to limit the power of government, without which the Constitution certainly could not have been ratified. Sadly, we have become a country in which the Bill of Rights has been raped, ravaged and misrepresented. The conditions of a society without such protection can be illustrated by the words of Patrick Henry, who said *before* the Bill of Rights was drafted:

"Here is a resolution [the formation of a central government without limits to its power] as radical as that which separated us from Great Britain. It is radical in this...our rights and privileges are endangered, and the sovereignty of the states will be relinquished...The rights of conscience, trial by jury, liberty of the press, all pretensions to human rights and privileges are rendered insecure...A number of characters, of the greatest eminence in this country, object to this government for its consolidating tendency...The government will operate like an ambuscade. It will destroy the state governments, and swallow the liberties of the people."[20]

As Henry said it, so it has become; a society without diligent adherence to the principles protected under the Bill of Rights will quickly lose its liberty, erode the states' powers — and lose control of those elected to protect the public interest.

It should be clear at this point that the Founding Fathers drew heavily on their Anglo-Christian background in developing their ideals toward government. They believed there is a nature to things; that "the natural law system can be best understood in terms of certain doctrines developed out of it. Underlying these doctrines was the belief that this is an orderly universe whose order is reasonable and can be understood by the application of reason. What makes it orderly is the underlying natural order. Undergirding this is the belief that there is a law for man and a law for things, that everything has its own nature embedded in it, that these things account for perceived regularities, and there is a remarkable harmony pervading all of Creation."[21]

Said Russell Kirk,

> "...to guide the sovereign; the chief of state; the legislator; the public prosecutor; the judge...there endures the natural law, which in essence is man's endeavor to maintain a moral order through the operation of a mundane system of justice...[But] natural law is more than a guide for statesmen and jurists. It is meant primarily for the governance of persons — for you and me, that we may restrain will and appetite in our ordinary walks of life. Natural law is not a harsh code that we thrust upon other people; rather, it is an ethical knowledge, innate perhaps, but made more clearly known to us through the operation of right reason."[22]

It is from these principles that the concepts of life, liberty and the right to property arise. Man has the right to come and go as he pleases, to use his abilities to the fullest possible extent, and to keep that which he produces with his own hands, his own tools, and his own mind (providing that he does not impugn the rights of others in the process). The right to property extends from this, and is the bedrock principal upon which free Republics are formed. It is for this very reason that our rapidly eroding private property rights are so alarming. A nation that is not free to use its land as it sees fit, is no longer a free nation.

This concept was brilliantly defined by Clarence Carson in *Basic American Government:*

> "Justice requires the continuation of real property in land as a right once it has been established. In the nature of things, all life — individual and social — depends upon being able to use land. Since no two bodies can occupy the same space at the same time, and no two persons can carry into effect the will to make contrary uses of any plot of land, some sort of distribution of land must be made. Justice requires that the person(s) having the best claim by tenure, through improvements made, by inheritance, or by purchase have title to particular plots of real property."[23]

Mark Anthony

Law of Man
What Our Government Has Become

Make no mistake, the linchpin of freedom is the right to own and improve property. This concept has deep roots in the Declaration of Independence, the Constitution, the Bill of Rights and the Ten Commandments. Pat Robertson, presidential candidate in 1988, placed this right in wonderful perspective,

> **"God's order recognizes the sanctity of private property. The eighth commandment, 'You shall not steal' means that the God of Jacob forbids a citizen to take what belongs to another citizen...What a man had accumulated was his. In God's order there are no schemes of wealth redistribution under which government forces productive citizens to give the fruit of their hard-earned labors to those who are nonproductive...**
> **When the framers of the U.S. Declaration of Independence spoke of the pursuit of happiness, they obviously had in mind the ability to work, to accumulate private material possessions, and to pay for the type of lifestyle such possessions made possible. Remember, though, our founders guaranteed the pursuit of happiness, not happiness itself. No government has the wealth or power to guarantee happiness...**
> **Every single utopian vision of world order requires a severe restriction on people's ownership of property and the enjoyment of its fruits. God's world order says that every man should be free to own private**

property free from the fear of theft by his fellow citizens or the confiscation by a greedy government."[24]

One does not have to look far to find egregious abuses of private property rights, illegal search and seizure and wanton redistribution of wealth. "Since 1985, federal, state and local governments have seized the property of over 200,000 Americans under asset forfeiture laws, often with no more evidence of wrongdoing than an unsubstantiated assertion made by an anonymous government informant...Privacy is vanishing beneath the rising floodtide of government power. Government officials have asserted a de facto right to search almost anybody, almost any time, on almost any pretext...The number of federally authorized wiretaps has almost quadrupled since 1980, and the Federal Bureau of Investigation is trying to prohibit the development of new types of phones that would be more difficult to wiretap...The law has become a tool with which to force people to behave in ways politicians approve, rather than a clear line that citizens can respect in order to live their lives in privacy and peace...residents in Chicago, Washington D.C., and other cities submit to de facto prohibitions on handgun ownership imposed by the same governments that grossly fail to protect citizens from private violence."[25]

The juxtaposition of what *was* (meaning, what should be), and what has *become,* is clearly illustrated by the following three quotes. The first two are by John Locke (1632-1704). Locke's *Second Treatise on Civil Government* is one of the finest works on natural law ever written and was enormously influential to the Founding Fathers. Historian Clarence Carson wrote, "Locke began his political theory by reasoning from a state of nature...By 'state of nature' thinkers generally meant that state in which man would be *without* government, whether such a state ever existed or not. The state of nature, Locke wrote, is a condition in which all men are in

> **'a state of perfect freedom to order their actions and dispose of their possessions and persons as they think fit, within the bounds of nature, without asking leave or depending upon the will of any other man.'"**[26]

Locke also said:

> "The great and chief end, therefore, of men uniting into commonwealths, and putting themselves under government, is the preservation of their property; to which in a state of nature there are many things wanting."[27]

And what has become...

In *Lost Rights, The Destruction of American Freedom,* James Bovard writes,

> "Politicians and the courts have created an overwhelming presumption in favor of the government's right to seize control over private land; seize possession of private homes, boats, and cars; and even seize the cash in people's wallets. While the dispute over property rights is often portrayed as merely an economic contest, the power of government officials to seize private property directly subjugates citizens to the capricious will of those officials.

Private property marks the boundary between the citizens and the State. The degree of respect the State shows for property rights will largely determine how much privacy, autonomy, and independence the citizen has."

What have we become? Is there no semblance of sanity? Are there any remaining vestiges of Natural Law? We have digressed to a criminal justice system that lets offenders go free after serving minute portions of their sentence; a judicial system that throws out cases on petty technicalities that somehow impugn the *"rights"* of the criminal — and who has the real criminal become? A 1992 Justice Department Newsletter reported, "Like children in a candy shop, the law enforcement community chose all manner and method of seizing and forfeiting property, gorging ourselves in an effort which soon came to resemble one designed to raise revenues."

Law enforcement officials now rely on a technicality that allows them to bypass the property owners' rights by suing the property itself. "Since the Bill of Rights recognizes the rights only of citizens and state governments, not the rights of chunks of land, or bottles of wine, there are almost no due process restrictions on government's attacks on property."[28] Now, one finds such pathetic lawsuits as *U.S. v. 667 Bottles of Wine*; or how about that landmark case: *U.S. v. One Ford Tractor, Mdl VC715V, Unit OH22B, Engine OH16A, its tools and appurtenances thereon; One Towner Offset Disc, Model A248, Serial Number 24C665, its tools and appurtenances thereon.* In the latter case, court documents note the owner of said equipment "did knowing take and aid and abet

95

the taking of an endangered species of wildlife, to wit, Tipton kangaroo rats."

The tractor inadvertently ran over five rats.

The equipment was seized by the U.S. Fish and Wildlife Service and the owner was threatened with a $300,000 fine. Have we digressed this far, that a man's rights are less important than those of a rat?

In 1990, the Justice Department's Executive Office for Asset Forfeiture, decreed, "It is the Department's position that *no advance notice or opportunity for an adversary hearing is statutorily or constitutionally required prior to the seizure of property, including real property.*"[29] Said Cary Copeland, the department's director, "Asset forfeiture is still in its relative infancy as a law enforcement program," and the FBI expects a 25 percent increase per year between 1992 and 1995.

The government has aggressively used environmental and zoning laws to prevent private citizens and businesses from using their property as they wish. In 1972 the Federal Water Pollution Control Act was passed. In it was an obscure act that prohibited "discharging dredged or fill materials into navigable waters without federal permits." In 1975 the Army Corps of Engineers expanded the definition of navigable waters to include "other U.S. waters." In 1977 it was redefined again to include "wetlands."

By 1987, "'navigable waters' had evolved into land that needed only to be 'occasionally wet.'"[30]An area could be considered a 'navigable water' if it contained the right kinds of plants and soil. *According to the current Corps of Engineers wetland delineation manual, visible water is no longer necessary.*"[31] This affirmation came from the Federal Manual for Identifying and Delineating Jurisdictional Wetlands, released by the EPA and the Army Corps of Engineers just after George Bush took office in 1989. Candidate Bush promised "all wetlands, no matter how small, should be preserved."

> "The new manual was written in secret; officials of several agencies met behind closed doors and effectively decided between themselves to claim jurisdiction over the property of hundreds of thousands of American landowners. This was in stark violation of the federal Administrative Procedures Act, which requires public notice and comment before a major federal regulation acquires the force of law.
>   Under the 1989 definition, land that was dry 350 days a year could be classified as a wetland...Fairness to Land Owners, a Maryland advocacy group, estimated that the new definition magically increased the amount of wetlands in the United States from roughly 100 million acres to up to 200 million acres. The vast majority of these new 'paper wetlands' were owned by private citizens. Robert J. Pierce, an Army Corps of Engineers official who helped to write the 1989 manual, later observed, 'Ecologically speaking, the term wetland has no meaning...For regulatory purposes, *a wetland is whatever we decide it is....* '"[32] (My emphasis)

"Any time the Army Corp or EPA think a parcel of land is beneficial to wildlife," said Justice Department attorney William Laffer, "they arbitrarily apply the wetlands definition to prohibit the owner from using the land."[33] As a result, "Many private property owners who make their living off the land, and have for generations, are being told that they can no longer engage in normal ranching or farming activities. They have lost the ability to use their land to support their families,"[34]noted Rep. Bill Brewster of Oklahoma. Most nauseating, the abuse of private property rights is a source of intense pride for many bureaucrats. "On November 25, 1991, William Reilly, chief administrator of the Environmental Protection Agency, held a press conference to brag that the EPA had 'once again had a record year for enforcement...Environmental crime is no less a crime than theft or blackmail or assault. And more assuredly, if you do the crime you'll do the time.' The federal government's war on violators of wetland regulations was part of Reilly's achievements — and an example of racking up a political body count of violators of unclear, contradictory, and constantly changing federal rulings."[35]

Liberal elitists have taken centralized government planning to the next degree. Private property rights, once the foundation of free societies, now come at a dear price; and can be taken away at the pernicious whim of the local zoning board.

Allow me to quote liberally some examples of property rights abuses, from one of the finest works on the subject: James Bovard's *Lost Rights, The Destruction of American Liberty.*

"A publication of the American Planning Association, an association consisting primarily of government officials, asserted, 'Under its zoning power, a local government has the authority to entirely prohibit all business enterprises from operating in residential districts...'"[36]

"A 1991 zoning ordinance allows the city of Camarillo, California, 'to abate any problem that diminishes property

98

values,' as the *Los Angeles Times* reported. Camarillo city manager William Little explained: 'It's broad enough to cover virtually anything. But we are very judicious in what we go up against.' Little's remark exemplifies *how zoning to protect property values gives government officials almost unlimited power to restrict the use of property — thereby defeating the whole notion of property rights.*"[37]

"The federal Advisory Commission on Regulatory Barriers to Affordable Housing (known as the Kemp Commission) reported in 1991 that zoning and other restrictions add up to 35 percent to the price of a new home. The National Association of Home Builders estimates that *government regulations knock over one million home buyers out of the market in the nation's twenty-five largest metropolitan areas...*"[38]

"Sylvia Lewis, editor of *Planning* magazine, observed in a 1991 article, 'You can think of planning as a giant Monopoly game — with the board representing all the land in town and the moves representing the rules of land-use law. But in real life, as opposed to the games, the rules are always changing.' Zoning rules are binding only on citizens, not on governments, who can make hundreds of thousands of exemptions, variances or revisions to their master plans each year. And because zoning officials in most states effectively have absolute immunity against lawsuits from property owners, there is little to restrain their creativity."

"The reigning principal of legislation in the former Soviet Union was, 'Everything is prohibited which is not specifically permitted.' The American Planning Association recommends a similar rule to subjugate American Citizens:

"As a matter of legislative drafting, it is good practice to include a general 'violations' section in zoning regulations that, in part, says, *'It shall be a violation of this ordinance to make any use of property not expressly permitted by this ordinance or a permit or other approval granted hereunder....'"* (My emphasis)

"As zoning expert Dick Cowden observed, 'Anyone who buys property and hopes to alter its use is considered, almost by definition, to be in violation of a land-use plan...'[39] Zoning forces average citizens to beg politicians and bureaucrats for permission to use their own property."[40]

Criminal Behavior: Nature Or Nurture?

Before the 1994 election Joseph Sobran wrote, "This election year, we're hearing lots of liberal scare-talk about the 'Christian right.' Do they move out of neighborhoods when conservative Christians move in?" This led me to reflect on one of the basic tenets of liberalism. That is: delinquent, abhorrent, anti-social, criminal behavior is caused by the inner city poverty experience.

So I ask you: "Is crime the cause or the consequence of poverty?" If one is to assume that crime is a consequence of one's surroundings rather than a product of a cognitive thought process, then one must also believe that all human behavior is based on nature rather than nurture. Conversely, this argument would mean that all children born to wealthy families lead lives of resplendent virtue and happiness. Of course, we know that is not the case.

Vanishing Republic

This is precisely why transferring wealth from rich to poor will never elevate the poor out of poverty if they stay mired in the same patterns of irresponsible behavior and dependency.

One of the main elements that differentiates humans from all other animals is that a great deal of animalistic behavior is instinctive. It is done by nature rather than nurture. An animal does not make a cognitive decision as to whether or not it will stalk its prey. It must, lest it starve. Similarly, humans nurse when they are infants. But I think it's safe to assume that most sixteen year olds do not awaken and cry for their mothers' breast.

So why do we treat abhorrent criminal behavior as the unconscious result of substandard living conditions?

The other element separating man from beast has been theorized by Professor Walter Williams: Animals do not have rights in the same sense as humans because animals do not have the ability to respect the private property rights of others (neither do liberals, but that's another matter). So am I guilty or insensitive if I call a vandal, or a thief, or a rapist an *animal?*

We cannot bring a semblance of law and order back to our society until we recognize that we as humans *make our own circumstances.* We are *not* slaves to our environment, meandering through life, tossed by the whim of some cosmic force. We are a product of the cognitive decisions that **_WE_** make on a daily basis. The greater good of society can no longer afford to apologize for those who have *chosen* to fail.

Since the 1960s, our judicial system has been virtually destroyed by three foundational principles of liberalism: a) that we must

101

focus on the "root causes" of crime, like poverty, racism, abuse and neglect, and lack of economic opportunity; b) that our focus must be on "rehabilitation" rather than punishment; and c) that we must always be cognizant of the *criminals' "rights."* The fallacy of each of these theories can be found in natural law. Any person of right reason can see that the root cause of crime is immorality dangerously mixed with a lack of personal responsibility and devoid of respect for private property rights.

As Benjamin Franklin declared:

"What can laws do, without morals."

The key factor that differentiates man from all other creatures is that a moral man has the ability to respect private property rights. An animal does not take into consideration private property rights before it defecates on your carpet or destroys your furniture. As for criminal "rights," it is patently offensive to presume that derelicts and criminals have the same rights as those who respect natural law and the private property rights of others. Under natural law, man has the right to life, liberty, property and the pursuit of happiness — under the express condition that man does not infringe upon those same rights of any other human being. If one violates that law, he or she does maintain certain rights: such as the fourth amendment right against unreasonable search and seizure; the fifth amendment right of due process of law; the right to a speedy and public trial; a trial by jury, and reasonable bail, as specified in the sixth, seventh and eighth amendments — but the criminal certainly does not retain the same rights as those of a law abiding citizen.

Of the issue of "rehabilitation," it should be clear by now that rehabilitation without swift and certain punishment is an exercise in futility. Such rehabilitation would not be necessary in societies that have the courage to adequately punish offenders. "In 1980, nine percent of arrested murderers were juveniles; but by 1990, this had burgeoned to 14 percent. Today, juvenile criminals account for about one-sixth of murders and rapes, and one-third of robberies, burglaries, and thefts."[41] In this regard, we are certainly more compassionate with our animals than we are with our criminals.

Allow me to explain. When you bring an animal into your home, and that animal is destructive, which would be more compassionate: to sternly and forcefully punish the animal once or twice, thus having the lesson quickly learned; or moderately punish indefinitely, lacking purpose of intent. To do the latter is not compassionate, as you have now condemned the animal to a life of continual punishment, as the pattern of behavior is never broken. If society wants to be truly compassionate to criminals, may I suggest swift, certain and strict punishment. "One detailed study, undertaken in Chicago, indicated that even modest confinement — less than a year — was enough to reduce serious juvenile offenders' later arrests by nearly 60 percent...The key to reducing later arrest was control. An intensely supervised, tightly restrained individual was less likely to return to crime even after the restraints were released; he had learned the price."[42] How many of us know first hand examples of parents who failed to discipline their

103

children under the perfidious guise of compassion, only to mutually share in lifelong regret?

Statistics bear this out. The following data are from Wayne LaPierre's *Guns, Crime and Freedom:*

> "In 1960, 738 people were in prison for every one thousand violent crimes. By 1980, after the apologists had had their way for two decades, the number had plunged to 227. Our criminal justice system was firmly in the grip of those who believed in the limitless possibilities of 'rehabilitation' and who opposed punishment. This collapse of the concept of punishment, specifically imprisonment, was accompanied by astonishing increases in crime. From 1960-1969 the violent crime rate in America increased by over 200 percent, in the decade following by over 225 percent. At the same time, of course, we were spending record levels in the 'war on poverty...'"[43]

> "During the decade of the 1980's, we started to climb out of this punishment trough. By 1992, 423 people were in prison for every one thousand violent crimes..."[44]

> "For the first time in two decades, crime rates actually began to fall. From 1980-1992, *the ten states that had the highest increase in their prison population relative total FBI index crime (including murder, rape, robbery, aggravated assault, burglary, theft, motor vehicle theft and arson) on average experienced a decline in the crime rates of more than 20 percent. The ten states with decreases or the smallest increases in their imprisonment rates averaged almost a 9 percent increase in their crime rates...* "[45]

> "Dr. Michael Block, professor of Economics and Law at the University of Arizona and a former member of the

United States Sentencing Commission, has shown that for every 10 percent increase in the certainty of punishment for those convicted of a violent crime, the violent crime rate can be expected to fall by 7 percent."

"If the number of violent criminals sent to prison were to increase by as few as nine thousand each year, almost 140,000 violent crimes would be prevented annually."[46]

One of man's most basic rights under natural law is the ability to protect himself and his family. Yet, gun control laws eliminate that right, and history shows that when man takes away such basic freedoms, there will always be a horrible price to pay. Wrote author Tom Clancy, "Criminals seek opportunity...If we take steps to allow them greater opportunity, that is, if we legislate the right to self-defense out of existence, we should assume that crime will increase."[47]

And so it has.

With the Sullivan law, New York has enacted one of the strictest gun-control policies in the nation; yet that city has one of the highest homicide rates: twenty-three per thousand. At the same time Switzerland, which requires by law that every adult male keep a fully-automatic firearm is his home, has one of the lowest, at only 1.1 per thousand.

"Switzerland...has a higher rate of firearms possession than the United States. It was the only European country that the Germans were afraid to invade in both world wars, knowing as they did that every man was armed. The armed Swiss have never been victimized by anybody...

"The Swiss have maintained their freedom for seven hundred years. Every Swiss male is required to keep this rifle and ammunition at home, to participate in group training, and to enter shooting matches.

"The citizen is not a soldier, because Switzerland has no standing army. Rather, the citizen is a member of the militia — the body of citizens trained to arms. At a certain age, the rifle is kept as private property. Swiss citizens are entitled to purchase and own all the firearms and ammunition they wish. Target shooting is the national sport, and the whole community participates in regular shooting festivals.

"In 1990, there were only thirty-four firearm-related homicides in Switzerland. Three times more persons were killed while mountain climbing. Murders tend to be committed by foreigners rather than Swiss."[48]

The underlying issue is not self-defense, it is trust.
A government that does not trust its citizens with firearms,
is indeed, itself not trustworthy.

In Federalist #46, James Madison wrote:

"Americans [have] the right and advantage of being armed — unlike citizens of other countries whose governments are afraid to trust the people with arms."

This point is critically important to the context of our discussion. In every *formally* free society which has succumbed to government aggression, the first two rights taken away are the right to private property and the right to keep and bear arms. At the Virginia convention to ratify the Constitution, Patrick Henry said:

"Guard with jealous attention the public liberty. Suspect every one who approaches that jewel. Unfortunately, nothing will preserve it but downright force. Whenever you give up that force, you are ruined."

Certainly, gun control is not about crime-prevention.

The elimination of one's right to self protection has led to a higher incidence of crime in every jurisdiction in which it has been tried. Crime is a moral issue, and a personal responsibility issue — the firearm is not a threat in and of itself. If one makes the irresponsible decision to drink and drive, it matters not whether that person gets behind the wheel of a Yugo or a Ferrari; someone will surely suffer. And when that person does hurt someone, we punish the driver, for he or she is the responsible party. Yet, when someone acts irresponsibly with a firearm, we punish the gun and every law abiding citizen who owns one.

In a piece about government's destruction of our Constitutionally granted freedoms and personal property rights, Professor Walter Williams wrote, "If they ever come to take Williams' guns, you'll know that Williams is dead."

I realize such rhetoric is cliché. The gun control nazis have a field day with anyone who disagrees with their utopian intent. They have somehow failed to realize that such rhetoric is not about gun ownership. *It is about the defense of our other vanishing Constitutional Rights.*

Dr. Williams' statement indicates the importance of our Second Amendment rights, *as it is the bulwark that stands guard against the erosion of the other nine.* How important is it? Let me phrase that another way. What is the *number* of the Amendment that addresses this right?

It should be noted that the Second Amendment does not simply state that law abiding citizens shall have the right to "keep and bear arms." The tone is much stronger than that. It says, "the right of the people to keep and bear arms

SHALL NOT BE INFRINGED."

That being understood, I take you back to the days that these legendary ruminations were born — fostered in the minds of men who sought to repel the further incursion of the *"Imperial Government"* that was the British Empire; a revolution begun in large part by an attempt to strip the colonists of their guns.

When the Bill of Rights was drafted, its intent was to limit the power the government would have over its people. Did Madison, et al., "brainstorm" — did they simply throw a bevy of Amendments into a hat to be randomly assembled into an unstructured mass?

No. They did not.

Did they choose to reference the Amendments by letter...*Amendment A, Amendment B* and so on.

No. They did not.

Rather, they put something before each Amendment...
a NUMBER...

And these numbers are used to delineate the order of importance. The order of importance was in accordance to the examples of oppressive governance that they observed throughout history. These enumerated rights are hierarchical — each succeeding right based on the framework clearly established by the preceding one.

And so you have the divine inspiration bestowed upon us by our forefathers — written in a time when true power was in the hands of the people, so that they may defend themselves from the incursions of omnipotent governance...whether it be the British Empire, or ours. Jeff Snyder wrote:

> "As the Founding Fathers knew well, a government that does not trust its honest, law-abiding taxpaying citizens with the means of self-defense is not itself worthy of trust. *Laws disarming honest citizens proclaim that the government is the master, not the servant of the people....*"[49] (My emphasis)

Is there any reason to trust so-called representatives of the people who endorse gun control? Over the years, they have written laws in violation of a Constitution they swore to uphold. They have given themselves control over virtually every aspect of our lives. They have fabricated a bureaucracy that daily tramples the Bill of Rights as if it is nothing more than the whimsy of a political "focus" group. Government has the ability to ruin lives and destroy businesses, yet it will not trust us with the ability to protect our loved ones.

For just as the First Amendment guarantees our freedom of speech, or to peaceably assemble, or to petition the Government for a redress of our grievances — So does the Second Amendment guarantee our right to keep and bear arms, should those rights ever be infringed.

Said Benjamin Franklin,

"They that can give up essential liberty to purchase a little temporary safety, deserve neither liberty nor safety."[50]

I'd like to end this chapter with two powerful quotes. Nothing so adequately illustrates the horrible consequences of a government disarming its people.

"**Before a standing army can rule, the people must be disarmed; as they are in almost every kingdom in Europe. The supreme power in America cannot enforce unjust laws by the sword because the whole body of people are armed and constitute a force superior to any band of regular troops that can be, on any pretense, raised in the United States.**"
— Noah Webster

"**This year will go down in history. For the first time, a civilized nation has full gun registration! Our streets will be safer, our police more efficient, and the world will follow our lead into the future!**"
— Adolph Hitler, 1935

Part II

Comprehending The National Debt And The Budget Deficit

"A democracy can last only as long and until a majority of the people discover that they can vote themselves largess (or large gifts) out of the public treasury and then they will continue to elect the politicians promising the most and the end result will be a fall of that democracy due to economic ruin and chaos."
— Lord Alfred Frazier Tyler,
British university professor,
over 200 years ago

Chapter 6
THE MYTH OF DEFICIT REDUCTION

Government never shrinks.
— Anonymous

"The budget before Congress contains $500 billion dollars in deficit reduction." How often have we heard that? We read George Bush's lips in 1990 and Bill Clinton's again in 1993.

Apparently, "$500 billion in deficit reduction" is a government euphemism for tax increase. It's become clear in recent years that there is no such thing as a "federal budget cut," or "deficit reduction," or whatever else your friendly congressman wants to call it. When our leaders use the term *"Budget Cut,"* that does not mean that they are going to spend less money on that particular program in the future. It means there will be *less of an increase.*

John Cogan, the Director of The Office of Management and Budget in 1988-89, was quoted as saying, "the Ways and Means and Finance committees deliberately legislate future spending increases they have no intention of granting, so that they can later reduce them and say they have 'cut the budget.'"

In order to fully appreciate the deception and disingenuousness of the federal budget tango, let's use a typical family budget as a metaphor — with one exception. We will be substituting *$1 billion dollars* for each dollar. Let us assume that you or your spouse have become unemployed. This may be due in part to the uncertainty your employer faces — how high corporate taxes are going to be raised...how much health care reform will cost...or, for

112

how many years the Clinton Administration decides to make taxes retroactive. Then again, it could be because your employer is a Subchapter S Corporation, and his five employee small business has magically elevated him to the status of "one of the rich who had a free ride in the 80's."

Now, he's forced to cut the payroll in order to make his "contribution."

You realize that having only one income, you are facing a *budget deficit,* and you will need to postpone some needed and worthwhile *investments.* You will simply have to make some "spending cuts."

You and your spouse have agreed that the first step you will take in your *deficit reduction package* is to eliminate your cable bill, which is $25 dollars — excuse me — $25 *billion* dollars per month. So, by eliminating the cable bill, we have cut our cable budget by $25 billion.

However, the federal government's budget does not work that way. When your congressman (that old "deficit hawk") uses the term budget cut, he does not mean reduce. He does not mean eliminate. He means *LESS OF AN INCREASE.*

Let us equate this twisted logic to our family budget example. Our current cable budget was $25 billion before we implemented our deficit reduction package. Next year, our cable budget calls for us to add H.B.O., Cinemax and Showtime, which will increase our budget 100% to $50 billion dollars. Your spouse shows the "courage to change" and introduces legislation that will cut Cinemax and Showtime, but will still add H.B.O. next year.

This will mean that next year's cable budget will **_increase_** $10 billion dollars to $35 billion. Yet, your spouse cheerfully informs you of the "courageous choice" to cut the deficit by $15 billion.

Welcome to the world of *Baseline Budgeting.* The subject has received considerable attention recently; but if you're not familiar with it, here's how it works. Instead of creating a budget from scratch each year, thus eliminating any unnecessary expenditures, or sunsetting outdated programs, Washington starts the budgeting process *using last year's budget as the foundation.* This is call the **"Current Services Baseline."**

The cable example we used is exactly how the Clinton Administration arrived at $496 billion in projected deficit reduction based on the 1993 budget. These projections are quite curious.

Their own numbers indicate that the Federal Deficit will increase by more than $900 billion between 1993 and 1997.

The bottom line is this: The Clinton Administration justified the largest tax increase in the history of the world by telling the American people that their economic plan would decrease the budget deficit by $500 billion over 5 years. It wasn't true when George Bush made the same claim in 1990, and unfortunately, it is not true now. These are rosy projections, and each year when Congress reworks the budget they hope that you'll forget about the cuts they promised you the year before.

I suppose we're going to do this every three years. I can't wait to see how they try to sell it in 1996.

Fool Me Once, Shame On You. Fool Me Twice, Shame On Me. Fool Me Five Times...

No, my friends, the noble task of raising taxes for the sake of deficit reduction is not a new idea. You see, the tax hike approach to deficit reduction has failed in 1981, 1982, 1984 and 1990. Washington logic mandates that we try it again. Those first four times must have been an economic fluke. We'll call it *"Keynesian Revenge."*

Editorialist Paul Craig Roberts noted that in 1981 David Stockman convinced President Reagan that "scaling back personal income tax rate reductions from 30 percent to 25 percent and delaying their implementation until the second half of his term would permit a balanced budget in 1984." The result was the deficit estimate for 1984 jumped from zero to $128 billion.

In 1982 the Tax Equity and Fiscal Responsibility Act (TEFRA) was designed to reduce the deficit to $59 billion by 1987 by taking back most of the previous year's tax reductions for business. The result was the 1984 estimate was raised to $229 billion. And within a short time the rosy projections of $59 billion in 1987 grew to a deficit estimate of $280 billion.

The Deficit Reduction Act of 1984 (DEFRA) took back even more of the tax cuts to business. The promised result — $100 billion in deficit reduction. Once again the tax hikes failed to reduce the deficit.[51]

I detect a pattern emerging.

I will *not* accept the assumption that some flawed data infiltrated the Reagan economic team's budget numbers, causing such erroneous projections. If this were the case, then why did it happen on three separate occasions?

They simply spent more than they had. As a conservative, I agree that it was vitally important to rebuild the military industrial complex which was summarily dismantled during the Carter Administration. But, this is still no excuse for a government to spend more than it takes in. The men and women of the Republican party have absolutely no right to deride the budget deficits of Democratic Administrations simply because *their* deficits are steered towards social programs.

Continual deficits are wrong. Period. Unless, and until we have bipartisan agreement on this issue, we are simply assessing percentages of blame.

I do not want to be in the position of explaining to my grandchildren why they are forced to finance budget deficits from a previous administration, be it Carter, Reagan, Bush or Clinton.

In 1990 George Bush signed legislation that was supposed to balance — *yes, balance* — the budget by 1995 and produce a $20 billion *surplus* in 1996. All the while, Congress, at the behest of Senate Majority leader George Mitchell, failed to pass along a capital gains tax cut. Instead, they rocked the American people with a $165 billion tax increase.

The following chart indicates the deficit projections given at the time.

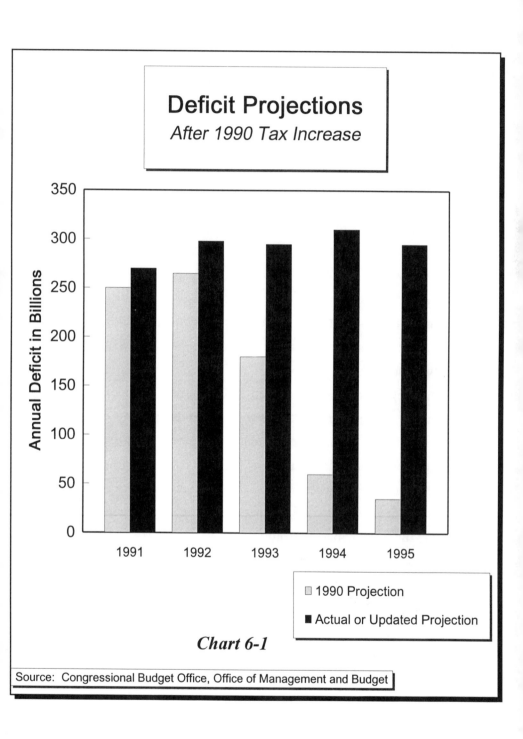

Deficit Projections
After 1990 Tax Increase

Annual Deficit in Billions

350 — 300 — 250 — 200 — 150 — 100 — 50 — 0

1991   1992   1993   1994   1995

□ 1990 Projection

■ Actual or Updated Projection

Chart 6-1

Source: Congressional Budget Office, Office of Management and Budget

Mark Anthony

In 1993 Bill Clinton got his wish and saddled the American people with a *$612 billion tax increase, the largest in world history,* under the guise of deficit reduction. And what will be the impact? Notes Mr. Roberts, "The plan *says* it will add **$916 billion** to the national debt over the next four years — and that's if everything works as advertised." (Meaning, interest rates remain low.)

If we have any *more* deficit reduction, we'll be broke.

Over the last fifteen years, our government has had ample opportunity to show some budgetary restraint. The Grace Commission began its work examining government waste in January of 1982 at the behest of President Reagan. The Commission was composed of leaders of industry such as the chairman and CEO's of Coca-Cola, Motorola and Merck, among others. The Commission exposed 2,478 specific areas of waste or mismanagement offering suggested improvements to President Reagan in 1984. Their proposals were given insultingly little attention; not by the President, not by his economic advisors, nor by the Congressional leaders of the Democratic or Republican parties. The majority of the Commission's suggestions were nothing more than basic common sense. For example: at the time, the federal government had 322 incompatible accounting systems. How formidable is it to recognize such inherent idiocy?

I have little faith in the government's sincerity to enact any significant deficit reduction, if they do not have the ability to accurately count what they have — what *you* have paid for. The conclusion to be drawn is that this is patently done on purpose.

If you ask any businessperson what his or her overhead is, you will get an itemized list. You ask the government that question, and they say "I dunno."

In order to grasp the scope of America's fiscal woes, realize that these are only *annual* deficits. Our political leaders have taken to patting themselves on the back if they cut a few billion dollars here or there. This is akin to fixing a small leak in the ceiling when the entire roof is about to cave in. We'll discuss the national debt a little later, but first let's take a look at some of the contributing factors to the debt.

Chapter 7
The Sources Of The Debt
Entitlement Spending

"In order for a single mother to get her welfare 'paycheck' she must meet two conditions: 1) she must not work; 2) she must not marry an employed male."
— Robert Rector,
The Heritage Foundation, 1993

"We tried to provide more for the poor and produced more poor instead. We tried to remove the barriers to escape poverty, and inadvertently built a trap."
— Charles Murray, *Losing Ground*

"Why be thrifty any longer when your old age and health care are provided for, no matter how profligate you may be in your youth? Why be prudent when the state insures your bank deposits, replaces your flooded-out house, buys all the wheat you can grow? Why be diligent when half your earnings are taken from you and given to the idle?"
— David Frum, *Dead Right*

Over thirty years ago, President Lyndon B. Johnson pledged to attack poverty "in all its forms" and "drive it underground." As a liberal, he could not have been expected to know the folly of his statement — that with his vow, he ensured the overwhelming proliferation of that which he sought to destroy. For it has been proven time and again that you subsidize things that you *want* to occur — and thus was born what are now known as "entitlements."

Vanishing Republic

Five trillion dollars later, and welfare still hasn't been "driven underground" — *only now* it consumes 5 percent of America's gross national product instead of 1.5 percent. *Only now,* the illegitimacy rate in the black community is 68 percent — up from less than two percent in the 1950's. *Only now,* the illegitimacy rate among whites is 22 percent, up from three percent in 1963. *Only now,* entitlements consume 50% of the entire federal budget.

> *Quite simply, the American Government*
> *has become nothing more than a drug dealer —*
> *and the dependent masses, its junkies.*

What are the fruits of such misguided compassion. *The Wall Street Journal* noted "more than 10% of this nation's people are on food stamps and nearly half of its babies are born on Medicaid. The New York Post recently found 1 in 7 New Yorkers to be on the dole in some fashion, and in Los Angeles County the number may be 1 in 5."

Said Paul Harvey, "The poverty industry is now our nation's biggest business...giving to poor people $184 billion a year."

And still, to this day, liberals fail to see the futility of their actions. Congressman Louis Stokes (D-Ohio) said, "If you want to get rid of welfare in America, create jobs."

Just like that.

Apparently, in Washington, D.C., one need only think "happy thoughts."

As charts 7-1 and 7-2 show, the growth of entitlement spending foreshadows ominous fiscal problems. In 1995 entitlement spending will rise to $795 billion. That same year, net interest payments are projected to be $244 billion, as the majority of the spending is debt financed. At the same time, discretionary spending — the amount left over for other government programs — has shrunk from 65.6% of the budget in 1962 to 34.1% in 1995.

Medicare and Medicaid alone consumed almost a *quarter trillion* dollars in 1992. A government spokesman told author Martin Gross that "the Health Care Financing Administration — Medicare and Medicaid — pay about 40% of the entire cost of running a typical hospital."

It has been proven innumerable times that the government is not able to efficiently administer such grand social plans. Between 1991 and 1993 Medicare spending rose 23%. Yet, the number of beneficiaries increased by only four percent. The amount of resources lost to fraud and abuse is estimated at between *$20 billion and $40 billion a year.* I believe these numbers to be frighteningly optimistic.

Even more fiscally apocalyptic — relevant to any discussion of huge new entitlement programs like health care reform — is the difference between the original projections and the actual cost for these programs.

Entitlement Spending
1962

Entitlement Spending
1995

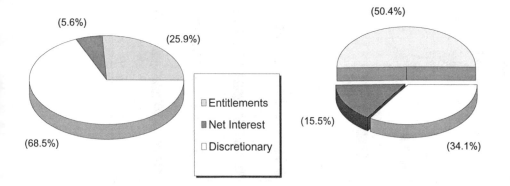

(5.6%)

(25.9%)

(68.5%)

- ☐ Entitlements
- ■ Net Interest
- ☐ Discretionary

(50.4%)

(15.5%)

(34.1%)

Chart 7-1

Source: Congressional Budget Office

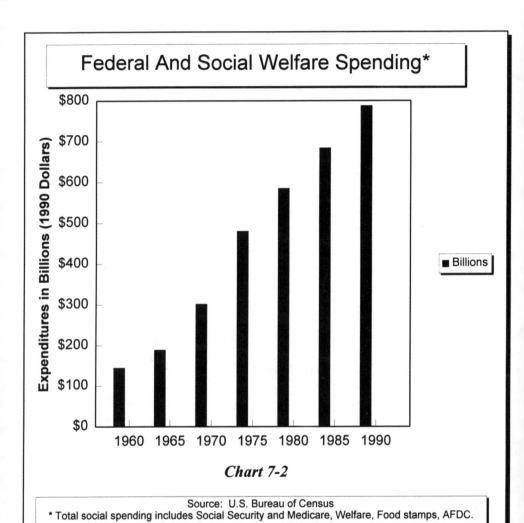

Federal And Social Welfare Spending*

Expenditures in Billions (1990 Dollars)

■ Billions

Chart 7-2

Source: U.S. Bureau of Census
* Total social spending includes Social Security and Medicare, Welfare, Food stamps, AFDC.

The AFDC Travesty

When a newborn child bounds helplessly into the world; wet and cold, and no doubt frightened — if he knows such emotions — he is greeted with a warm, gentle, soothing hand. The hand lovingly cleans him until his face shines bright red cheeks. The hand wraps him in soft clothes. The hand caresses his beautiful head, soothing his fears.

The hand belongs to Uncle Sam, for Medicaid now pays for nearly half of this country's births.

California Congressman Henry Waxman, and numerous other congressional "Poverty Pimps," have massaged and stroked, molded and formed a Medicaid law that provides prenatal, obstetric and one year's follow-up services to more than 40% of America's pregnant mothers. "The child," notes *The Wall Street Journal*, "immediately becomes a Medicaid beneficiary."

The Aid to Families with Dependent Children (AFDC) program disbursed $19 billion to 3.75 million families in 1988. It has grown to include 14 million people in 4.97 million families at a taxpayer cost of $25.8 billion in 1993.

How can this be? Can it be possible that well over 40% of America is below the poverty line? Of course not. But, Uncle Sam, er, the American Tax Payor, has deep pockets. Regardless, is it necessary to lavish such misplaced compassion on those who do not need such financial assistance?

Liberalism derives its empowerment by ensnaring the poor in its web of dependency, and thus, the only way to further increase its power base is to intermingle the welfare state with the middle class. Affirmed Thomas Sowell, "power is what liberalism is all about and 'compassion' is just one of the words used to get that power."

Oh, this all began innocently enough. Reducing the percentage of "low birth rate and problem births was good economic as well as social policy," Congress said. And thus, new avenues of entitlement were opened. Households making 133% of the national poverty line are eligible. In South Carolina, for example, the bar rises to 185% — nearly twice the level of poverty — resulting in 49% of all births being covered under Medicaid.

The problem is further enhanced as eligibility is "based on the month prior to application," which makes cyclical economies like logging, farming and mining susceptible to a deluge of government paid births during the down season. North Dakota's Medicaid birth rate is 43%. Idaho is at 42% — and, surprise, surprise — this is up from 6.7% in 1987. This compassionate system spawns 1.2 million illegitimate births every year.

As usual, the slings and arrows of liberalism take their toll on capitalism and personal responsibility in slow and well intentioned steps. The ubiquitous caring and compassion is soon replaced with governmental bureaucracy — at the expense of personal property rights, free-market forces and self-reliance. Liberals take this slow, deliberate action completely by design — for they know all too well that if they are to jam socialism down the American public's throat, they will surely choke on it. But if they cut it up into small pieces and compassionately hand feed it, America will swallow it whole.

Destroying The Family...
Declaring War On The Black Father

*"The first priority of any serious program against
poverty is to strengthen the male role in poor families."*
— George Gilder

If we wish to understand why America has a welfare crisis, and a crime crisis, and an illegitimacy crises, it is necessary to work backwards to unearth the problem. We have developed a welfare system that rewards complacency and dependence; and so we have a welfare crisis. We have built our judicial system around the needs and rights of criminals, instead of the law abiding society; and so we have criminal activity run rampant. We have rewarded continued illegitimacy; and so we are awash in unmarried mothers.

Imperial Government, as an abhoration of natural law, does not understand the human spirit. The human spirit does not crave a handout; it thirsts for an opportunity. Yet, we have crafted a welfare program that is the joke of the civilized world and an insult to all that for which America stands.

At the root of the welfare tree is Aid to Families with Dependent Children. From this misguided attempt at compassion do the chains of subservience grow. How does one qualify for this *Great Society* program? Simply be irresponsible enough to have a child out of wedlock, and the floodgates of government benevolence open. Everything from medical care to Food Stamps to supplemental food from the Women, Infants and Children (WIC) program, to legal assistance, subsidized housing, subsidized electricity and job training, Pell grants for education and Head Start for children.

AFDC beneficiaries receive a monthly cash payment of $500 on average, plus Medical care through Medicaid, federal housing through HUD (Housing and Urban Development) or Section 8 vouchers that can be used to obtain private housing up to $1200 per month. Food Stamps are administered through the Department of Agriculture, subsidized electricity via the Department of Energy, and job training by the Department of Labor.

The degree of overlap and duplication is daunting. In all, there are seventy-eight federal welfare programs administered by the various agencies. The Census Bureau defines "poverty" as a family of four that earns less than $14,700. However, many programs allow beneficiaries a much higher income. For example, the Weatherization Assistance Program administered by the Department of Energy offers families with incomes under $18,000 per year a benefit of around $2,000 to insulate their homes, while the Low Income Home Energy Assistance Program (LIHEAP) allows a family income of up to $22,000 per year. The Women, Infants and Children program offers food baskets (over and above Food Stamps) to families with incomes up to $27,000.

We used to celebrate the nuclear family. Now we celebrate illegitimacy through reward. If a woman has a child out of wedlock, she will receive her benefits. In all states but New Jersey, she will receive additional benefits if she has more children.

How does she lose her benefits? By marrying a gainfully employed male (earning more than $10,400 per year).

What demonic, twisted sociologist came up with this scheme?

Vanishing Republic

The Office of Economic Opportunity in Washington found a direct correlation between increased welfare benefits and decreased employment incentives in even the *smallest* increments. They were able to statistically show the decline in employment with each additional dollar spent.

The University of Wisconsin found that an increase in welfare benefits of $200 per month caused illegitimate births to skyrocket by 150 percent!

Is this how we define compassion — by incentivizing illegitimacy?

Is it surprising that 90 percent of the five million families receiving AFDC benefits are headed by unmarried mothers? Or that researchers at the Kennedy School of Government found that the average stay on the public dole is 12 years — with 20 percent staying on more than *fifteen* years?

And what legacy have we wrought?

The Children of AFDC families have an illegitimacy rate 300 percent higher than normal, continuing the cycle of misery and dependency. If they do marry, they have a 92 percent higher divorce rate. They are two to three times as likely to use drugs, engage in criminal activity and commit suicide.

The federal government is not only forcing the taxpayers to foot the welfare bill, but also forcing them to contribute to the demise of their fellow citizens. This is both destructive and immoral. Government has told the black male that he is no longer needed. He is free to procreate as he pleases with no responsibility.

Mark Anthony

In *A Call For Revolution*, best-selling author Martin L. Gross notes:

> "The Census Bureau has classified 35 million persons as 'poor.' They exist in 70 percent of the households that receive help. An educated guess is that there are 23 million people — about 9 percent of the nation — somewhat dependent on welfare.
> By dividing those 23 million into the $318 billion, [spent annually] we get $14,500 as the cost of the average welfare client. That comes to $58,000 a year for a family of four! It's 80 percent higher than the average working family's income of $36,000, which generally comes from two wage earners."

But, it's extremely important to understand that subsidizing an activity can encompass many forms other than simple monetary support. Subsidy can occur in the form of the relaxation of normally acceptable societal standards. If society removes the stigma of illegitimacy, it has subsidized the behavior for the sake of "tolerance." If society removes the stigma of alternative sexual preferences, it has likewise subsidized the activity by normalizing the behavior. As Senator Moynihan accurately stated, "We have defined deviancy down," and therefore society has come to accept that which was previously unacceptable.

And so you have the blueprint how liberal government establishments nurture a growing dependency class, paralleled by rampant societal decay.
1. The government subsidizes the activity that it wants to occur.

2. It accelerates the objectionable activity by normalizing it via a willing media, dominated by those sympathetic to its goals.
3. It entrenches the activity by removing the social stigma normally attached to the activity.

Is it any wonder that we now have more crime, more poverty, more homelessness and more illegitimacy than before we embarked on the *"War on Poverty?"*

You can fill in the blanks with anything you want...crime, illegitimacy, abortion, the breakdown of the family, moral decay. Unfortunately, for you and me, this simple three-step recipe works every time it is tried.

Incentives That Enslave

"Since 1960, births to unmarried teenagers have increased 200 percent. On average, today's sexually active 18 year-old girl has already had as many partners as a woman in her 40's."
— Columnist Don Feder

"During the Bush years, the federal government earmarked a paltry $7 million for a program called Adolescent Family Life (AFL). It was the only program funded by the federal government that taught abstinence and mentioned the option of adoption for unintended babies. The Clinton administration has proposed to eliminate it."
— Columnist Mona Charen

Mark Anthony

The foremost example of the deadly combination that exists between relaxed societal mores and government subsidy is illegitimacy. Charles Murray, fellow at the American Enterprise Institute, wrote: "illegitimacy is the single most important social problem of our time — more important than crime, drugs, poverty, illiteracy, welfare or homelessness because it drives everything else." Illegitimacy accounts for nearly "30% of all live births."

Just prior to World War II, 19% of all black births were illegitimate. That figure now stands at 68%. The number for white children is 22% and climbing rapidly. Former Secretary of Education, William Bennett, agrees: "Most proposals now on the table miss the essential point of welfare reform — not to ensure tougher work provisions and job training but to go after, root and branch, a system that fosters illegitimacy and its attendant social pathologies."

Both men are correct in agreeing that economic support should be cut off for single mothers who continue to bear children. Interestingly, Mr. Bennett quoted President Clinton, who said, "He (Murray) did the country a great service. I mean, he and I have often disagreed, but I think his analysis is essentially right...There's no question that (ending welfare for single mothers) would work. The question is...is it morally right?"

Mr. Clinton later contradicted that statement at the introduction of his welfare reform proposal in Kansas City, Missouri, in June of 1994. Reporter Ron Suskind of *The Wall Street Journal* wrote, "This trend, especially concerning teen pregnancies 'will not be turned around overnight,' he (President Clinton) said, *'but be sure of this: No government edict will do it.'*"

Are you kidding me? *It's government edict that caused it!*

As usual, liberal folly is not open to debate — the Clinton welfare reform proposal was lacking one notable provision. They refused to employ a "family cap" that would remove increased government subsidies for welfare beneficiaries who bear additional children.

Conversely, would you care for an example of a Clinton administration "edict" that promotes out-of-wedlock births? James Bovard noted, "an unmarried couple, each with two children and $11,000 in income, would lose $5,686 in Earned Income Tax Credit benefits by marrying, according to Tax Notes Magazine. So much for a pro-family policy."

"Making illegitimacy more inconvenient, what economists would call raising its opportunity cost, is the key to reducing out-of-wedlock-births."
— Douglas Besharov, of
the American Enterprise Institute

If we are to ever solve America's welfare problem, we *cannot* continue to measure compassion in the amount of money that the federal government *gives* to people. We must measure compassion as the end result of our policies. If the aim of welfare programs is to elevate the poor into a state of prosperity, then the program is a failure by any means. And if it *is* a failure, why does Congress call it an "entitlement" and therefore untouchable during budget debate?

They do so because entitlements are *not* about compassion, or about rehabilitating the poor.

> *For decades liberals have purchased the minority vote via the welfare system. They have addicted generations of families to squalor and indignity — and they refuse to cut back the programs because they will be forced to give back some of that vote.*

I ask you: How did Americans cope with life before FDR and "two chickens in every pot," or Lyndon Johnson's "attack on poverty in all its forms?" Simple. Americans did what they had to do, in order to get by. They worked a second job. They saved their money. They enlisted the help of family, friends and their church. You see, when you're flying without a net, you put forth the extra effort that is necessary because there is no federal assistance to catch you when you fall.

Unfortunately, liberals panic when they are confronted with talk of personal responsibility. Their solution is to increase spending, and expand social welfare programs. "If we still have poverty, then we are not doing enough," they say. But, poverty is not a symptom of a lack of jobs or economic activity; it is precisely a symptom of social spending. The evidence is irrefutable.

> *For every increase of one percentage point in social spending as a percentage of Gross Domestic Product, there is a corresponding half percent increase in unemployment.*

Vanishing Republic

Let me return for a moment to President Clinton's question: "Is it morally right (to terminate welfare programs)?" Conversely, is it morally right to take away from achievers in order to redistribute the fruits of their labor to those who produce little or nothing? Biblically speaking, no it is not. Societal values prior to The New Deal and The Great Society held the belief that achievement is to be rewarded, for that is the only means to stimulate the underachievers to elevate *themselves.*

We, as a society, must return to these values; but it is imperative that government stop undermining our efforts. Said William Bennett, "social science evidence is in: illegitimacy is the surest road to poverty and social decay. And welfare subsidizes and sustains illegitimacy." A *Wall Street Journal/NBC* poll taken in June of 1994 indicated an overwhelming consensus in agreement with Mr. Bennett. Seventy percent "think that babies-for-benefits is a major or moderate reason why people are on welfare."

Unfortunately, Health and Human Services Secretary, Donna Shalala, disputes the contention that welfare mothers intentionally bear additional children in order to increase Uncle Sam's subsidy. What other reason *could* there be? Are we to believe that poor unwed mothers continue to become pregnant because they *enjoy* the experience of poverty-stricken, single parenthood? Of course not. They continue to bear children because the government subsidizes their procreation.

The time to act is long overdue. The black community has already been devastated by illegitimacy and crime fueled by welfare programs; and the white community is on the verge of the precipice. Remembering that the white illegitimacy rate is 22%,

135

Charles Murray makes a critical point: "The historical fact is that the trendlines on black crime, dropout from the labor force, and illegitimacy all shifted sharply upward as the overall black illegitimacy rate passed 25%."

A Federal Fix — And Uncle Sam's Buying

"Senator William Cohen, a key proponent of reforming SSI and the related Social Security Disability Insurance program, notes that taxpayers send $160,000 a year in checks to a Denver bartender who uses the money to run a tab for 40 friendly alcoholics."
— Columnist Tony Snow

The Supplemental Security Income (SSI) program certainly knows how to throw a party. This well intentioned progeny of New Deal thinking was intended to help the "aged, blind and disabled" when it was conceived in the early 1970's. It was intended to supplement the income of those hard working Americans who had given their bodies to a lifetime of hard labor, who — no longer able to perform — were forced to retire at an earlier age than say, a person who pushed a pencil all his life.

SSI and SSDI are perfect examples of how government entitlements are designed to feed on themselves by forcing a growing number of beneficiaries into patterns of dependency. As with all entitlements, these programs were seemingly innocuous at their inception. But this illustrates why government welfare programs must be debated upon principle, not compassion.

Liberals use the rhetoric of compassion in order to sneak the proverbial "camel's nose under the tent," as their willing accomplices in the media label detractors as "mean spirited," incompassionate, bigots.

And thus, a new entitlement is born.

In time, liberals are not content with the seductive intoxicant of free government money. They summarily recruit new "welfare junkies" by forcing them into the cesspool of public assistance.

There are frightening data to support my contention. A full 30% of all working Americans between the ages of 60 and 64 are categorized as being "incapable of gainful employment." A *Wall Street Journal* editorial quoted a draft paper written by federal retirement analyst Robert Ipolito. Ipolito wrote, "[Social Security Disability] creates an incentive to quit the work force too early. Unlike those who work until age 65, workers who qualify for disability retirement receive their unreduced Social Security annuities at much earlier ages. And they get a free medical policy (Medicare) after two years on the program."

Now, you can add to the list of disabled 250,000 people who collected $1.4 billion in SSI benefits in 1993 simply because they are alcoholics or junkies. Congress no doubt offered this appropriation in order to facilitate payment to drug treatment centers to assist in the addict's rehabilitation.

Think again.

A General Accounting Office study found that 172,000 of these addicts were not receiving treatment. I find the statistic appallingly low in that there is no reasonable framework in place that could possibly monitor rehabilitation compliance. Congress, in its infinite wisdom, *did* install one "safeguard": they will not pay the check directly to the addict, it must be made to a "payee." But, the "payee" can be anyone from a relative, to a fellow junkie, to Joe the bartender, to the guy who runs the local check cashing establishment (outside of which the "disabled" person's dealer has conveniently set up shop).

Further compounding the problem is it can take up to a year to process an addict's application for SSI disability payments. Once approved, the checks are made retroactive, meaning that $4,000 to $6,000, and sometimes up to $15,000, has summarily been dropped into the hands of a newly recovering — or in most cases still using — alcoholic or drug addict. That, my friends, is the federal government's interpretation of compassion. Said Bob Cote, director of a Denver homeless shelter, Washington is "helping people commit suicide on the installment plan."

You subsidize things that you want to occur.

This is *not* compassion. That's the most important point. I have found that analogies based on a typical family show most clearly the insanity of welfare programs, so let's return to the family metaphor. The federal government has, since LBJ's Great Society, played the role of parent (or "Big Brother," if Orwellian prophecies are your cup of tea). And if the Great Society is the parent, then FDR's New Deal is certainly the grandparent. You see, this particular school of parenting is thus: A wealthy man (Congress) sends his prodigal sons (the unfortunate lower middle class and the poor) to an exclusive school (Constitutional Government University) which has the world's best Capitalism Department.

There's just one little snag — they don't want to go to class or study, or otherwise pull their weight in order to earn their degree like the other students.

The more productive students pay their own tuition. *Yet, they're assessed an inexplicable fee (federal, state and local taxes) over and above that which is necessary to pay* their *tuition cost.* While these students are busy studying, the delinquent students goof off. Their study habits are bad, you see. So, being a compassionate — and deep pocketed — parent, (the government) decides that the children will make it if only they are provided some additional assistance.

Obviously, the poor students' problem is not a matter of responsibility. Rather, the parent (Uncle Sam) has come to the conclusion that their "children" need a helping hand (entitlements).

So, Uncle Sam shows compassion the only way he knows. He takes the extra tuition (taxes) that is levied against the productive students, and gives the delinquent students the funds to purchase the services of any tutor (social worker) they choose.

Unfortunately, Uncle Sam demands absolutely no accountability. The children, who have already proven that they are *irresponsible,* have been given the *responsibility* to spend the subsidy in the manner in which it was intended.

So, they take the money and continue to goof off. The children, not being stupid, realize that if they use the subsidy in order to work with a tutor (social worker), the resultant rise in their grades will signal the termination of their subsidy (welfare checks).

Regardless of the outcome, you (the government) have concluded that you are a more compassionate and loving parent than those who demand hard work from their children. (Those parents demand more from their children because the moral code that they have instilled in them will simply produce nothing less.)

You feel that you must continually show your compassion by annually increasing the ill-advised subsidy (transfer payments).

So now, *you ask the responsible citizens, er, students, to pay even more of a premium on their tuition than they already have.*

Food Stamps...For Food (and drugs, and alcohol, and prostitution and...)

"Show me a government handout, and I'll show you something that encourages irresponsibility."
— Bob Cote, director of a Denver homeless shelter

"Food stamps have become a second currency used to pay for drugs, prostitution, weapons, cars — even a house. Says Cathy E. Krinick, a Virginia deputy commonwealth attorney, 'Food stamps are more profitable than money.'"
— Daniel R. Levine

The food-stamp program consumes $24 billion of taxpayer money annually, a sum exceeded only by Medicaid in the welfare hierarchy. The program has swelled to its current level from a modest $173 million in 1968. Now, more than eleven times that amount — two billion dollars (more than eight percent of the entire food-stamp budget) — is lost to waste, fraud and abuse; making it one of the most widely misapplied of all Great Society giveaways.

The idea behind the food stamp program is to provide enough monetary assistance so that the recipients would be able to purchase a quantity of food which is in accordance with the government's basic daily nutrition requirements.

But guess what? The beneficiaries receive that 100% — *plus three percent.* This additional three per cent is given at a taxpayer expense of $850 million per year, which itself is five times the $173 million total allotment in 1968, the year of the program's inception. In a typical food-stamp scam, a junkie will buy drugs from a dealer at fifty cents on the dollar. The dealer will then mark the stamps up to, say, seventy-five cents on the dollar and sell them to an authorized merchant. The merchant will then redeem them at face value.

Unfortunately, the federal government has made food stamps very easy to obtain but has not established a framework to adequately monitor abuse. The Food and Nutrition Service (FNS), a branch of the United States Department of Agriculture, has only 175 men and women assigned to overlook the practices of 213,000 authorized dealers. Of these, Mr. Levine points out, "3200 are expected to be illegally exchanging stamps for cash...A USDA audit in 1992 found that there were 'no effective procedures' to prevent disqualified retailers from continuing to accept and cash food stamps."

Mark Anthony

Run For The Border

*"For its fiscal year 1994-95, California estimates
public costs for illegal immigrants at $2.5 billion...
Once born, the children of illegals are automatically
U.S. citizens, entitled to the full range of social
benefit programs."*
— Randy Fitzgerald

Applying the above logic, if someone entered your home illegally, rather than expelling the transgressors or summoning the police to aid in doing so, you would have to provide them with three hot meals per day, food, shelter and educational expenses.

Absurd, isn't it! Is this analogy any different from current immigration mandates? Estimates suggest that over 300,000 illegal aliens arrive in the United States each year.

In Los Angeles County public hospitals, two-thirds of the births are to illegal aliens. Said Randy Fitzgerald, "nearly one-quarter of those receiving Aid to Families with Dependent Children (AFDC) in the county are children of illegals or of former illegals now under amnesty." This is not only an abomination to all American taxpayers, but also an affront to hard working, law abiding, *legal* immigrants. AFDC benefits alone will reach the one billion dollar mark in Los Angeles County by the turn of the century.

And it will certainly get worse.

Congress continues to make senseless laws and then mandates the funding to states in clear violation of the Tenth Amendment. In 1986, by virtue of the Omnibus Budget Reconciliation Act, illegal aliens must be provided free emergency medical services. A young

142

woman may conceive a child in Mexico, then just before the delivery she can slip across the border to give birth to an *American* child. The child is immediately eligible for AFDC, and his mother will receive all the commensurate benefits, food stamps, housing, et al.

What the Immigration and Naturalization Service refers to as *Chain Immigration*, causes the problem to increase exponentially. Once the American child reaches age twenty-one he may apply for permanent residency status for his parents and siblings. As the parents and siblings become citizens *they* may "sponsor" other family members, who in turn sponsor still more family members...

The Supreme Court has upheld such inanity. In 1982, the court ruled that public education cannot be denied to children even if they are living in the country illegally.

Lest you think this problem is unique to border states like California, Florida and Texas, be advised that the states pay only half the Medicaid fees, the rest is picked up by you and me. The overall costs are staggering. Estimates of illegal immigration range between one and three million per year, with legal immigration approaching the one million mark. A June 1993 Rice University study estimated the *direct* cost of illegal immigration at $7.75 billion in 1992. The total annual cost — when one factors in welfare, job training, unemployment benefits and the estimated 900,000 jobs taken away from legitimate American citizens — was a whopping $14.7 billion in 1993, with growth estimates as high as $180 billion annually by the end of the decade.

It goes without saying that those who would illegally enter a foreign country in order to take advantage of the public dole, are obviously not of high moral character. It should surprise no one that 450,000 illegal aliens are behind bars, or that they represent a full 25 percent of the entire federal prison population.

Did You Know You Were Once Homeless?

"The term 'homelessness' must not be allowed to mask what is really going on: a proposal for a major expansion of federal housing assistance."
— Howard Husock, director of case studies at
Harvard's Kennedy School of Government

"Housing Secretary Henry Cisneros unveiled a $30 billion plan today that he said would revamp the nation's public housing projects."
— Associated Press, April 20, 1994

Mr. Husock cites a draft report called, *"Priority: Home! The Federal Plan to End Homelessness,"* which calls for $15 billion in funding annually for homeless programs. The liberal fix employs its customary bedrock principal: "If throwing federal money at the problem hasn't worked yet, we simply need to throw *more* money."

The most accurate estimates suggest that there are about 600,000 homeless Americans. Yet homeless advocates routinely place that figure closer to *seven million!* The key to increased federal funding is to magnify the problem by employing questionable data.

When I first moved to Central Florida, I stayed with my brother and his wife for a short time while I looked for other housing. In homeless advocacy parlance: I was homeless. Similarly, a single parent living with a relative would earn homeless classification. In addition, says Mr. Husock, "someone without sufficient savings to pay several months' rent if he were to lose his job, can be classified as being in danger of becoming homeless." That same person is also in danger of being hit by a dump truck while he crosses the street, but we don't count him as a motor vehicle fatality before the fact. It's ludicrous for the government to attempt to ward off the hands of fate, via increased subsidies.

I am not implying that there are not those who are mentally ill and *should* be directed by society into a qualified treatment facility.

But, homeless activists refuse to believe that the majority of homeless people are homeless because they have *chosen* to drop out of society. It has been shown time and again that many homeless people make their way through the welfare system, yet regardless of how much assistance they receive, they return to the streets.

Recycling Welfare

"But we have to make a beginning. We can't let millions continue in a cycle of dependency."
— President Clinton, in a speech unveiling his welfare reform plan

Mark Anthony

"The main problem with U.S. welfare is that benefit levels are so high that people can only with difficulty be induced to leave the rolls...Families with incomes up to about $23,000 a year become eligible for welfare."
> — Tom Bethell, Washington correspondent for
> *The American Spectator*,
> quoting Robert Carleson, former
> U.S. commissioner of welfare

Just as in 1988, both sides of the aisle are equally responsible for their excursions in welfare reform yielding the exact *opposite* of its intended effect.

Prior to the 1994 election, Republicans have historically sought a consensus on welfare reform; ostensibly in order to avoid the perception of being obstructionist. I heartily disagree with that practice. Right is right and wrong is wrong. The Republican party must have the courage to say "No" to the expansion of the welfare state, and the conviction that the American people are intelligent enough to understand why they did it.

In the bipartisan 1988 bill, the few welfare recipients who do find work are entitled to remain on Medicaid for an additional year. I find it ironic that a federal government that aims its legislative power at fostering "fairness" would implement a system that allows these newly employed welfare beneficiaries to work alongside others who *pay* for their health care benefits.

Once again, it is painfully evident that Congress' definition of compassion forces the welfare population into patterns of dependency. "The new Republican bill would cause another such expansion, because it would allow those on welfare who join the work force to 'disregard' up to 50 percent of their income before it disqualifies them from receiving benefits," wrote Tom Bethell. And that is exactly how a family that effectively earns up to $23,000 per year can continue to qualify for welfare.

"Even the best job training programs have had little success in reducing welfare rolls. Five percent reductions... are considered major accomplishments."
— Douglas Besharov, of
the American Enterprise Institute

Both welfare reform proposals floated during the 103rd Congress (1993-94); President Clinton's and the one espoused by Republicans, were nothing more than jobs bills. I ask you: If the intent is to "end welfare as we know it," why are the American taxpayers being asked to ante up ten billion dollars? And why does ten billion dollars of additional federal spending offer only "reform" that applies to less than half of all welfare recipients by the turn of the century?

If the government simply transfers welfare recipients from one entitlement program to another, what inroads will those billions make?

Health and Human Services Secretary Donna Shalala contends that shuffling welfare recipients between training programs and subsidized make-work jobs is "humane," and is not out of phase with Mr. Clinton's pledge to "end welfare as we know it."

Donna, wake up and smell the welfare state. It stinks.

Remember CETA, The Comprehensive Employment and Training Act of the Carter administration? Billions of dollars were wasted so that Congress could find out what is painfully obvious — government jobs programs don't work.

Mr. Besharov cites four case studies compiled by the Manpower Demonstration Research Corporation that took place in West Virginia, Illinois and two in Southern California. *They found that "In no site did the work requirement reduce welfare payments."*

In early 1994, Amitai Etzioni, founder of the Communitarian Network, wrote, "rather than cutting cash benefits at once and thus 'incentivizing' welfare clients to seek work, the House GOP bill provides for a kind of severance pay: two years at an educational watering hole...anyone can join, including those who are currently employed but poorly paid, those who want to be retrained — and those who simply want to take classes."

There can be no argument that Mr. Clinton's plan to reform the welfare system would only serve to expand it. For example, the Clinton plan authorizes an additional $2.8 billion for government education programs; $1.2 billion in subsidies for government jobs, and $2.7 billion more for day care.

The Clinton proposal would recycle between 350,000 and 400,000 welfare recipients into government funded public-service jobs. *The Republican plan (103rd Congress) would provide at least 700,000 such jobs!*

Can we agree that the proliferation of welfare in America is due to forcing the lower middle class and the poor into patterns of dependency, and is fueled by the failure to demand any assemblance of personal responsibility? Can we further agree that in order to fix the system, we must reduce absurd benefit levels that have become a deterrent to self-reliance, and instead make people responsible for their own success or failure? If common sense leads us to agree on the previous two questions, then how can recycling a welfare recipient into a government subsidized job — where no threat of being laid off or fired exists regardless of lack of performance — teach that person responsibility?

The fallacy inherent in all socialistic, government sponsored rhetoric is that government can create jobs. Government is not capable of efficiently training people for jobs in the private sector. Seventy cents of every dollar funneled through Washington is lost to fraud, abuse and bureaucracy. Government jobs training programs should be scrapped and turned over entirely to the private sector. If training programs are the answer, why not offer a tax deduction to businesses to hire and train welfare recipients? The welfare recipient would then get "on-the-job" training, and the profit motive inherent in a capitalistic free-market would ensure that the trainee receives *quality* training.

Privatization is the simple answer to many "big government" problems. Government cannot do anything (other than national defense and law enforcement) in an efficient and cost-effective manner.

Not convinced?

California is one of 30 states that has training programs similar to those contained in the 1993-94, Clinton and House GOP plans, which attempt to integrate welfare recipients into the working world. *Of the 33,000 participants, only three percent more found* *jobs than those that received **no** government provided "training, education and job placement."*

The [UN]Earned Income Tax Credit

"Following sharp expansions in 1990 and 1993, the Earned Income Tax Credit is now far more of a direct handout than a tax refund. The program will cost more than $16 billion this year — more than the federal cost of Aid to Families with Dependent Children."
— James Bovard

Cost-effectiveness was never considered. The General Accounting Office found that the EITC was only responsible for a *one percent* drop in the poverty rate. Yet, the Internal Revenue Service estimates between 30% and 40% of EITC benefits are extended to those who are legally ineligible to receive them; further proof that government is incapable of "lifting someone out of poverty."

Those making up to $27,000 are eligible for the EITC. In an attempt to intermingle the welfare state with the middle class, the government has forced the bread-basket of America to subsidize its neighbors. In theory, a conservative should welcome any form of tax relief. But, this break does nothing but provide minimal relief on the backs of those who make just a little more — or *less* — in "real" dollars. For example, an annual income of $27,000 is just above the poverty level for New York residents; but in the rural south, that sum garners drastically increased buying power. As author Martin Gross noted, "in Arkansas, $27,000 is a good living, as shown by then-Governor Clinton's salary of only $33,000. Even today, the Lieutenant Governor makes only $29,000, and the Speaker of the Arkansas House only $14,000."

This is specifically why wealth redistribution is unfair *and* immoral.

Dr. Walter Williams offers this poignant analogy:

> "Taxes represent government claims on private property...
> suppose I see a lady sleeping on a grate in downtown
> Pittsburgh. She needs housing, food and medical care.
> Suppose further that I walk up to another citizen with
> a gun and demand $200 from him. Having gotten
> his $200, I purchase housing, food and medical attention
> for the woman. Would I be guilty of a crime? Yes, of
> course. I would be guilty of theft regardless of what I did
> with the money. Is there any conceptual distinction
> between that act and Congress sending its agents out to the
> same citizen demanding $200 from him and using it to help
> out the same lady? I assert that there is no conceptual
> distinction between those two acts.   And if pressed for
> one, the only distinction I can find is that the first act is
> illegal theft. The second act is legal theft. It is theft
> nonetheless because what rightfully belonged to one person
> was forcibly taken and given to another to whom it did not
> belong."[52]

Mark Anthony

Unfunded Mandates

The Tenth Amendment
"The powers not delegated to the United States by the Constitution, nor prohibited by it to the States, are reserved to the States respectively, or to the people."

In discussing the welfare nightmare, to look at federal spending alone is to miss an integral part of the misery. We must also consider a uniquely Washingtonian policy called "unfunded mandates." Nothing brings a smile to a beltway veteran like forcing others to finance his utopian good intentions. Those warm and fuzzy feelings in the pit of his stomach are very expensive for you and me.

The dictionary defines the word "mandate" as follows: *"A contract by which one party agrees to perform services for another **without payment**."* A mandate is simply a tax levied on the American people indirectly, by forcing state governments to pick up the tab.

Apparently, the federal government is not content to simply bankrupt itself. It has a more ambitious agenda than that; and when budgetary constraint does not permit the spending that it craves, it simply forces the states to pay for it. Washington gives your money away with the typical strings attached: loss of sovereignty and fractured balance of power. With the proliferation of unfunded mandates, Congress erodes the States' rights, while spending them into insolvency at the same time.

Vanishing Republic

The *Wall Street Journal* noted that "during the 1980s, Congress passed roughly 27 major statutes with new regulatory burdens for state and local governments...the Congressional Budget Office estimates that regulations imposed on local government between 1983 and 1990 cost up to $12.7 billion." The National Conference of State Legislatures (NCSL) offers a slightly more gloomy rendering: the 103rd Congress introduced 115 bills, designed by federal bureaucrats, staffers and special interests, all on the States' nickel. Such fiscal irresponsibility lends concerns not only regarding the national debt, but also the ever-growing burden on the Colonies, *er,* States.

> *In 1994, 42 cents of every dollar will go to pay the cost of government at all levels. Current estimates of the cost of unfunded mandates range from a low of $100 billion to a high of $500 billion annually. In New York City alone, the annual cost of AFDC and Medicaid (which are shared mandates), exceeds $3 billion; not to mention the cost of numerous other welfare programs.*
> *The National Governors Association estimates that by 1995 federal mandates will consume 28 percent of all state budgets.*

Many would like to eliminate this practice. Sen. Dirk Kempthorne (R-Idaho) and Gary Condit (D-California) have sponsored legislation that would allow the states to ignore any federal programs that contain unfunded mandates. Many of the GOP majority would further empower the States by turning many federal programs into "block" grants which allow the States to administer assistance depending on the particular needs of their

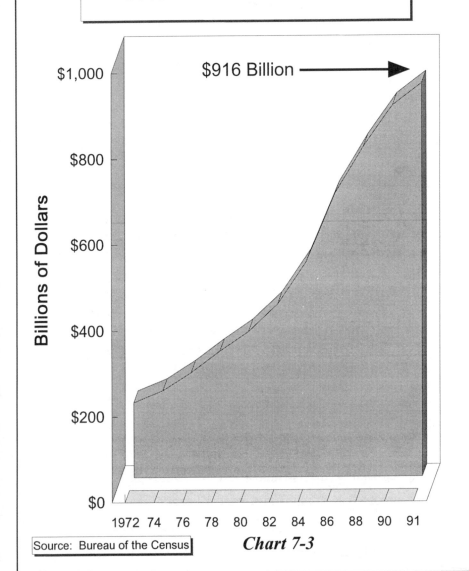

Growth Of State And Local
Government Debt 1972-1991

$916 Billion ⟶

Billions of Dollars

$1,000
$800
$600
$400
$200
$0

1972 74   76   78   80   82   84   86   88   90   91

Source: Bureau of the Census

Chart 7-3

citizens.

Chart 7-3 indicates the magnitude of debt at the state and local level. You may be wondering what the American public has received in return for its considerable benevolence?

Welfare Reform is covered in Chapter 16, as some of the economic principles discussed later in the book play an integral role.

Part III

Reforming The System

Chapter 8
Government Waste
Why Big Government Can't Work

"A government that is big enough to give you all you want is big enough to take it all away."
— Barry Goldwater, October 1964

"What is this oozing behemoth, this fibrous tumor, this monster of power and expense hatched from the simple human desire for civic order? How did an allegedly free people spawn a vast, rampant cuttlefish of dominion with its tentacles in every orifice of the body politic?"
— P.J. O'Rourke

"The Federal government is the world's largest: power producer, insurer, lender, borrower, hospital system operator, landowner, tenant, holder of grazing land, timber seller, grain owner, warehouse operator, ship owner, and truck fleet operator. The Federal government owns and operates 436,000 nonmilitary vehicles. It has over 17,000 computers, 322 accounting systems, and over 100 payroll systems."
— J. Peter Grace, chairman,
President Reagan's Private Sector Survey
on Cost Control (the Grace Commission)

"I don't think you can spend yourself rich."
— George Humphrey

Big government, by definition, is wasteful. Big government cannot work. It has no choice.

Why?

Because *Big Government Is The Antithesis Of Capitalism,* and as such, all of the efficiencies, economies of scale, and performance incentives that are the basis of "profit motive" are removed.

For example, in the area of efficiencies and performance incentives, a stark contrast exists between a government department and a large corporation. Both may have very large staffs, with sizable budgets, but that's where the similarity ends.

Let's compare the Department of Agriculture with, say a computer software company. Large corporations, like government agencies, are broken down into many smaller departments. Each department has its own operating budget.

The budget for each corporate department is decided based on an identifiable, written goal. That goal is part of a larger "mission statement," which serves to objectively define the direction of the corporation. This is meaningful as it is highly inefficient to set out on a journey without knowing one's destination. Furthermore, the budget for each department is balanced against the probable return on investment of the capital equipment and human resources allocated to that department. A company would not allocate one million dollars in equipment and employee-hours to produce a product or service that would only generate $200,000 in profits year after year.

In the final analysis, if the department meets its goals, *and* produces its project at or below budget, *it will be rewarded with a larger budget next year.* A free market economy demands — through the very nature of competition for customers that defines it

— that flawed concepts change in order to become viable. If the department does not meet its goals, management will be forced to take a different course of action next year. If the department continues to fail to meet its objectives, that particular program risks being cut entirely. If the company as a whole continues its ineptitude, it will have too many non-performing assets, and will eventually go out of business; or be bought by a more efficient company.

In a government agency, each department gets an annual budget as well. However, its budget is *not* based on the previous year's efficiency. It is not based on any predetermined departmental goal. In fact, it *has no goal* other than to perpetuate itself by spending all of the money that is allocated to it, regardless of how inefficiently or irresponsibly it does so.

This is due, of course, to baseline budgeting. An increase in the budget of any government program is predicated only on it spending its entire budget — efficiently or otherwise — the year before.

J. Peter Grace, chairman of the Grace Commission, wrote, "The [U.S.] government handles some $6.8 billion in transactions a day...but despite these enormous sums the government is years behind the private sector in developing modern budgeting and accounting systems. Nor is it familiar with the common business techniques of cash, loan, and debt management."

Imagine if Ford Motor Company operated in this manner. After the Edsel had been introduced, it proved to be an abysmal failure. The showrooms and warehouses were stacked to the gills with Edsels because Ford couldn't give them away. So, the next year,

Ford not only continued to produce Edsels, but also increased the budget resources allocated to building them! Imagine, if Ford did this year after year, decade after decade. Imagine, millions of Edsels, sitting in warehouses all over the country, no one wanting to buy any of them. Yet, billions upon billions of resources were continually dumped into the Edsel program.

Well, it's been happening for years. In 1887 the Interstate Commerce Commission was created to oversee the railroad industry. It seems difficult to justify a $30 billion annual expenditure when the only railroad news one hears is the bi-monthly Amtrak derailing. The ICC is hopelessly obsolete, yet the government continues to plow billions into it. Likewise, the Rural Electrification Administration (REA). By the 1960's 98% of rural America was on line. Yet, the REA has over $30 billion in loans outstanding. In 1991 it lent out $1.7 billion more and continues to spend two billion dollars annually — all to homes that have had electricity for decades. Remember that the next time your Representative tells you America can't afford to spend two billion dollars a year on the Space Station.

Here is another example.

In the early 1900's America had roughly five million farms, and the Department of Agriculture had 3,000 employees to take care of them. Today, the amount of farmers has dropped to just over two million, with at least half of them part-timers. Only 500,000 of those run ongoing commercial farms. Yet the number of federal farm employees has swelled to over 60,000.

How much does the Department of Agriculture cost American taxpayers? Try *$65 billion* per year.

What else is happening down on the farm?

Milk. It does a body good — but not the taxpayer's wallet. During the 1980's milk subsidies totaled $17 billion. The real "kick in the utter" is that these subsidies cost consumers an additional $40 billion in increased milk prices during that time.

The Farmers Home Administration (FmHA) was called "the largest direct lending institution in the Federal Government." That assessment was made by the Inspector General of the Department of Agriculture in a 1991 report to Congress.

Should Congress have been surprised? The FmHA "has lent more than $172 billion to farmers and rural communities since 1935." Then, the Agricultural Credit Act of 1987 compassionately "forgave" an estimated $10 billion in loans. They didn't work out a settlement option, or restructure the loans; they simply wrote off all or part of many of them. As of 1992, 37% of the loans were delinquent.

Congress so graciously released loans underwritten with your tax dollars, yet the loans to farms and rural homeowners were heavily subsidized to begin with. How heavily? Some, all the way down to one percent!

Between 1980 and 1992, the American taxpayer's tab for "Farmfare" was estimated at over $190 billion dollars. James Bovard wrote in his landmark book *Lost Rights,* "Subsidies are the twentieth-century method of humane conquest: slow political coups d'état over one sector of the economy and society after another. Government subsidies have become a major factor in squeezing out unsubsidized developers, unsubsidized schools, unsubsidized theater producers, and unsubsidized farmers."

Could anyone argue that paying someone to *not* do something is morally wrong? This is not meant to be an assault on the American farmer. The forgotten losers in the increasing intransigence of federal control are farmers who *want* to produce a product and can't. It is obvious that the federal government has taken an honorable profession and led it down the primrose path to dependency and destruction, all at the expense of middle-class men and women who have to get up five or six days a week to go to work — working at jobs with often uncertain futures, caused by an entire economy that is overburdened by those who choose to do nothing.

Take for example the "0-92" subsidy. It allows farmers to plant *nothing at all* at taxpayer expense. Says the Congressional Budget Office, "Current law allows participants in U.S. Department of Agriculture price-and income-support programs to receive 92% of their deficiency payments even though they do not plant any of the program crops (the 0-92 program available for wheat and feed grain producers)."

Meanwhile, we are paying for other Americans to *buy* food through the Food Stamp program. *With an annual budget of $24 billion, one in ten Americans has his groceries paid for by the other nine.*

What we have then is a system that at the same time pays farmers not to plant or sell groceries, then pays welfare recipients to buy groceries. Meanwhile, the American taxpayer pays higher food prices to subsidize the farmers, and higher taxes to underwrite the Food Stamps.
(Refer to Chart 8-1)

162

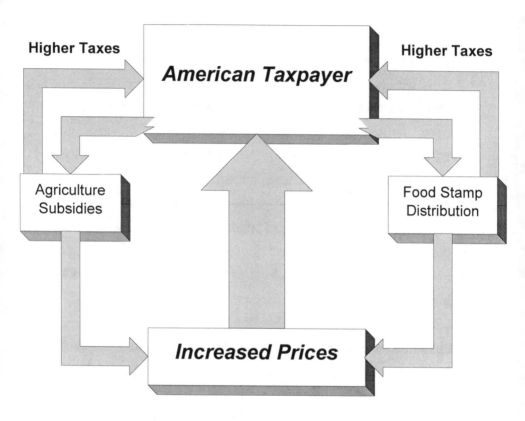

At the same time, the American Taxpayer is asked to:
- a) pay farmers not to grow or sell food
- b) pay welfare recipients to buy food
  and
- c) absorb higher food prices and increased taxes to subsidize both

Chart 8-1

A Fitting Metaphor

What better way to express how bloated, inefficient and idiotic the government machine operates than to compare a typical small business with the way Uncle Sam conducts his.

David Hale, chief economist of Kemper Financial Companies in Chicago, wrote, "If we add Subchapter S returns and sole proprietorships returns, about 89% of all tax returns with significant business income are subject to personal tax rates."[53] Clearly, small business is the engine that drives the American economy, and the business owners and the people that they employ are the main financiers of federal government largess.

How fitting to compare the plight of the weary entrepreneur with the bureaucracy he's forced to support.

In our fictitious small business, the first thing that we need is a location. So, we'll speak to an average real estate investor about leasing some office space. (He's in rough shape himself. The real estate market bottomed out when most of the tax advantages of owning property were stripped in 1986.)

The real estate investor operates several moderate sized office properties. He explains that tenancy has continually declined since the peak Reagan economy in the late 1980's. He assumes it is because of the destructive effect the Bush tax increase in 1990 as well as the Clinton tax increase in 1993 had on small business, which comprises the bulk of his tenants. He further assumes the regulatory burden enacted by the Bush and Clinton Presidencies added to the small businessman's plight.

He is right.

Vanishing Republic

The real estate investor shows our fictitious small businessman a nice office suite — there are plenty to choose from, as the building is at only 40% capacity. Our small businessman likes the suite and signs a lease. As they part company, the small businessman contemplates the fate of the barely solvent real estate investor. He certainly won't be purchasing any *more* office buildings, what with his current vacancy rate.

Uncle Sam doesn't have such problems. The General Services Administration keeps an eye on his buildings. Of course the federal government does not need to concern itself with trivial matters like cost/benefit analyses; it simply continues its unabated consumption. As such, the federal government now has over 15 million square feet of *vacant* space. Yet, the GSA still spent two billion dollars on additional office space in 1992. It spent another billion on "repairs and alterations." It also handed out over $100 million of taxpayers' money for the building needs of private institutions. Unfortunately, your business was not one of them.

Next, our small businessman needs electricity. Assume that the going rate in his area is 10 cents/kilowatt hour (more if he lives in the northeast). The electric bill is one of his primary concerns, as it will be one of the main components in his operating budget. Would it surprise you to know that you are not only paying for *your* electricity, but also subsidizing cheap electricity for many other Americans?

Think about that the next time you pay your electric bill. You, the taxpayer has bought and paid for the multi-billion dollar hydroelectric program. Yet, only six percent of the country receives low-cost federally subsidized electricity in return.

Furthermore, the five federal power administrations that in turn wholesale the power to their customers owe the treasury a combined $10 billion. Of course, they have a repayment deal that is beyond the reach of the average citizen. You see, the power administrations are repaying the loans at 3.25% interest — while the government borrows at roughly eight percent interest; a loss to the banker (the American taxpayer) of an additional $475 million.

The entrepreneur in our example has given it some serious thought, and decided it would be wise to take out a loan to assist in his start-up expenses. So, he goes to his local bank, delivers his personal financial statement, his business plan, as well as his sources of collateral, only to find that his banker is under extreme federal scrutiny to lend money only to those who are eminently qualified. In other words: he can get a loan, only if he doesn't really need it. Let's take a look at how the federal government lends money — *at your expense.*

The federal government is lending your money and providing government backed insurance to almost everybody. FHA, VA, Farm Loans, FDIC backed deposits; there is almost $7 trillion in outstanding loans and insurance, and the default rate is staggering. The OMB estimates that over $350 billion in loans may default by 1998. Historical evidence indicates that it may be much higher. Martin Gross, in his 1992 bestseller, *The Government Racket, Washington Waste From A to Z,* popularized an especially egregious use of federal loan dollars — the Export-Import Bank. The Eximbank is "a strange government operation in which we loan foreign companies money so they can buy our exports." The

1992 budget indicated the Eximbank experienced "large losses over the past decade."

How large?

The bank had a $2.3 billion operating loss. It had $9 billion in direct loans outstanding as of 1992 and expected a 66% default rate, leaving the American taxpayer with a $6 billion loss. How can a bank post a $2.3 billion operating loss? Simple. *It lent money to its Foreign customers, at below market interest rates (i.e., less than what the bank paid for the money it lent).*

I've scoured the Constitution and can find nothing regarding below-market loans to Foreign entities.

"Surely, it would be easier to obtain a Small Business Administration loan," our entrepreneur says to himself. "Certainly, if the government can make ill-advised loans to foreign entities, knowing that two-thirds of the loans will default, they would consider my business a good risk," he says.

Wrong.

You see, Uncle Sam thinks big, and our interpretation of the word 'Small' is considerably different than his. An audit of SBA loans found that the typical firm had about one million dollars in revenue. As a matter of fact, companies with assets of $20 million can qualify for SBA loans.

"Look at the bright side," he says to himself. At least these companies are good credit risks.

Wrong again.

In 1990, the SBA had $1.1 billion in bad loans.

At the same time the federal government was telling our entrepreneur that he was not worthy of a loan, the SBA was using his tax dollars to pay for the bad loans that it made to other *"Small"* businesses.

Still undaunted, our courageous small businessman proceeds to his next destination: the local auto dealership to lease a few business vehicles. The cars represent an enormous investment, not only in cost, but also in responsibility. If the vehicles are not used in a productive manner, the monthly payments cannot be made, the vehicles will be repossessed, and he no longer has any means to deliver goods and services to his customers.

Maybe the government has a vehicle it can spare.

It has *more* than a few. The federal government is swimming in vehicles — over 190,000 non-postal, non-military vehicles. Of course, a car is not a car without a driver. The government has an abundance of those too; about 12,000 to be precise.

How much does the world's largest taxi service cost?

Over three billion dollars to purchase the vehicles, $750,000 million in annual depreciation, over a billion dollars in repairs and general maintenance, not to mention assorted overhead that nears another $200 million.

And our entrepreneur is worried about making a few measly car payments.

Realizing his prime objective is to turn a profit, the small businessman has expediently decided to lease one less vehicle than he really needs — the one that would have served as his personal business vehicle. Instead, he has chosen to take the subway to work each day. This is not without cost, but it is considerably less than the payments and upkeep of another vehicle.

Doesn't he wish he could ride the Washington Metro?

Vanishing Republic

The Metro's funding was aided by $7.7 billion in federal funds. How much of that will be recouped in ridership? Not much. In 1991 a bill was introduced in the Senate and signed into law by President Bush that provided *free* ridership to federal employees up to $250 per year. What a deal. The taxpayers not only paid 70% of the cost to build the Metro, but also they're stuck paying the fare for federal employees who have pensions of which the average middle class American can only dream.

Oh, well. Life goes on. So, the small businessman goes to the local furniture store to pick out some office furniture. The cost is prohibitive, so he decides to lease the furniture.

The federal government, on the other hand, has more furniture than it can ever use. It has warehouses full of perfectly good furniture. But does that stop the rabid consumption. Of course not. It's your money they're spending.

The best estimates of the General Services Administration place the annual figure near two billion dollars in new furniture purchases — *and that doesn't even include the Department of Defense.*

After putting a great deal of his future at stake, the entrepreneur has decided to enlist the services of a consultant; a specialist in his field. Can he afford outside counsel? His cost/benefits analysis indicates that the guidance he is purchasing may mean the difference between success and failure.

Meanwhile, an audit by the General Accounting Office found an astounding amount of federal consulting is being paid for with your tax dollars. The GAO discovered that $4.9 billion is spent annually on outside consultants — a figure that may well be as high as $20 billion. Amazingly, the government already has over 3,500 regular consultants at a cost of more than $35 million a year.

Where does the money go?

Here's a sampling: $308 million by the Agency for International Development; $44 million by Commerce (some commerce; they take your money and spend it on consultants); $99 million by Energy; and $60 million by Education.

Despicable.

One of the suggestions the entrepreneur's consultant offers is to keep a keen eye on his "overhead," which they both plot and budget. They have found a reputable printer, at a fair price, to handle forms and promotional items.

I'm sure you're wondering how the federal government handles the flood of paperwork that the bureaucracy creates? The Government Printing office spends well over one billion dollars a year. The 5000 employees of the GPO produce over $150 million of printing in government owned and operated facilities. An audit determined that at least half — $75 million — could be saved annually by turning the job over to commercial printers; and although more than half of the GPO's machinery sits idle during an average work week, auditors found a considerable amount of weekend-overtime is performed.

The fact of the matter is: the federal government really has no idea what its overhead is. Congressman Lamar Smith of Texas attempted to find out the answer in the early 1990's. The best estimates came in at roughly *$270 billion* a year. With at least another $170 billion surreptitiously buried under the budget heading, "Other Services." (Remember, these are early *1990 numbers;* as we'll discuss later, the figures are much higher now.)

Small businessmen I talk to know where virtually every penny of their overhead goes. This can be accomplished with any one of the new breed of financial/bookkeeping computer programs on the market. Yet, the Office of Management and Budget — with a veritable army of accountants stacked like cord wood — cannot provide such data.

I'll volunteer to buy the OMB a copy of *Quicken* if it will help.

And what about travel expenses. Our courageous, small businessman takes no-frills flights — often the "red-eye" — and only when his profit margin allows it.

This is in sharp contrast to *"Uncle Sam Airways."* The always frugal Feds own 1,406 *non-military* airplanes of over 100 different varieties — and these are only the civilian planes. This costs a nifty two billion dollars a year, plus another billion when depreciation and maintenance are factored in. Not surprisingly, the government deems it necessary to *lease* another 5,000 planes at an annual cost of $100 million.

Oh, and one last item. Today's businessman has another bogeyman to mind. The new environmental bureaucracy. He dare not soil the hallowed ground or pollute a body of water, or violate the "human" rights of a defenseless tree. Many a business has been laid to waste for such transgressions. Never fear; the government has the darndest idea to clean up Mother Nature — the "Superfund."

Knowing what you now do about government waste and the temerity with which your tax dollars are squandered, the very thought of a federal program called *"Superfund"* ought to make you hang onto your wallet with both hands.

The Environmental Protection Agency began Superfund in 1980. The program was designed to clean up 1,250 contaminated industrial sites with fifteen billion dollars allocated for the program. By 1991, only 65 cites had been completed, and $10 billion had been spent.

But, it gets worse.

The EPA will spend a projected $40 billion dollars to complete the original sites, and since the program is unbearably behind schedule and hopelessly over budget, the only logical solution is to add an estimated 900 *more* sites to the list during the 1990's. What's the tab for the EPA's perpetual money pit? About $125 billion — and we know how accurate the original projections were.

It should be abundantly clear that although the average American must have the discipline to live within his means or risk the consequences that await the losers in a free-market economy, the government has exempted itself from such fiscal responsibility.

The federal government endlessly consumes without regard to feasibility. The government continues to take, never acknowledging the loss of personal freedom that such confiscatory tax rates mandate. Is it right for Americans to scrimp and save to own the home of the their dreams, or to send their kids to college while the government remains mired in hideous waste?

Is there any stopping its expansion?

Vanishing Republic

According to the Institute for Policy Innovation, "the number of workers in the public sector — 18.6 million — is greater than the number in the entire manufacturing sector."

Is this the government the Founding Fathers had in mind when the *Federalist Papers* were written in order to help ratify the Constitution Of The United States?

Where in the Constitution is the federal government granted the authority to take a dollar out of your pocket, waste seventy percent of it, then give the remaining thirty cents to someone else?

Is it within the Constitution Of The United States to allow the government to accumulate massive debt, payable to foreign institutions, which ultimately compromises our sovereignty? Can any member of Congress look you straight in the eye and defend a multi-trillion dollar national debt, as continues to be proposed?

At this time, four points should be made emphatically clear:
- The charade being handed down by Washington — the notion that it is terribly difficult to find additional spending cuts — is preposterous. A prudent individual could find more than enough real spending cuts than would be necessary to balance the budget. Theoretically, it would be simple. In practice — well, that's another matter. The problem is the entrenched bureaucracy. The more people who have their hands in the government's pocket, the more difficult it is to

173

reform the system that created this debacle. This was patently done by design. The upcoming chapters on reforming the way that Washington spends money will provide a step-by-step method to bring about actual reform.

- The American public and the American economy have had an enormous burden affixed to it in order to feed the appetites of irresponsible governance and abominable federal spending. The populace does without so that the government may continue to consume.

- There are powerful forces in Washington: lawyers, lobbyists, bureaucrats, consultants; who do not care if the freedoms that we collectively refer to as *"The American Dream"* are destroyed. The government will be able to outlast the fallout of any economic implosion. Just as the federal government cemented its omnipotence during the great depression, as it was able to pick up the pieces and capitalize on the weakness and dependency of the American people, so too will government — under the guise of compassion — take the opportunity to further erode our rights and freedoms as global economic conditions worsen.

- Always, remember —

THE GOVERNMENT HAS NO MONEY OF ITS OWN
It only has that which it has taken from you.

Chapter 9
The Collapse Of American Freedom...
The National Debt

"Of all the dispositions and habits which lead to political prosperity, Religion and Morality are indispensable supports. In vain would that man claim the tribute of patriotism who should labor to subvert these great pillars of human happiness, these firmest props of the duties of men and citizens...And let us with caution indulge the supposition that morality can be maintained without religion. Whatever may be conceded to the influence of refined education on minds of peculiar structure, reason and experience both forbid us to expect that national morality can prevail in exclusion of religious principle."
— George Washington, 1796

"Can the liberties of a nation be thought secure when we have removed their only firm basis, a conviction in the minds of the people that these liberties are the gift of God?"
— Thomas Jefferson

What, you may ask, do the principles of "Religion and Morality" have to do with the ominous specter of the national debt?

Allow me to share with you an editorial piece I've written:.

Dangerous Debt...Endangered Freedom

My friends have asked me, "Why do you devote so much of your writing and speaking addressing the issue of taxation?"

175

Because the primary threat to personal freedom is big government which is *fed* by confiscatory tax rates.

"How do taxes invade my freedom?" you may ask.   It is very simple. You are no longer free to spend that which the government has taken away from you. This has a tremendously detrimental effect on personal freedom.

When a government confiscates almost 40% of a nation's income through taxation, and billions, if not trillions more, through regulatory proliferation, millions of citizens no longer have the freedom to own the home that they would like.   They no longer have the freedom to send their children to private school.   They may not have the freedom to offer as much to their church.   They may not have the freedom to drive the type of car they would like, or the freedom to take the vacation they would like — all, so that the government can take a dollar out of *your* pocket and give it to someone else.

But, there is a much bigger issue than freedom to consider.   The future of our nation is at stake.   For, the more government takes away, the more it spends.   As of April 25, 1994, the national debt was Four *Trillion*, Five Hundred and Fifty Eight *Billion,* Three Hundred Forty Eight *Million,* Six Hundred and Ninety Eight *Thousand* dollars.   Not to mention, the trillions more that have been *"borrowed"* from the Social Security **Trust** Fund.

Yet, there are still those who believe that the economic collapse of The United States can never happen.   "We are the richest nation on earth," they say. "Prosperity is our birthright." This apocryphal security makes one fallacious assumption.   Our government was founded on principles clearly outlined by God.   Over the last 200 plus years, *He* has systematically been stripped from the American culture.

Through the ages, every Godless society has fallen.   Why do we feel that *we* are the exception to that rule?   How can a nation that has so clearly embraced Godless, omnipotent government, still claim Divine Providence?

Am I crossing the line clearly drawn by the First Amendment? Am I attempting to integrate church and state?   Absolutely not. But I will not stand idly by while the elements of morality, religion, virtue, discipline and responsibility — all which are fundamental to the establishment of our democracy — are disemboweled from our proud American heritage.

William J. Bennett put it quite eloquently:

> "...No one demands doctrinal adherence to any religious beliefs as a condition of citizenship, or as proof of good citizenship, here.   But at the same time we should not deny what is true: that from the Judeo-Christian tradition come our values, our principles, the animating spirit of our institutions.   That tradition and our tradition are entangled.   They are wed together.   When we have disdain for our religious tradition, we have disdain for ourselves."

Said John Adams, one of our Founding Fathers: "Our Constitution was made only for a moral and religious people.   It is wholly inadequate to the government of any other."

How Large Is The National Debt?

Any analysis of the national debt must be broken down into two parts: "on-budget" debt, and "off-budget" debt. Or, more accurately, the debt that the government will admit to and that which it attempts to conceal. And this is where the numbers get a little frightening.

"On-budget" debt, as of November, 1994, was approaching $4.7 trillion. But unfunded liabilities like money *"borrowed"* from the Social Security Trust Fund, as well as future obligations for military and civilian government employee pensions, add at least another six trillion dollars to the total.

Larry Burkett, author of *The Coming Economic Earthquake,* wrote, "with a real national debt (current debt plus future liabilities) in excess of $10 trillion, the total debt is actually greater than the GDP." Conservative estimates indicate that more than six trillion dollars in additional debt will be added by 2004.

Creative Accounting 101

Let's talk about "off-budget" spending for a moment — I'll wait while you grab some *Tums.* You may not know this but the Postal Service is "off-budget." It loses over one billion dollars per year (not to mention some of your mail). Direct loans from The Export-Import Bank and Small Business Administration are off budget, as well as loan guaranties such as The Federal Housing Administration, Veterans Administration, Rural Electrification and Student Loans. Federal deposit insurance programs are also "off budget"; they consist of the Federal Deposit Insurance Corporation, The Resolution Trust Corporation and The Office of Thrift Supervision. Other "off-budget" programs are: The Federal Home Loan Mortgage Corporation (Freddie Mac), Federal

National Mortgage Association (Fannie Mae), Student Loan Mortgage Association (Sallie Mae) and Federal Agricultural Mortgage Association (Farmer Mac). These are known as government sponsored *enterprise loans.* If the borrower defaults on these loans, the taxpayers pick up the tab.

Some enterprise.

Without a doubt, the most potentially devastating federal insurance program is the Pension Benefit Guarantee Corporation which insures close to $50 billion in pension benefits. If a company becomes insolvent and cannot meet its pension obligations, the PBGC simply gives it *your* money instead.

Social Security Trust Fund. Now, there's an oxymoron. In 1983, Congress increased contributions to the fund through higher withholding taxes, in order to ensure adequate funds to meet future obligations. Congress concluded that the changes would give the Trust Fund in excess of one trillion dollars in assets by the year 2010 — the year baby boomers would begin to retire (at that time there will be only 3.2 contributors for every recipient). But, like a junkie who wins the lottery, the newly found resources would simply perpetuate their vise. The thieves capitalized on the windfall then lended themselves *your* money! They raided the till and replaced the funds with *Non-Marketable Treasury Bonds;* a valueless instrument, of purely nefarious intent established solely to allow bureaucrats to transfer *your* money out of the Trust Fund. They spent your nest egg and replaced it with piles of IOU's that will one day be worth approximately the paper they are printed on.

To date, they have stolen over one trillion dollars from various trust funds. To add insult to injury — almost for spite — *the*

179

government counts the money it has stolen from the trust funds as REVENUE instead of a liability in order to conceal the enormity of the national debt! The blatant arrogance; that they can throw your money around with impunity, then lie to you about the grave danger we are in by surreptitiously hiding enormous future obligations by declaring them "off-budget" is truly repulsive. Imagine if you or I attempted such "creative" accounting. Assume you and I were applying for a home mortgage, and in listing our current debts, we left off all our credit card bills and installment loans. Upon completing our credit check, the banker discovered our omissions, and thus concluded that we were immanently disqualified from obtaining such a lavish home because our debt ratio is much too high to have any possibility of meeting the payments — the future obligations of the mortgage. We then looked the banker in the eye and told him, "you can't count those items; they're 'off-budget.' As a matter of fact, those debts we owe to Visa and MasterCard and CitiBank — why, they're not obligations at all — they're *INCOME!*"

Needless to say, we would get thrown out on our lying derriere.

> *The federal government, which would be guaranteeing the mortgage we sought, will not allow us to conduct business in such a deceptive manner — and we shouldn't allow the government to conduct business that way, either.*

Chart 9-1 illustrates the projected growth of the national debt. It does not even take into consideration future unfunded liabilities.

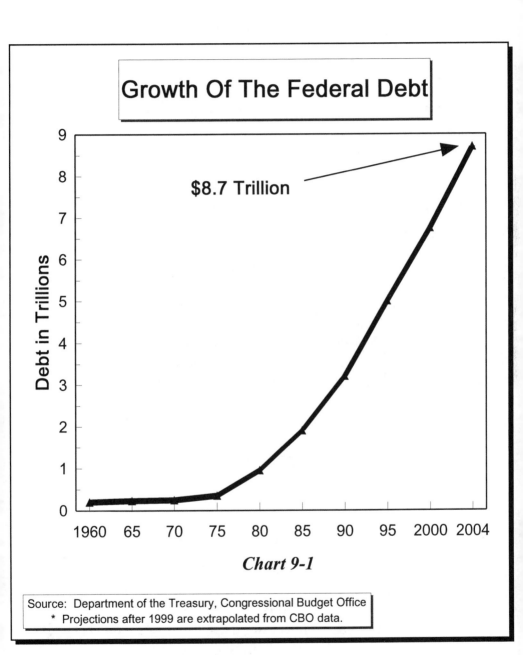

Growth Of The Federal Debt

$8.7 Trillion

Debt in Trillions

1960 65 70 75 80 85 90 95 2000 2004

Chart 9-1

Source: Department of the Treasury, Congressional Budget Office
* Projections after 1999 are extrapolated from CBO data.

Mark Anthony

The Interest On The National Debt

"Interest 'payments' is a misnomer. The interest is not actually being paid. It is being borrowed and added to the debt. So, in reality, we are paying interest on the interest from previous years."
— Larry Burkett

"There's no honorable way out of the situation. All that's left for us is to plead. America on its knees to its debtors...You might want to ask your member of Congress to explain how the government expects to pay any of its other expenses if everything it collects in personal taxes and more, is needed to pay interest to debt holders. Another thing you might ask your favorite politician: what he or she proposes to bargain away when our foreign debt holders: German, Saudi Arabian, Japanese and British, come demanding their money back? A government's ability to guarantee certain freedoms and liberties rests on that government's independence; which our country is close to giving away, if it hasn't already."
— Harry E. Figgie Jr.,
Gerald J. Swanson, Ph.D., *Bankruptcy 1995*

"The rich rules over the poor, and the borrower becomes the lender's slave."
— Proverbs 22:7

Thomas Jefferson said "every nation is enfeebled by a public debt...and their present political weakness stands as a monument of the unavoidable consequences of that fatal system."

Interest payments in 1993 consumed 57 percent of all individual income tax revenues. This is up dramatically from 19 percent in 1982.

In all this budgetary alphabet soup, one key point is missed. According to the nonpartisan Congressional Budget Office, our $4.7 trillion national debt will surpass five trillion dollars by 1996. The CBO projects annual deficits in excess of $200 billion well into the next century.

Why is this so alarming?

Interest payments on the on-budget portion of the national debt went over the $200 billion mark in 1993 and is projected to rise to $253 billion by the end of 1996. Furthermore, the interest on the debt will reach over one trillion dollars by the time a child born in 1994 turns age ten. We simply cannot continue to write checks that our children will *never* be able to cash.

At that point, *all personal income tax revenues will not be enough to pay the interest.*

Then, what happens?

Imagine, if your personal debt were so high that your entire income was not enough to pay the interest alone. What do you think the chances are that a bank would continue to lend you money? If anyone were foolish enough to lend it to you, I guarantee he or she would demand much higher than "market" interest rates in order to offset the risk. Do you expect the Japanese and European bankers to react any differently?

Rising interest rates accelerate the cycle making it impossible to pay down the debt because each one percent rise in interest rates adds approximately $40 billion to the existing debt; which is why our fiscal future is so apocalyptic.

Given this scenario, what choice would our country have? The government could either default on the debt or monetize the debt.

The first option is out of the question.

So, what does *"monetize"* mean?

It means *print enough money to pay the debt;* resulting in hyperinflation. When the Treasury needs additional revenue, it has two sources. The Treasury can sell bonds, notes or bills, in which case investors pay dollars to the Treasury in exchange for Treasury securities. Monetizing the debt is another matter entirely. A key role of the Federal Reserve is to monitor the money supply, and as such, the Treasury has the ability to "sell" its debt to the Federal Reserve. The Federal Reserve writes the Treasury a check; the check is deposited in a member bank; and *viola* — money is created, and the Treasury gets its funds. This practice comes at considerable cost. A rise in the money supply brings with it inflation. The credit markets are then forced to raise interest rates so that *their* investments will not lose value. As inflation erodes the dollar, consumers also see inflation eroding their buying power. They then choose to make purchases today that they may not have otherwise made. For example, at 10% inflation, an automobile costing $20,000 today will cost $22,000 next year, and $24,200 the year after that. This in turn, breeds artificially high consumer demand, further driving up prices. Interest rates continue to climb, adding approximately $40 billion to the national debt for each one point rise. Thus, hyperinflation feeds on itself, being virtually impossible to control.

Anyone care for a $10,000 loaf of bread?

It can't happen, you say? Tell me why?

Because the annual deficit is only a small percentage of the Gross Domestic Product? Such perverse logic is the folly of fools.

If all tax revenues were not enough to pay the interest alone on the national debt, interest rates would skyrocket, inflation would explode and the dollar would plummet. The writing's on the wall. Federal spending has been debt financed for years. The dollar was at a post World War II low in the summer of 1994. Is it any wonder that many countries are hesitant to extend additional debt to a nation perched on such a precipice?

But remember — we were only talking about "on-budget" debt. There is another $6 trillion in off-budget debt when you consider the money "borrowed" from Social Security, as well as unfunded future federal pension obligations.

Charts 9-2 and 9-3 illustrate current and future interest payments on the debt.

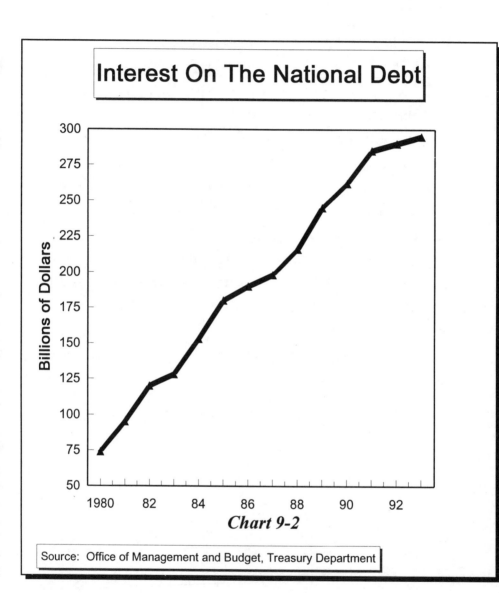

Interest On The National Debt

Billions of Dollars

Chart 9-2

Source: Office of Management and Budget, Treasury Department

Projected Interest On The National Debt

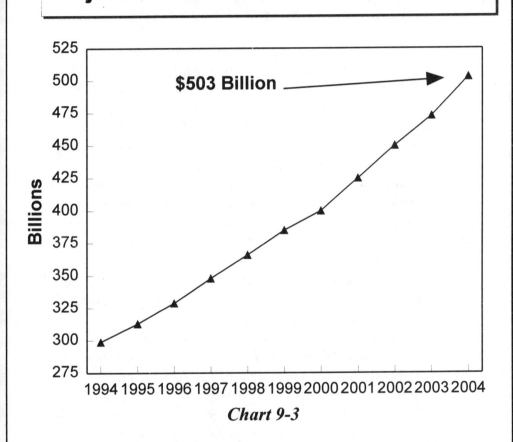

$503 Billion

1994 1995 1996 1997 1998 1999 2000 2001 2002 2003 2004

Billions

525
500
475
450
425
400
375
350
325
300
275

Chart 9-3

Source: Congressional Budget Office

Chapter 10
The Ways Of Washington:
Complicated, Inefficient, Bureaucratic, Wasteful And Myopic... By Design

"The foreboding is of what citizen anger must now overcome: a huge new, entrenched governing elite, one that in some ways approaches those who misgoverned Rome. Over the last half century, a Washington swollen by expansions in peace and war has become what ordinary citizens of the 1780s and even some architects of the U.S. Constitution feared — a capital city so enlarged, so incestuous in its dealings, so caught up in its own privilege that it no longer seems controllable or even swayable by the general public.

There is no point in mincing words. Aging great-power capitals often become parasitic cultures. The term "parasite" was frequently used in seventeenth- and eighteenth-century criticisms of the Spanish and Dutch capitals. Washington, in different ways, is beginning to resemble those wayward governmental centers of previous declining empires, from Greece and Rome to Hapsburg Madrid and The Hague...the parallel...is chilling — and is also a warning. The lessons of history could not be more relevant. Too much of what happened then is happening again now...

As Washington has entrenched, the old two-party system, revitalized by once-a-generation bloodless revolutions at the ballot box, no longer works... Washington is too big, too rich, too pride-set in its ways as arbiter of the postwar world, to accept another of the

upheavals and housecleanings that Thomas Jefferson
predicted would be necessary every generation.... "[54]
— Kevin Phillips, *Arrogant Capital,*
Washington, Wall Street, And The
Frustration Of American Politics, 1994

"When all government, domestic and foreign, in little as
in great things, shall be drawn to Washington as the
center of all power, it will render powerless the checks
provided of one government on another, and will become
as venal and oppressive as the government from which we
separated."
— Thomas Jefferson, 1821

The *"overhead"* of the federal government is estimated at *$356 billion per year.* *"Other Services,"* a category that appears in virtually every nook and cranny of the federal budget — everything from travel, equipment, overhead, personnel, pensions, consultants and decorating — is a national scandal popularized by Martin Gross in *Government Racket Washington Waste From A-Z.* Gross notes "'other services' is the government's open-ended slush fund. While Congress may argue about a billion here and a billion there, agency bureaucrats can dip into this pot for whatever reason, whenever they want. The amounts will be secret."

The Tax Foundation reported that in 1994, forty-nine cents of every dollar of personal income (less transfer payments) will go to government at all levels.

The Federal government alone consumes 24% of our nation's Gross Domestic Product.

There are 150 different jobs training programs scattered across 14 government agencies.

The Federal government bestows 606 categorical grants costing $225 billion to state and local agencies. Not surprisingly, 98% of the programs come with strings attached.

While the Clinton administration crowed about annual deficits falling below the $200 billion a year mark (as if we should be proud that Washington *only* spends $200 billion per year more than it takes in) Treasury Department figures place the annual deficit for 1993 and 1994 closer to $340 billion annually.

The Cato Institute found a nearly one-to-one ratio between rising state taxes and federal aid over the previous four decades of one party Congressional rule.

Can we all agree that something needs to be done — *fast?*

The number of Federal employees increased from 75,000 at the inception of the New Deal to over 165,000 in 1940. But even that ballooning of the bureaucratic army was nothing compared to what would come in the next 50 years.

Washington was not only the seat of power of the United States, but also became the seat of power for the entire world. And as with all world powers that preceded it, from Greece, to Rome, to the Dutch and Spanish and British empires; several decades of incredible growth followed as the world cast its attention to the planet's premier capital city. Washington, D.C., was not only the center of politics, it was the center of commerce, as well.

The presidential election of 1964 pit left versus right, or rather right versus wrong. Lyndon Johnson triumphed, ushering in liberal Great Society programs that built on the New Deal legacy. But the social welfare programs that were popular (at least in the minds of the voters) in a time of great need were not so popular in a time of great prosperity. And so, in 1968 Richard Nixon swept into office, as the Republican party sought to undue the Johnson legacy. Congress, which had been controlled by the Democratic party for decades, quickly sought to consolidate its power. House rules were reformed, lobbyists and interest group peddlers were given sway, myriad committees and sub-committees were added while their staffs exploded in numbers, as Democrats in the House insulated their power in preparation for an unprecedented war with the Republican controlled Executive Branch.

A fourth branch of government, the lawyer-lobbyists was born; from whence the roots of our ungovernable ruling class sprung. Quickly, the tide of influence turned from the voters to the interest groups who provided the elite body of legislators unfathomable power.

In *Arrogant Capital,* Kevin Phillips wrote:

> "As the federal government's agenda grew during the 1960s and 1970s, Washington drew power brokers and courtiers in numbers that began to constitute another of history's danger signals. Some of the parasites were government employees, but given private-sector demands and late-twentieth-century civil service restraints, the notable expansion in the Washington parasite structure during the 1970s and 1980s came from *outside* the federal government — from an explosion in the ranks of lawyers and interest-group representatives out to influence Uncle Sam, interpret his actions, or pick his pockets for

themselves or their clients. The gunslingers, card sharks, and faro dealers were checking into Gucci Gulch."[55]

Phillips recognized the "transfer-seeking sector" raised Washington to the highest per capita income area in the United States; "seven of its jurisdictions" are "now on the list of the twenty U.S. counties with the highest median family income." The D.C. area also has the dubious distinction of having the highest income spread between the top and bottom tenth of wage earners — $101,831 versus $12,661 — itself a microcosm of the ruling elite, and those of us forced to fund their excess.

Another warning sign of impending doom (as history tells us) is a capital city filthy with lawyers (excuse the pun). Members of the D.C. bar totaled over 61,000 in 1993 up from less than a thousand in 1950; *a 60,000 percent increase in just over thirty years!* Not even ancient Rome, poised on the brink of ruination, exhibited such corpulent excess.

The Two-Party Stranglehold

"All parties degenerate into aristocracies of self interest."
— John Taylor, 1814; in a letter to John Adams

"We are currently in the process of a massive shift from
a representative to a participatory democracy...The demise
of representative democracy also signals the end
of the traditional party system."
— John Naisbitt, *Megatrends,* 1982

Vanishing Republic

Each year when we file our tax returns, millions of Americans dutifully check-off to contribute one dollar to the Presidential election. In 1992 the Federal Election Commission which disburses the booty gave $11 million dollars to each party to engage in mirth and revelry at their respective conventions, in order to announce what we already knew.

After that, Messrs. Bush and Clinton each received $55 million to purchase mudslinging ads and promote campaign promises the victor would break once in office. Ross Perot also qualified for FEC funds but declined.

American politics has become a "duopoly" in which more and more the choices are two heads of the same coin. Many conservative Republicans, and disenfranchised Democrats — unhappy with the leftist interests that have betrayed them — voted for the Independent candidate, Mr. Perot.

But there appears to be a considerable representative inequity.

The National Elections Center at the University of Michigan found that 37 percent of Americans consider themselves Independents (up from 23 percent in 1953), while only 36 percent label themselves Democrats and 29 percent Republicans.
  If this is the case, why do we only find one or two "token" Independents in Congress at any one time?

Let's examine some of the reasons for the inequity.

A recurrent indicator of an Empire in decline is the entrenchment of two parties, sometimes hundreds of years old, virtually eliminating the realistic formation of a competing third party.

The Democratic and Republican National Committees are powerful, efficient, well-organized *Corporations.*

What?

That's right. Corporations. Both are incorporated in Washington D.C. In 1991-92 the Republican National Committee took in $192 million and the DNC $104 million, as well as $52 million and $37 million respectively in their "non-federal" accounts.

Also interesting to note is that the American taxpayers (even the 37 percent who call themselves Independents) pay for party leaders and their staffs. On the Federal payroll are the House Majority and Minority Leaders, the Majority and Minority Whips, and the Majority and Minority Chief Deputy Whips. The Majority Leader has a staff of 26 party workers, plus 3 foreign affairs advisors (*what?*) — all compensated from the federal payroll — at an annual cost to the taxpayers of one million dollars.

The Democratic Party Whip makes do with only 17 party workers. The total staff for the six Majority and Minority leaders is 90 employees.

But the "Party" is not over, yet.

The Democratic Steering Committee has eleven federal employees.

The Democratic Caucus has twelve federal employees.

The Republican Conference has 42 federal employees.

The Republican Research Committee (they should research the Constitutionality of taxpayer funded party employees) has six federal employees.

The Republican Committee on Committees — I'm not making this up — has one federal employee.

Vanishing Republic

In all, the House has 160 party workers on the federal payroll while the Senate has a whopping 201. Equally egregious, party leaders get an additional $14,800 on top of their normal $133,600 salary. Not bad work if you can get it. The total taxpayer tab for all these party staffers is a cool $20 million a year.

Unfortunate barriers have been erected to curb third party growth. While the Democrat and Republican parties have automatic placement on the ballot at all levels of government, Independents have purposely been shut out by the legislators from both parties, who, by and large, have written the rules governing state and local elections. Inordinate support and effort is needed for a third party to find its way onto the ballot. In California, more than 750,000 signatures are needed in order for an Independent to be placed on a statewide ballot. In Florida, 180,000 signatures are required — all on separate cards — and a 10 cent "validation" fee paid for each name. Similar obstacles exist in many other states.

Callous political analysts expect such strong-arm tactics from the liberal wing of the Democratic party, whose partisanship is legendary, but this should not be expected from the Republican party based on its historical planks. The Republican party supposedly stands for laissez-faire, free-trade, inclusion, and freedom to pursue excellence without the cumbrance of government shackles — with the apparent exception of allowing an equal playing field for Independent candidates.

These views will certainly not curry favor with my Republican friends.

Mark Anthony

To them, I ask: Is the reason conservatives firmly believe in free trade not due to the fact that competition makes one stronger?

Of course.

Then, why should competition among our aging party structure be any different? In a free and open market — whether it be in the exchange of trade, or the exchange of ideas — will not the more salient, viable entity always win? And won't all parties involved — their structure, practices and pursuits be enriched as a result?

Surely, the formation of a third party hurts the Republican establishment more than the Democrat — but only initially.

One must understand the disenfranchised voter.

Who are the disenfranchised?

They are a coalition of conservative Republicans who feel the party has compromised its conservative values during the Bush and Clinton years, both socially and fiscally in order to build a working consensus with the majority party. The disenfranchised conservatives are joined by so-called moderate Democrats, confounded by the welfare state, frustrated by big government and alienated by the shift to the left of the Democratic governing elite.

In both cases, these Independents are simply varying degrees of conservatism, who will intermesh in the rejuvenated Republican party.

If one has the courage to look beyond the horizon, he or she will see that competition from a third-party will force the Republican party to return to its roots. Limited Constitutional government, social responsibility, and an economic environment in which all who wish to succeed, will have the unchained opportunity to do so.

Yes, if one has vision, he or she will see that I and many other conservatives are tired of liberal Congressmen in Republican clothing. If you are going to act as a liberal — if you are going to vote as a liberal — then please change your party affiliation or form another party. Allow those of us who love America and the Republican party tradition — as well as the conservative values that it stands for — to do what is necessary to save the Republic.

The Vanishing Republic is long past consensus building. Just as we demand a principled stand from our legislators, we too, must stand on principle — a principle that isn't swayed by the prevailing winds of political correctness.

PACs, Elections, Lawyers And Lobbyists

"We have lost our way, but there is a way forward. To remake America, we must understand that it will not happen without citizen intervention. To expect the political class to commit suicide by overseeing the needed reform and downsizing of government is naive."
> — Martin L. Gross, *A Call For Revolution,*
> *How Washington Is Strangling America —*
> *And How To Stop It,* 1994

"[T]he Government of the uncontrolled numerical majority, is but the absolute and despotic form of popular governments."
> — John C. Calhoun

"We don't allow government officials to participate in matters in which they have a direct financial interest, yet we allow members of Congress to draft the rules for elections that determine whether they will keep their jobs."
> — Trevor Potter, chairman of the Federal Election
> Commission, in a speech to the Conference on
> Campaign Reform, July 29, 1994

Therein, lies the problem. The Founding Fathers envisioned a Republic in which the people were directly represented, yet had a reasonable ability to remove those representatives in order to serve as a check on their power. The Founding Fathers could not have envisioned that those men and women, after taking the oath of office, would construct a system of Political Action Committees, gerrymandered districts, manipulative lawyers, lobbyists and special interests that spawned such a bastardized system of *"representation"* — allowing certain legislators the divine birthright to a "safe" seat in Congress.

The very nature of the word Republic is that power comes from the people, and that power is exercised by the representatives the people have chosen.

Madison said,

> *"We may define a republic to be...a government which derives all its powers directly or indirectly from the great body of the people, and is administered by persons holding their offices during pleasure, for a limited period, or during good behavior."*

Yet such profound notions have been replaced by the burning desires of the individuals who we sent to represent us. A freshman House member told Trevor Potter, chairman of the Federal Election Commission,

> *"The only thing members care about more than campaign finance, is redistricting. They would never voluntarily relinquish control over their political futures."*

Obviously, left to their own devices, any election reform drafted by the men and women who served to corrupt it, would be substantially watered down and festered with loopholes.

When the final numbers were tallied, over *one billion dollars was spent on electoral races at all levels in 1992.* The average House winner spent $550,000; the average Senatorial winner, a robust $4 million. In total, $678 million was spent in Congressional races alone.

The results?

Ninety-three percent of incumbents won. It should surprise no one that they outspent their opponents by a hefty eight-to-one margin.

Election reform begins by reforming the laws that govern Political Action Committees (PACs). *Financial World* magazine noted in an April 1991 article that between 1990 and 1996 $350 million in PAC money would be spent in each House of Representatives election — '92, '94, and '96; and $600 million during the Senatorial elections in 1994; for a total of $1.65 billion. Said Ellen Miller of the Center for Responsive Politics, "In a country which calls itself a democracy, clear and fair elections with politicians not bought by special interests ought to be a priority."

How much influence does the average citizen have with his or her Congressperson? The answer is debatable. But I can assure you that it is insignificant in relation to the influence peddled by the nearly 4,700 PACs. How much PAC money is given to Congressional challengers? Very little. PACs place their money (and the influence it buys) on the nose of the horse with the best chance of winning   The challengers are of no use to the lobbyists that feed the bureaucracy until they become part of it.

PACs may give $10,000 per candidate; $5,000 for the primary race and $5,000 for the general election.   PAC contributions totaled a whopping $269 million in 1992, with the average House member garnering $260,000 in PAC money.   In all 40% of all House election funding came from Political Action Committees. The flow of money was so overwhelming the candidates could not spend it all — the elections ended with a $76 million surplus in PAC funds.

One form of PAC shenanigans is a particular affront to the Founding Fathers' vision of American democracy; the so-called "Leadership" PAC. Leadership PACs allow your elected Representatives to spread a little cheer and goodwill at election time.   Oh, they surreptitiously appoint a trusted associate to manage the PAC and give it a jolly patriotic name like former Congressman Dan Rostenkowski's "American Leaders Fund." But what's really occurring is Congress is using PAC funds to grease their fellow Representatives, both allies and adversaries, to the tune of $5,000 a piece maximum in order to influence legislation.   In 1992 Rostenkowski gave a total of $203,761 to 13 candidates, including $8,500 to state and local politicians.

Massive loopholes exist in current laws regulating individual contributions as well. The maximum allowable individual offering is ostensibly $1,000 to a presidential primary candidate, and $20,000 to his or her favorite party. An individual may also give up to $5,000 to a PAC. But the really big contributions come from a practice known as *"soft money."* An individual may give over the $20,000 limit to a national party committee, so long as the money is used for non-federal "party building" activities, such as get-out-the- vote campaigns. In 1992 "soft-money" contributions to the Democrat and Republican parties totaled $63 million at the federal level, in addition to that given to state parties.

Wrote Kevin Phillips,

> "Soft money is, in its essence, a giant slush fund administered by the two parties. The Center for Responsive Politics, in its study of how eighty-three million dollars were fed into the 1991-92 election cycle, used the appropriate title 'Soft Money, Real Dollars.' 'Soft Money, Real Clout' would have been just as descriptive, given the extraordinary opening for influence seekers. To no one's surprise, the combined finance, insurance, and real estate sectors led the soft-money list, giving a total of $17.2 million — $10.9 million of it to the Republican National Committee, $6.3 million to the Democrats. Within this group, the securities and investment business ranked as the biggest single industry, with $7.0 million. The individual leaders were Merrill Lynch, Goldman Sachs, Forstmann Little, Kohlberg Kravis Roberts, and Morgan Stanley (and all except Forstmann Little gave to both parties)...
>
> "The 1990s have seen a bipartisan flowering. In June 1992 the quarterly magazine of Common Cause ran a cover story, 'George Bush's Ruling Class: Who They Are, What They Gave, What They Got,' describing the 249 top contributors who gave $100,000 or more to the GOP's 'Team 100.' Fred Wertheimer, the president of Common Cause, summed up their access to favoritism as effectively 'destroying the country's existing anticorruption laws.' Then in April 1993, when it was clear that the Clinton

administration was merely favoring a *new* portion of the existing political-governmental elite instead of living up to its election-year housecleaning promises, the *New Republic* described the old-boy and old-girl network of the new Clinton administration as representing 'Clincest' because it was so full of Yale Law graduates, well-connected lobbyists, Harvard professors, and Rhodes scholars: 'The Rhodes scholar Mafia is just the beginning. In Clinton's Washington, the worlds of the government, law and academia are now structurally enmeshed. Most everyone seems to have gone to school with each other, is married to each other, writes about each other or lobbies each other. And boasts about it. Is there any way out of the web?'"[56]

This is the frustration the American people face: Washington has become a special interest football game. On one side is the moneyed business elite — financial interests — plying their influence to benefit the *Fortune* 500 and the Wall Street Barons who play the money game. On the other side are limousine liberal, Rhodes scholar, wealth redistributing poverty pimps. Regardless of the final score, no matter which side wins — the American people lose.

Shadow Campaigns And Special Interests

"I can't say that PACs are buying these elections, but you'd have to be a fool to believe that they aren't buying something."
— Senator William Proxmire,
(D-Wisconsin) 1957-1989

Vanishing Republic

In a loophole only a beltway veteran could think of, 24E contributions allow wealthy partisan loyalists to run a shadow campaign — *with no spending limits* — for the candidate of their choice. Under 24E, an individual may run a campaign for his or her chosen candidate, so long as he or she does not have the cooperation of the candidate, or otherwise help him or her directly.

Yeah right.

No wonder recent polls show that 60% of American citizens believe that special interests are controlling Washington. Charles Lewis, founder of the Center for Public Integrity, a lobbyist watchdog organization, said, "In the mercenary culture of Washington, money and power, access and influence, dominate politics and public discourse. The lobbyist is to Washington what the investment banker was to New York in the Eighties. There are huge sums of money to be made and no real controls."[57]

The imminent danger sign is the exponential increase in *foreign* lobbyists in and around Washington. In 1979, the list of foreign interests with paid lobbyists in Washington numbered just over 400. In the 15 years hence, that number has *tripled.* Author Pat Choate compiled a list of 200 former high level government officials, from National Security Advisors, to presidential aids, to Congressmen, who were listed as foreign agents — mostly for Japanese interests. In fact "47 percent of former U.S. Trade Representatives had been lobbyists for the Japanese."[58]

The parallel to fallen empires of yore is unmistakable. *Step one:* During decades of unprecedented growth and prosperity under limited government laissez-faire policy, a thriving, abundant middle class emerges. *Step two:* The middle class is methodically strangled by the awesome weight of government taxation and regulation. *Step three:* As increasingly more power and influence is transferred to the empire's capital city, a political, lawyer-lobbyist culture buys and sells the nation's assets — its culture, savings and manufacturing base, its entrepreneurial spirit and individualism — to the highest bidder. *Step four:* National and international moneyed interests get fat on the wealth of the middle class, which quickly erodes.

In *A Call For Revolution,* Martin Gross graded the foreign lobbyist report card for the 1992 presidential election:

> "Unpaid Bush communications advisor James Lake is a member of the public relations-lobbying firm of Robinson, Lake, Washington insiders who represented Japan Auto Parts Industry Association, Mitsubishi, Suzuki, Minolta and others.
>
> "Another top 1992 Bush campaign aide, Craig Fuller, had until January 1992, been president of Hill and Knowlton, a public relations firm, where he represented the embassy of the People's Republic of China and reportedly was registered as a 'foreign agent' with the Justice Department at the time. His firm had handled many Japanese accounts including Toyota, Mazda, and the Japanese Ministry of Foreign Affairs...
>
> "Clinton had *eight* presidential advisors who personally, or whose firms, had worked for foreign governments or companies. Several were even registered 'foreign agents,' reveals the Center for Public Integrity. They include Thomas Hoog, a vice chairman of Hill and Knowlton, who like his Republican colleague, also handled the embassy of the People's Republic of China. His firm has had such clients as Fujisawa Pharmaceuticals and Hitachi.

"Clinton advisor Paula Stern, who had chaired the International Trade Commission, had testified before her old agency for the Japanese Display Industry. Clintonite attorney Samuel Berger, a partner in the prestigious Washington law firm of Hogan and Hartson and a former Carter administration official, was also a registered foreign agent. His firm represented no one less than the embassy of Japan...

"Being named to the presidential campaign staff was only the beginning of honors for former lobbyists. For Secretary of Commerce, Clinton chose Ron Brown, head of the Democratic National Committee and partner on leave from the powerful Washington law firm of Patton, Boggs, and Blow — whose clients included such Japanese subsidiaries in the United States as Fuji Photo Film USA, Hitachi Sales Corp. of America, Mitsubishi Electric Sales America, Toshiba Corp. US, and others.

"The trade representative chosen by the new President was Mickey Kantor, Clinton's national campaign chairman and partner in a law firm that has represented the Japanese electronics giant NEC."[59]

Three recent attempts to part the sea of lobbyists have been undertaken. The first came from president-elect Clinton who informed America that he would not allow his transition team — the men and women who helped select over 3,000 Clinton appointees — to lobby those people they had helped hire. *President Clinton mandated that this ironclad reform measure would be in effect for a corruption cleansing six months!*

Clinton's second attempt at reform was Executive Order #112834 which he signed on January 20, 1993. Upon leaving office, his political appointees would be barred from lobbying for five years; however, the ban would apply *only to their own agencies* or those that they had a relationship of "substantial responsibility." They would of course be able to lobby the rest of the beltway parasites.

The only honorable reform was offered by Senator Max Baucus (D-Montana) who sponsored S. 3203 which would bar senior campaign officials from lobbying for foreign interests.

Wake me when it gets out of committee.

The Influence Of The Financial Community

"Beyond America's transition from steel mills to mutual funds and stock exchanges, late-twentieth-century financialization has also depended on a second critical circumstance: the changeover by which money in the United States and elsewhere lost intrinsic value through the end of silver coinage in the mid-1960s and the end of dollar convertibility into gold in 1971. Once this happened, dollars, francs, and marks were worth only what the cold-eyed computers and markets decided, and politicians — and the bewildered electorate they sometimes represented — could not keep control. Fixing the value of currencies passed to the financial centers, and within the United States more specifically to the New York and Chicago stock and futures exchanges, and the leading banks and investment firms.

The interaction of economic volatility and billion of dollars' worth of computers programmed by the country's best mathematical and financial minds put the nation's leading financial organization into a catbird seat. This power rested on three pillars: The first was financial-sector ability to take advantage of how U.S. and foreign currencies, now lacking intrinsic or real value, could be played with as almost never

before.   The second, the firms' wherewithal to use their new electronic search-and-deploy capacity to probe every nook and cranny of both the U.S. and the global economies, every bourse and **bolsa**, *every market and contract, for transactions and profits that would have been ungraspable in the pre-electronic era.   And the third was Wall Street's command of profits and compensation levels high enough to excite lawyers and corporate executives, motivating them to help push more of the real economy into the orbit of finance."*
— Kevin Phillips, *Arrogant Capital*

I've quoted Mr. Phillips liberally in this chapter.   He has identified some brilliant similarities between the United States in decline, and fallen empires before it. The "financialization of America" is a large part of the equation.   Over $800 billion is traded daily on the world's currency markets, yet "only $20 billion to $25 billion was exchanged in support of global trade in goods and services."[60]

No longer are the slings and arrows of high finance the proprietary domain of conspiracy theorists and "new world order" inquisitors. The effects of financializtion are a symptom of a much greater problem, summed up by Phillips:

"For the first time in modern U.S. history, stock prices decoupled from the real economy, enabling the Dow-Jones industrial average to keep setting records even as employees' real wages kept declining...
Which brings us to a powerful historical caution about financialization: the evidence that it is not nirvana, but a late stage of great economic powers heading into trouble. Each of the countries we have been examining

Mark Anthony

[Ancient Greece and Rome, the Spanish, Dutch and British Empires] as it passed its peak, underwent a transformation in which finance found itself riding high, feeding on investment and speculation as manufacturing lost importance. As overall decline set in, these same great economic powers also displayed a strong service-sector trend...."

The declining manufacturing sector and the contrasting growth of the service sector — as well as government employees now outnumbering those in the manufacturing sector — should not be overlooked. The warning sign of a world manufacturing leader — *at one time the foremost creditor nation* — relegated to a service economy and the world's largest debtor nation, foreshadows ominous problems if we do not expeditiously reign in Leviathan.

But even as Phillips and other scholars of political science have correctly determined the effect of the financialization of America, *I believe they are only half right in deciphering the cause.*

It is true that the manufacturing sector has retooled its operation, in many cases to emphasize the financial aspect of some enterprises at the expense of the traditional manufacturing base. General Electric has unloaded its consumer electronics division in order to consolidate its considerable resources into General Electric Credit Corporation. Ford Motor Company has seen profits skyrocket from its subsidiary, Ford Credit Corporation; and General Motors has had similar profitability with General Motors Acceptance Corporation.

Vanishing Republic

What the analysts are forgetting is that in all the fallen empires, from ancient Greece to Rome to Edwardian England, to our present economic woes:

Massive, bureaucratic, regulation-riddled central government, has handicapped and penalized the productivity of the manufacturing sector. The manufacturing sector understandably has moved to less regulated, credit and speculative markets. Would this transformation have taken place without government intrusion? No. Why should the manufacturing sector continue to fight the Department of Labor, the EEOC, OSHA, and the EPA, when they can make greater profits in spectronic finance.

The second part of the equation is this: After government grew beyond its means, as it wormed its way into every facet of every business, no matter how large or small; as it transferred wealth from the achievers to the non-achievers; as the welfare state was sold by the elitists who would profit from it, as it developed layer after layer of bureaucracy and inefficiency, its appetite for debt financed deficit spending grew. Somebody had to trade and manage the enormous government debt. Not only did the government force assets out of the manufacturing sector with its oppressive governance, but also offered a carrot as well. Billions were to be made off Uncle Sam's colossal appetite, and the giants of American industry were only too happy to oblige.

The final piece of the transformation occurred as the financial community sought greener pastures in the vibrant economies overseas. This, too, mirrors the decline of Empires before us. Investment bankers seeking greater returns in the world's growth areas, like the Pacific Rim countries — quite possibly the next Empire — have been pouring money into the enterprises of our Asian and European friends. During the five year period between 1988 and 1993 American investors' foreign equity holdings more than doubled from $101 billion to $210 billion.

209

Mark Anthony

The financial services sector has grown in size and influence, fed by government debt, until ultimately the servant would be the master.

As such, we now see leading government officials join the ranks of the financial elite: Goldman Sachs, the Blackstone Group, Lehman Brothers and the Carlyle Group. Former Secretary of State James Baker, as well as former OMB director Dick Darman, and former defense secretary Frank Carlucci have been associates with the Carlyle Group. Former defense secretary James Schlesinger and former deputy secretary of state George Ball teamed up with Lehman Brothers; while former commerce secretary Peter Peterson, Reagan OMB director David Stockman and former Treasury official Roger Altman hung their shingle at the Blackstone Group. Altman has since returned as deputy Treasury secretary, and was summarily bounced as a convenient Whitewater scapegoat.

The most notable commingling of the financial/political community is courtesy of Bill Clinton, who appointed Robert Rubin, co-chairman of Wall Street's most powerful firm, Goldman Sachs, as the chairman of the National Economic Council. Said Stephen Moore, fiscal studies director at the Cato Foundation, "If any Republican had ever tried to get anyone like Robert Rubin near the White House, he would have been savaged."

As the 104th Congress convened in January 1995, Rubin waited in the wings to succeed Lloyd Bentsen as Secretary of The Treasury.

Where was the media on this one?

Vanishing Republic

Capitol Hill — Who's Really In Charge Here?

"ADA [the Americans with Disabilities Act] was a perfect bill. Everybody was for it, and nobody had read it. Not even most of its sponsors."
— Sam Gerdano, former senior counsel to
Senator Charles Grassley (R-Iowa)

"In the Reconciliation Bill of 1989, [the proposed federal budget] the text was brought into the House at the last minute like a sacred icon. The oversize cardboard carton filled with over 1,000 uncollated, unindexed pages was gingerly placed down in front of the House, all wrapped up with cord.

'We were permitted to walk down into the well and gaze upon the bill from several angles, and even to touch it,' recalls Congressman Chris Cox of California. But no one knew exactly what the bill contained. There were no copies, and no one could read it. They could only look at it in the box, then vote up and down, yes and no."
— Martin L. Gross, *A Call For Revolution,* 1993

This is how your elected officials spend a trillion of your tax dollars.

The Founding Fathers, when they fashioned their vision of the ideal constitutionally federated republic, did not intend to have the people's representatives insulated by another level of government — lawyers, lobbyists, congressional aides and permanent committee staffers.

The breakdown of Congress as a legitimate representative legislative body can be attributable to five predominant abuses:

211

- The use of House Rules to block worthwhile amendments to legislation, and stall any reasonable reform proposals.
- The proliferation of excessive committees.
- The army of Congressional aids and committee staffers which has added another inefficient, myopic layer of bureaucracy.
- The practice of writing sweeping, yet vague and thoughtless, laws only to let federal regulatory bodies and the courts decide the final implications and limits of the legislation.
- The formation of the *"Iron Triangle"* that exists between powerful committee chairmen, the special interests they legislate, and the regulatory agencies that monitor compliance.

House Rules

"The Democratic majority in the House is like a baseball team that always plays at home and changes the ground rules for each game. If an opposing team is known for using squeeze plays, then bunts are ruled out. If the visitors are a bunch of heavy hitters, then shots over the wall are called ground-rule singles. The House Rules Committee draws up a fresh set of ground rules for nearly every piece of important or controversial legislation considered on the floor."
— Eric Felton, *The Ruling Class,*
Inside The Imperial Congress, 1993

We've all heard the sentiment that forty years of one party House rule has corrupted a once great institution. But many do not know exactly why. The leading cause: the Majority Party has ruled with a veritable iron fist.

In the Senate, a single member may raise virtually any piece of legislation he or she wishes. However, in the House, strict rules prohibit which amendments reach the floor for a vote. Several proposals throughout this book, such as the A-Z Spending Cuts bill or numerous Term Limit proposals were simply bottled up in committee by the Majority Party which appoints the chairs of those committees.

Should a bill make it out of committee, there is a back-up line of defense the Leadership may employ — the House Rules Committee. For example, an overwhelming majority of Americans are in favor of a presidential line-item veto. House Leaders, led by (Former) Speaker Tom Foley would never willingly give such budgetary authority to the Executive Branch, so they watered down the proposal with an alternate called "Enhanced Recision" which allows the President to make "recommendations" to Congress which would still exercise final approval of the appropriation.

David Mason, director of the U.S. Congress Assessment Project at The Heritage Foundation, noted, "in recent years, the Rules Committee has increasingly and severely restricted Representatives' ability to amend bills. In the 95th Congress (1977-1978), only 15 percent of the special rules restricted amendments which would be otherwise permissible under the permanent House rules. During the last two years, [1993-1994] 79 percent of special rules disallowed amendments."[61]

Chart 10-1 illustrates the proliferation of House Rules obstructionism.

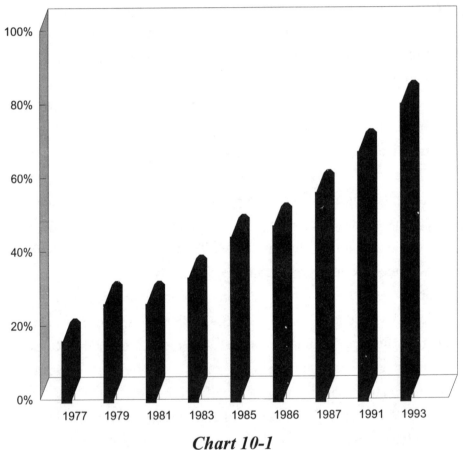

House Rules Committee Employs Politics
The Growth of Restrictive Rules

Chart 10-1

Source: Vital Statistics on Congress, 1993-1994

Rules abuses not only abound in number, but also in range of implementation. Appropriations bills normally do not need approval of the Rules Committee in order to reach the floor. However, in 1994, Democratic leaders sent the Legislative Branch Appropriations bill to the Rules Committee which imposed a special rule that allowed only six of the 53 proposed amendments to be heard, with the watered down measures "affecting less than one-third of one percent of the funds in the bill. More serious proposals — for a five percent across-the-board spending cut to eliminate franked (free) mail and calling for an audit of House operations — were not even allowed to be debated."[62]

The Proliferation Of Committees, Aides And Staffers

"Much of the staff went to the burgeoning committees, creating a shadow bureaucracy, one that helps explain why cutting spending is so hard in Washington: For every corner of every federal program, there is not only a gaggle of bureaucrats desperate to protect and expand their turf, there are one or more congressional staffers who also have a stake in the program's existence. The bigger a program a staff aide oversees, the more power and importance he has. No aide, then, wants to allow, let alone propose, cutting spending in a program under his control...

"...committee staffers become what congressional scholar Michael Malbin calls 'unelected representatives' making decisions routinely affecting hundreds of millions of dollars...

" ...John Jackley, a former congressional staffer and author of **Hill Rat,** *tells of a conversation with a staff aide unimpressed by the tale of an investment banker who had bet one-million dollars*

on a single hand of the game Liar's Poker: 'I can do ten mil with report language and not even have to ask the chairman,' he said. 'Who cares about keeping the money?...It's a lot more fun to shove a hundred mil up someone's a-- and then knock off for the rest of the day for a cold one.' For many young congressional staffers, government is not something one does for the people, but rather what one does to the people. "[63]

— Eric Felten, *The Ruling Class,*
Inside The Imperial Congress, 1993

"People asked me how I felt about being elected to Congress, and I told them I never thought I'd give up that much power voluntarily."[64]

— Congressman Norman Dicks (D-Washington)
on his transition from being an 8 year aide to
Senator Warren Magnuson (D-Washington)
to an *elected* member of the House of
Representatives

Each member of the Senate has 42 aids, while House members have to make do with 18 full-time and 4 part-time staffers. *The total number of Congressional staffers approaches 12,000!* In addition, legislators have a veritable army of committee staffers. The combined total approaches 4,000. Committee staffers are often paid over $100,000 per year, with the staffers of the party leadership paid even more. The combined support personnel for the 535 members of Congress now exceeds 30,000.

Why are there so many?

Because Congress has roughly 300 committees.

This is an absolutely unworkable bureaucracy, and it ultimately distances our elected officials from the very people they are supposed to represent. Many members of Congress spend their time running from committee to committee, often missing sessions of the more trivial ones. This conflagration of lawmakers, allegedly doing the people's work, is costing the people about a billion and a half dollars a year.

While your representatives are spending so much of their time sitting on numerous committees with grossly overlapping responsibilities, their newly empowered committee staffers are busy writing legislation. The American public has finally come to the awareness that Congress rarely reads the legislation it votes on. Now they're finding out their Representatives usually don't *write* it either.

Senators have personal aides assigned to their respective committees. *"S. Res. 60"* aides, as they are called from the 1975 legislation that authorized them, have enormous power — elected by no one — accountable to no constituency except the leather loafered lobbyists that purchase their meals.

The end result is fragmented, inefficient power.

The Department of Defense and the Department of Housing and Urban Development are each under the jurisdiction of *over 100 different committees and subcommittees.* Our tax dollars are sent into the abyss while committee staffers — the true authors of appropriations bills — and high powered beltway law firms representing the moneyed special interests, fight for the booty. The growth of the parasite culture since 1975 has been unprecedented. Even during the historic government expansion under FDR's New Deal, House members only had two or three aides.

217

Mark Anthony

When I discuss matters of political reform with friends and family, they are invariably stunned to find out that their elected representatives have so little to do with the inner workings of Washington. Although a majority of Americans believe special interests are running Washington, they're shocked when they're exposed to the degree to which it has risen.

In *The Ruling Class*, Author Eric Felten dubbed Kevin Kelly as the "Mayor of HUD." Mr. Kelly is the top staffer on the Senate Appropriations Subcommittee which is responsible for approving spending for the Department of Housing and Urban Development. Although legally, Mr. Kelly is answerable to Senator Barbara Mikulski (D-Maryland) — in practice he is answerable to nobody, not even the Secretary of Housing and Urban Development. Jack Kemp, a conservative Republican, was appointed as Secretary of HUD and assigned the responsibility of cleaning up the department. It was Kemp's goal to award the department's discretionary funds to those most worthy, on a competitive basis rather than a political one. His staff developed a point system in order to award funds to those with the highest merit, attempting to put a stop to the gravy train. Congress sought to block Kemp's reforms by using the power of the one (unelected) man who could: Kevin Kelly.

Kelly initially agreed with Kemp's point system, but then set himself up as the "gatekeeper for congressional pork projects." Kelly didn't put their requests in the appropriations bill, but in the committee report that accompanied it. Committee reports may not be changed once they leave committee.

Frank Keating, Kemp's General Counsel at HUD, informed him that it was within his authority as secretary to ignore "line-item projects in the committee report." Kelly responded the following year. He "placed an item in the appropriations bill requiring the Secretary to adhere to recommendations in the accompanying committee report. Kelly also punished Keating for giving the Secretary the advice about ignoring line-item projects by deleting the funding requested for nearly 50 lawyers that were to have been added to his staff."

Kelly was not through yet. Years later, Keating was denied a federal judgeship on trumped up allegations which had the unmistakable fingerprints of a rancorous committee staffer and his appreciative congressional accomplices.

Kelly continued to thwart Kemp's attempts to clean up HUD and reorganize its slothful bureaucracy. Wrote Felten,

> "Key staffers like Kevin Kelly rarely leave, thus becoming the institutional memory of their committees. If Sen. Mikulski loses or gives up her position as chairman of the subcommittee, her successor will inherit Kelly. And he will be happy to do so. Kelly is the only person who, practically speaking, can write his subcommittee's appropriations bill. Along with the power that comes from being the only mechanic who understands the machinery, staffers like Kelly enjoy leverage over pet projects and the power to put people out of jobs. If this doesn't make them the most important people in Washington, it at least makes them think they are."

219

Mark Anthony

Vague Laws — Regulatory Nightmares

Political Scientists have coined a new phrase to denote the powerful "sub-governments" that have sprung up within the beltway. They are known as "Iron-Triangles." On one hand are powerful committee chairmen and co-chairmen, as well as their staffers, who write vague laws. The other two points of the triangle are the federal bureaucracies the congressional committees oversee and the large corporations/special interests the bureaucrats regulate.

Away from the public eye, often in stark violation of "sunshine" laws, the bureaucrats and business leaders bribe and cajole, negotiate and barter; divvying up the tax dollars of the average Joe and crushing the competition offered by small entrepreneurial interests.

Little do they know or care about the ramifications of their legislation. And when legislation threatens personal implications, the guilty amendment will surely be discarded in committee. Any attempt at Congressional reform is treated like cancer on the corrupt body politic.

During debate on the Americans with Disabilities Act, Senator Orrin Hatch (R-Utah) wanted to offer tax credits to small businesses to compensate them for the inordinate compliance costs. Senator Lloyd Bentsen (D-Texas) objected, and as such admitted that no one actually knew what the cost of the legislation would be. "We have no estimate of how much the amendment will cost the federal government," he said. "Before we ask the taxpayers of

America to provide that relief, we should know what the cost will be."

Senator Charles Grassley then offered an amendment that would make the ADA binding on members of Congress as well. Grassley noted other sweeping legislation from which they conveniently exempted themselves: the Civil Rights Act of 1964, the Freedom of Information Act of 1966, the Age Discrimination Act of 1967, the Occupational Safety and Health Act of 1970, the Privacy Act of 1974, the Ethics in Government Act of 1978, and many more, ad nauseam.

Grassley supported the bill. His aim was to force Congress to determine the cost of the ADA, thus forcing some legislative accountability. The Grassley Amendment was supported on the floor — to do otherwise would be politically imprudent. But the effect was smoke and mirrors, as the teeth of the amendment would surely be stripped by the time it left committee.

And so they were.

In the final conference report the House was responsible for policing itself, and complaints against the Senate would never escape its hallowed halls. They would not be accountable to the legislation they just forced on the rest of the populace.[65]

Once the law was implemented it was hopelessly vague. Congress left it up to the bureaucrats and the courts to do what they themselves did not have the principle or fortitude to do. "Under the law, public accommodations (e.g., hotels, restaurants and such) have to be made accessible to the handicapped, but only if the changes are 'readily achievable.' Asked to define readily achievable, Senator Ted Kennedy explained that businesses would have to do what was 'easily accomplishable and not involving much difficulty or expense.'"[66]

What does that mean?

It means the Equal Employment Opportunity Commission would decide what the law means — they and their attorneys and Administrative Law Judges — oh, and also the moneyed interests who could afford to influence the regulators.

This is a practice known as "regulation-negotiation," better known as "reg-neg." Congress, knowing that the real authority to remove them from office lies with the powerful lobbies that fund the Political Action Committees, refuses to take a stand that would impugn the wishes of even the smallest special interest faction. Therefore, they purposely write vague laws (or instruct their staffers to write vague laws, as the case may be). It is then up to the bureaucrats to hash out the finer points in counsel with the lobbyists. But more often than not, it is the lobbyists who decide among their more influential members what the limitations of the law will be. Marriot Hotels lobbied hard for strict regulations on ADA; and why not? They had built their establishments to accommodate for the legislation for the last ten years.

Such is the danger of reg-neg and the inherent peril in allowing Representatives to relinquish their obligation to the people in favor of those who can afford the price of admission to "Gucci Gulch." The result is a two-tiered economy. Large corporations actually increase their market share as government regulations run amok. They have the resources and the corporate attorneys to sort through the bureaucratic jungle while their less capitalized competitors are consumed by it.

How Congress Reforms Itself — or... Why We Have To Do It Ourselves

"In framing a government which is to be administered by men over men, the great difficulty lies in this: you must first enable the government to control the governed; and in the next place oblige it to control itself."
— James Madison

Nineteen-ninety-two...The 103rd Congress welcomed 110 new faces. Fourteen states put the question of term limits to the voters, and 14 states overwhelmingly approved the measure. A "New Democrat" was moving his family into the White House. This would be the era of reform.

Or would it?

A non-partisan administrator was given the task of cleaning up the House of Representatives. Several months later he resigned in disgust. His version of reform did not conform to that which the House Leadership had in mind.

The Joint Committee on the Organization of Congress, a bi-cameral panel of 24 members, was started equitably enough by appointing "moderates" Lee Hamilton and William Gradison of the House as well as David Boren and Pete Domenici of the Senate. Then Democratic Leaders George Mitchell and Tom Foley and their Republican counterparts, Bob Dole and Robert Michel, held their breath and stomped their feet until they all agreed to appoint partisan loyalists to the other 21 spots.

And where were all the reform-minded freshman? "Not one of the Senate members had served less than a decade in Congress...Of the 110 freshman Representatives — over a quarter of the House — only one, Representative Jennifer Dunn, was appointed to the Joint Committee; and her appointment was possible only after Gradison's resignation from Congress."[67]

The partisans bickered back and forth to no avail. A line item veto was not even considered; nor were reductions in Senate staff. A reduction in the number of committees each Senator would sit on was proposed, but was later knocked out by the Senate Rules Committee. They also scuttled the notion of applying employment laws to the Senate.

The House showed even less gumption to cut committees than the Senate. Democratic leaders also blocked any changes in floor procedures that were urged by Republicans. House leaders ensured that little if any reform would be produced by forcing most resolutions to go to both the House Administration Committee *and* the Rules Committee. Ultimately, "the House Rules Committee killed the review of House committees, leaving the entire internal bureaucracy of the House, its rules, structure, and personnel untouched by the reform effort."[68]

Any attempts at reform were averted even before the newly elected freshmen members arrived in Washington. Former Speaker Foley, Dick Gephardt and several other influential Democratic leaders diligently criss-crossed the country promising pork and prized committee assignments to all would be renegades, if they quietly fell in line behind the big kahuna.

And tow-the-line they did.

Plans for a mid-November 1992 conference "organized by and for newly-elected lawmakers" never took place. Rather, "the freshman reform task force was set up as an arm of the House Democratic Caucus. In so doing, Foley again split his freshmen from their Republican peers (who set up their own reform task force), steering the freshmen toward party affiliation rather than bipartisan cooperation."[69]

Recent Attempts At Budgetary Restraint — Or...Why The System Needs To Be Changed Before Any Reform Is Possible

"There are, to be precise, 536 of them; [Congress and the President] and they have hired about twenty thousand bright and energetic people to act as their accomplices and assistants. They pay themselves, and they help us very well, by the way. And why not? It's your money they're living on. That, and the checks they bounce at the House bank and the loans they don't repay at the White House Credit Union. What could they possibly know of fiscal responsibility?"
— Harry E. Figgie, Jr. and
Gerald J. Swanson, Ph.D., *Bankruptcy 1995*

Figgie, who served on The Grace Commission, and Swanson conjectured in their book that their efforts were nothing more than "an old shell game, with a new chestnut." They felt the Reagan administration choreographed the entire exercise in order to foreshadow serious deficit reduction so that the administration could justify massive defense expenditures.

Their contention is debatable. Two of President Reagan's main objectives were to rebuild the military, which was devastated

225

during the Carter years, and to eliminate the threat of Communist Russia. I strongly support the military, and rebuilding our national defense was of critical importance to national security. President Reagan, as Chief Executive Officer, restored a pride and dignity in our country that I will always cherish. Furthermore, the defeat of the Soviet Union had scores of benefits.

However, if these noble efforts help serve to bankrupt our country, they will be remembered as hollow victories, indeed.

No intellectually honest individual can dispute the value of the Reagan military buildup, but the funding should have been offset by budget cuts. This is not entirely the fault of the Reagan administration. President Reagan surely would have made considerably larger budget cuts had Congress obliged him.

The same fiscal responsibility should be applied to President Clinton. The media have focused on the Clinton rhetoric of deficit reduction, never questioning the validity of the numbers. President Clinton has no right to embark on a mission of massive social spending unless his programs are offset by legitimate spending cuts as well. Although I disagree fiscally, morally and spiritually with the type of dependency breeding social programs the Clinton team desires, the fact remains that *they* have control of the White House between 1992 and 1996. It is the political prerogative of the Clinton administration to foster a legislative agenda that it believes in. My point is the White House should balance its wants with fiscally responsible spending cuts first, and then let our democratic system wrestle with enacting its agenda.

Obstructing the effort of the 103rd Congress to enact The A-Z Spending Cuts Plan, was — surprise, surprise — House Speaker

Tom Foley. Mr. Foley called it "probably the most poorly thought out proposal for the consideration of public policy that I've ever seen in many years — maybe the worst one ever."

His response is to be expected. In Speaker Foley's Congress, 79% of all bills have operated under a closed rule. That, my friends, is simply government by stealth.

Closed rule was also responsible for blocking the Penny-Kasich bill. On November 22, 1993, Penny-Kasich, which contained $103 billion of *REAL* budget cuts, fell by a 219-213 vote. The genesis of the bill has relevance regarding beltway liberals raffish view of the deficit.

President Clinton, needing the vote of Rep. Penny (D-Minnesota) in order to pass his 1993 budget, promised to find an additional $106 billion in spending cuts later that year. Mr. Penny, one of the more honorable men in Congress, voluntarily vacated his seat in 1994 after serving five terms (10 years). He felt that 10 years is the limit that one should serve, and, it should be noted, he was adequately frustrated by his peers who view such matters as fiscal responsibility, secondary to re-election.

Penny, therefore, stipulated that these must be "real" budget cuts, not ethereal baseline budget cuts. The resultant bill would have trimmed $103 billion in spending. President Clinton agreed. However, once the President's budget passed, his resolve disappeared faster than pizzas at a Jenny Craig convention.

The rhetoric surrounding the deficit reduction debate was filled with a more heightened degree of bombast than the norm. "The amendment as a whole is flawed and must be rejected," President Clinton wrote in a letter to House Speaker Tom Foley. Mr. Clinton also implored Congress to "not take risks with our now fledgling economy." Added deputy budget director Alice Rivlin, "substantial additional deficit reduction at this time could slow the growth of the economy at a crucial point."

Yet, there is something I fail to understand. In February 1993 President Clinton told America that he was going to have to renege on his promised middle-class tax cut because the deficit was $50 billion higher over five years than he was told during the campaign (it was later revealed by Rivlin in Bob Woodward's book, *The Agenda,* that the Clinton team knew all along what the real deficit numbers were). The result of the Clinton team's collective brain cramp was the imposition of a tax increase in excess of $600 billion — the largest in world history.

The implication is clear. A $50 billion budget gap posed a monumental fiscal crises which could only be remedied by $600 billion in new taxes.   If deficit reduction was so urgent, then why was the specter of Penny-Kasich — which would also have been implemented over five years, and *only amounted to 1 cent on the dollar of federal spending — such a threat to our "fledgling economy."*

Furthermore, a few weeks earlier, in October 1993 — less than *two months* after Mr. Clinton's 1993 budget passed — he was taking credit for a robust economic recovery (it should be noted that *not ONE SINGLE PROGRAM was cut from the 1993 Clinton budget,* yet federal spending increased roughly $200 billion dollars over the previous year — *some* deficit reduction). Then amazingly, the fledgling economy was defined as perilously fluttering on newfound wings as the debate turned to *real* budget cuts. Quite convenient, isn't it; to define economic growth by the legislative needs of the day.

Penny-Kasich would have used Medicare savings to cut the federal deficit. A bit of fiscal responsibility that would "fracture the growing consensus for universal coverage and cost containment," said the President. Replied Rep. Penny, "If you think Medicare is already a bottomless pit, wait until you see what happens with those new benefits."

When asked to elaborate on his theory, Clinton informed the public that although his 1993 budget plan promised America $500 billion in budget cuts, *he never said that he would use those funds to reduce the deficit.*

Huh?

Then why the tax increases? I thought it was because the $50 billion discrepancy they "discovered" was a threat to national security. Didn't the President tell us on January 14, 1993, that he was forced to abandon his promised middle-class tax cut because "we have a structural deficit that is too high. The American people would think I was foolish if I said I will not respond to changing circumstances."

Evidently, circumstances had changed again.

Said Rep. Penny, "Cutting the deficit is way down on his (Clinton's) list of priorities." He added, "Now I must conclude the President's only interested in budget cuts that will allow him to spend more elsewhere." Clinton, on the other hand, asked that we give his $500 billion in promised deficit reduction "time to work." Replied Rep. Penny, "How long do we have to wait for this promised deficit reduction?"

The political reality was simple: the Clinton administration knew that a vote for deficit reduction would make funding for their sweeping health care reforms all the more difficult.

So, instead of real budget cuts, we were offered this: Budget Committee Chairman Martin Sabo (D-Minnesota) offered an alternative plan consisting of $37 billion of "budget cuts." But don't start celebrating yet. As is typical of most "budget cuts," these measures will not shrink the deficit because they won't touch existing spending ceilings. Sabo's program, greatly lauded by the liberal media, would produce billions of phantom cuts in government bureaucracies.

The Death Of The Balanced Budget Amendment And The Birth Of A New Fiscal Policy — *"Carve And Spend"*

The battle on the hill over the balanced budget amendment has been fraught with hypocrisy since its inception. Liberals nonchalantly refer to it as a gimmick — although its chief sponsor in the Senate was Paul Simon (D-Illinois); not exactly a defender of the right. The amendment was designed to produce a balanced budget beginning in fiscal 1999. At such time, outlays of federal funds may not exceed revenues, and the national debt could not be increased. It would take a three-fifths majority of both the House and Senate to alter those requirements, except in the event of war or national emergency *(we already have a national emergency — that's why we need a balanced budget amendment)*.

Vanishing Republic

Washington Post Staff Writer Eric Pianin called the amendment, "a grand scheme promoted for years by Republicans and mostly conservative Democrats."

In early November 1993 Clinton said, "We must reject the temptation to use any budget gimmicks to hide from the specific choices that are needed for long-term economic renewal."

> *Ask your spouse about the logic — and long term benefits and peace of mind — of paying off your bills and becoming debt free? Why then, do liberal elitists act as if the very thought of balancing the budget is akin to being doused with honey and covered with ants? Their utter repulsion to deficit reduction is like a vampire's reaction to dawn's early light. Of what are they so afraid?*

Senator Robert Byrd, (D-West Virginia) former Chairman of the Senate Appropriations Committee — you may know him by his other moniker, "The King of Pork" — was instrumental in delaying the vote on the amendment until 1994. Apparently, Senator Byrd does not want any limitations on how he spends *your* money. He called the amendment "political sorcery" and, according to *The Washington Post,* claimed that it would destroy the Congressional budgetary process and undermine the economy.

Well, he's half right. The balanced budget amendment *would* destroy the Congressional budgetary process — the one that gave us a $4.7 trillion national debt. President Clinton followed Senator Byrd's remarks by saying, "I cannot put them in such peril [the balanced budget amendment] threatens the livelihoods of millions of Americans."

How sanctimonious.

In 1993 the amendment fell shy by eleven votes in the Senate and nine votes in the House. According to Clay Chandler of *The Washington Post*, "The administration's fiscal motto is neither 'cut-the-budget' nor 'tax-and-spend,' according to one White House official. Instead, their message is best described as 'carve-and-spend' — fund new policies by wresting money from other programs."

Carve-and-spend? Would you like to guess who the turkey is?

Then Speaker of the House, Tom Foley was quoted in the *Washington Times* on October 29 saying, "If all we do is assign every dollar of savings...to deficit reduction, we are not going to develop a policy of recycling federal programs into more efficient and effective investments. And I think that will tend to reduce to some degree the interest of the Congress in effecting those savings."

The message the esteemed Former Speaker implies is this: He and his Congressional brethren are more qualified to spend your money than you are. His remarks are the fiscal equivalent of using one credit card to pay off another. Whose interests are best served by such leadership?

And *can* we refer to such activity as leadership? To wit:

> *More than 100 members of the 103rd Congress favor term limits, yet Mr. Foley did not allow a single committee hearing on the issue.*

An unidentified senior Clinton administration official said that budget cutting right now would not be "wise or prudent." The mystery spokesperson also commented that "everybody on the economic team...feels we've come to a point where, we think, it is just not prudent to take risks with the recovery right now."

Maybe, I'm missing something. Where is the irrefutable correlation between national prosperity and huge federal deficits?

Mark Anthony

Chapter 11
Reforming Elections, Congress, The Budget Process and The Federal Bureaucracy

"When a man assumes a public trust, he should consider himself as public property."
— Thomas Jefferson

Election Reform

"Institutional developments and campaign changes have made members of Congress almost invulnerable to mass public judgments, while at the same time allowed them to manipulate the opinions of isolated constituencies and individuals.

Representatives cultivate individuals through casework, and narrow constituencies by direct mail and political action committee solicitations. The power to appease constituencies on an almost individual basis allows representatives to ignore larger issues and place the blame for inaction on the institution."[70]
— Rep. Pete Hoekstra, (R-Michigan)

Election reform begins with the Political Action Committee. Some commentators have espoused entirely eliminating the practice. I disagree. We do not need to eliminate participation in the electoral process simply because certain interests have abused the privilege. However, strict reforms of the PACs are required.

1. Corporate and special interest contributions to Political Action Committees would be strictly prohibited. The notion of

"one-person-one-vote" is a fallacy so long as well-financed entities have the ability to give thousands of dollars to a candidate. Their funds clearly purchase more than the equivalent of a single vote, and would be disallowed.

2. Individuals may continue to contribute to Political Action Committees, but with the following limitation: they may give to a maximum of three candidates per election, with a ceiling of $1,000 for the primary and $1,000 for the general election.

3. The so-called "Leadership" PACs would be banned. Candidates would be prohibited from contributing money to other candidates.

4. *Soft-Money* contributions would be strictly prohibited, as they are a barrier to the viability of third party candidates. If the Republican and Democratic parties wish to sponsor "get-out-the-vote" campaigns, they can do it with their own, already considerable, funds.

5. Eliminate 24E "shadow" campaigns. If a well-heeled constituent wishes to purchase the favor of "Senator Whiffenpoof," or any other elected official, let him move to a Communist country where they condone such activity.

Party Reform

1. Immediately remove all party staffers from the federal payroll, as well as bonus pay for Congressional party leaders. If they wish to maintain their party staff, let the party pay for it.

2. No Federal Election Commission funds will be given to the parties for their national conventions. They can buy their own drinks and pay their own hotel tab.

3. It would be strictly illegal for national party chairmen, or any other party official, to lobby or otherwise attempt to influence the Executive, Legislative or Judicial branch. The role of political parties is to aid in the election process of their chosen partisans, not govern the nation.

4. Direct primaries would be held in all states in order to allow Independent candidates a chance to represent their district.

5. The barriers to third-party access should be removed from the ballot in all states. One hundred signatures would be needed for statewide office, 500 for the House and 750 for the Senate. Additional fees and other barriers would be eliminated by appointing non-partisan election boards in all states. Loyalists of the two parties would no longer be allowed to write the restrictive state election laws currently in force.

General Reforms

1. All elections must be won by a majority. Forty-three percent of the vote is not a mandate for change, as President Clinton would have you believe. We can no longer afford to elect a President who is supported by less than fifty percent of the voters. In Senatorial and Presidential races, the top two candidates would engage in a runoff election thirty days hence in order to determine a majority victor.

2. In House elections, "Alternative Preference" would be used, as is done in Australia's lower house. The process is simple and could be easily tabulated using available computer technology. Voters would rank the candidates in order of preference; first, second and third. If a candidate receives more than 50% of the vote, the election is over and he or she is declared the winner. If no one receives a majority, the weakest contender is eliminated and his or her second choice votes are redistributed to the other candidates. The process is repeated until one candidate achieves a majority.

This system allows for third party candidates to have a realistic chance in House elections while preserving a more traditional method for Senate and Presidential elections.

3. All elections would include the choice *"None of The Above."* If "None of The Above" is the leading vote recipient in the first round of votes, all candidates would be eliminated and the process would begin anew.

This process reforms the current system in which both candidates are often two sides of the same coin. The notion that gridlock is detrimental, is not well thought out. It is simply the infantile ranting of liberal politicians, and their media allies, whenever the voting public does not see things their way. In politics, consensus means compromising one's principles. In order for the voters to have a choice, to have honest representation, we must demand that politicians take a clear stand on the issues.

Mark Anthony

We cannot, at the same time demand consensus building **and** *accountability from our leaders. The two are mutually exclusive.*

4. Impose term limits. Limit House members to five terms (ten years) and Senators to two terms (12 years).

5. Disband the Electoral College. Presidential elections should be strictly majority vote. Here's why. Under the current system, if a candidate receives only one more vote in a given state, he or she will receive all of the electoral votes of that state. The winner-take-all nature of the Electoral College gives the largest states inordinate importance — and it has been abused (*Read:* bought). California, New York, Texas, Illinois, Florida, Michigan and Pennsylvania have large numbers of electoral votes. These states also have some of America's worst welfare problems. Why? Because over the years, politicians have purchased the votes of the lower middle class and the poor, creating a welfare state that has caused devastation in these areas. As a result, taxes are raised on the *entire* nation in order to provide elected officials enough funds to continue to grease the wheels of the important electoral vote states. The numbers of voters in these states already have adequate numbers in the House of Representatives. To give such sway in presidential elections as well will compound the already crumbling infrastructure in these most populous of states.

6. Alter the role of the Federal Election Commission. All three dollar contributions would be distributed among candidates for House, Senate and Presidential elections. House and Senate portions would be determined by the size and population of the

constituency at stake. The FEC would disburse 25% of the funds to primary candidates, with 45% earmarked for general elections. This would allow 30% to be placed in a trust fund for run-off elections.

7. The candidates' personal campaign contributions would be limited to $2,500 for state and local office, $10,000 for the House and $20,000 for Senate and Presidential elections.

8. Candidates would be strictly prohibited from keeping campaign funds.

A Cautionary Word About The Initiative Process

Twenty three states have direct ballot initiatives. Populists are hailing the practice as a way to reform our corrupted government. "Give the power to the people," they say.

Let me remind you that 19th century socialist theory spawned the Progressive movement which began early in the 20th century. Progressivism begot unconstitutional "direct democracy" reforms such as the 17th amendment. The growth of Populism begot an environment where politicians could easily purchase the votes of a cultivated dependency class.

I suggest we defer to the wisdom of the Founding Fathers.

We are a Constitutionally Federated Republic. We are not a direct democracy.

Our problems have not evolved because the system doesn't work. It's because we have allowed the system to be bastardized.

We don't need to scrap the system; we need to return to our roots by implementing reforms that empower the citizens by purifying the representative process — *not by invoking mob rule.* To do so presents another unique set of problems.

The ballot initiative *can* be used for good government, as with Proposition 13, which rolled back excessive punishing property taxes in California.

It can just as easily be manipulated by a small, well financed group.

Limited Casinos were on the 1994 ballot in Florida. Although merits existed for both sides of the argument, they were totally irrelevant. My point is that a small group of some 60 entities spent an estimated $15 million — one of the largest expenditures of its kind in American history — in order to influence legislation. The power of the media has been harnessed to sway the outcome of the vote. The Limited Casino initiative failed, but the point remains: Do we want issues like Abortion or Drug Legalization put to a vote where more often than not, special interest bank accounts — and the size thereof — will determine policy.

I thought that was what we were trying to reform?

A more sensible approach is an "Indirect Initiative" process; several variations of which have been proposed by Rep. Pete Hoekstra (R-Michigan). Hoekstra has introduced three bills in the House that allow "voters to set issue agendas in national elections."

His first proposal would be a nationwide advisory referendum on term limits. "An advisory referendum is admittedly a 'test run' for initiatives; the results would be non-binding and Congress could choose to ignore — as it too frequently does now — the voters' choice. But the political dynamics of a national referendum, even one that is non-binding, are such that Congress will be hard pressed to avoid issues subject to such wide discussion."[71] In fact, this would force accountability. Legislators who recorded a vote opposite such overwhelming national sentiment would have no place to hide come election time.

Rep. Hoekstra's second bill is an indirect initiative process for *legislation*. Petitions would be carefully screened before gaining ballot access. If the initiative received a majority vote in three-fifths of the states, it would then go before Congress. Congress would have 15 months to act on the initiative. If it is approved and the President signs it, it would become law. If Congress passed a *different* version of the initial proposal, both versions would go to the voters for a second vote, with the majority version becoming law. If Congress does not act at all, the initiative would return to the ballot in the next general election. Voter approval on this second vote would automatically make the initiative law.

Hoekstra's final proposal is a mechanism to streamline the Constitutional amendment process. It would work similar to the previous suggestion, but the initiative would require a super-majority (60 percent) in three-fifths of the states. That being done, "the ratify procedures provided for in Article V of the Constitution take over."

Rep. Hoekstra's proposals are brilliant in their simplicity and function, while averting the "mob" rule which the Founding Fathers were so wary.

Reforming Congress

1. All tax increases would need voter approval via a national referendum. (I don't see this as a violation of my reservations regarding direct democracy. On the contrary. We are not forming policy via mob rule. We are simply placing limitations on government's appetite. This is absolutely in keeping with the spirit of the Constitution.)

2. Reform House Rules. The Rules Committee would no longer be permitted to restrict amendments from a floor vote. This practice has stifled fiscal responsibility, as well as any honorable attempts at Congressional reform.

3. Congress MUST OBEY ALL LAWS IT IMPOSES ON THE PUBLIC AT LARGE. Congress has irresponsibly released massive "Omnibus" legislation. They care not the regulatory or fiscal implications on the taxpayers nor the business community because they have no idea what their proposals will cost or whom they will destroy. By making Congress accountable to the laws they pass, as well as abiding the next three suggestions, they will carefully fashion responsible legislation.

The 104th Congress increased its accountability to "existing federal employee protection and anti-discrimination statutes, including wage and hour and family leave laws."

4. The Representatives themselves must write all legislation. In doing so we will tame the lobbyists and special

interests who control the real power brokers in Washington — the committee staffers who actually write the bills.

5. Congress must write clearly defined, specific laws. We can no longer afford to let lazy, overpaid Representatives write vague legislation, only to allow faceless bureaucrats to do the job of Congress.

6. Congress must READ all legislation (every page) before voting.

7. Congress must legislate ONLY. Show trials have become the domain of special interest witch hunts. The practice needs to be stopped.

8. Apply the Freedom of Information Act to Congress *retroactively.*

9. Reform the constituent service racket. In 1994 the approval ratings of Congress at large had plummeted to the teens, yet voters gave generally supportive (though declining) approval ratings to their own Representatives. This is not a statistical abhoration. It's a carefully cultivated result of the constituent service game. There are now over 1,000 Congressional *district offices.* Congressmen and their staffs have become glorified clerical workers. Government at all levels has become a bureaucratic nightmare. We don't send Representatives to Washington to track down missing Social Security checks. Now, the same people responsible for creating the mess are willing and able to ride in like a white knight to rescue their imperiled constituents. As former Rep. Vin Weber (R-Minnesota) said, "We create a government that screws you, and then you're supposed to thank us for protecting you from it." I don't think so.

We should cut the number of district offices to one per Representative. If citizens are faced with a bureaucratic monster, the answer is to put the beast on a diet, not build a bigger cage.

10. Drastically reduce Congressional franking privileges. Of the mountains of mail Congress generates, only eight percent is in response to a constituent complaint or request. The rest is self serving, promotional drivel. Cut the existing funding all the way down to 10% of the current level. Representatives can still do their jobs, plus have an additional two percent left over for Christmas cards.

Congressional Committees And Staffers

1. Cut Congressional employees at all levels from the current 30,000 to 10,000.
2. Cut the number of personal aides from 22 to 10 per member in the House, and from 42-20 in the Senate.
3. Trim the number of committees from 251 to 60.
4. Cut committee staffers from 3,700 to 480. Some reform suggestions slash the number of committees and staffers, yet maintain the same ratio. In doing so, you have trimmed the duplication and overlap, yet maintained the additional layer of bureaucracy by having an excessive number of staffers per

committee.   Both the number of committees *and* the ratio of staffers need to be cut.

The 104th Congress cut House committee staff by one third from the previous session and eliminated three committees.

5. Limit the salary of aides to $66,800 (half that of Congress).

6. Each Congressman will serve on no more than two committees.

7. Committee chairmen will serve no more than four years.

8. Eliminate "S. Res. 60" aides. Unelected, unaccountable, permanent staff aides would be a thing of the past. Committee staffers would be allowed to serve a maximum eight years.

9. No vote will be taken on any legislation until three full days have passed from the time the conference report is published and distributed to all members.

10.   All major legislation; Omnibus Budget Reconciliations, Crime bills and Welfare Reform packages would require a 10 day *"constituent consultation"* period.   In other words — GO HOME and find out what your constituents really want.

11. Reform Discharge Petitions.   The Discharge Petition is an archaic House rule that allows Representatives to posture one way in public while burying legislation in private. Recall that two main means exist by which the majority party may bottle up legislation. The first is to simply not allow it out of committee where it will die a slow death. The other is through restrictive

House rules that prevent some amendments from ever reaching the floor for a vote. The "Discharge Petition" allows for such tactics to be circumvented. If a majority (218 members) sign the petition, the bill is "Discharged" from committee and a vote is taken. However, Discharge Petitions have, until recently, been quite surreptitious. The petition was kept in the clerk's desk and could only be opened while the House was in session. If a member wished to sign the petition, he or she may bring neither pen nor paper to the clerk's desk, in order to maintain the secrecy of those who had (or hadn't) signed the Discharge Petition. Disclosing the names on it was ostensibly a banishable offense.

Until 1993, of course.

Representative Jim Inhofe (R-Oklahoma) — now Senator Inhofe — proposed a bill that would remove the secrecy of the names on Discharge Petitions. Ironically, it took a Discharge Petition to get his bill to the floor for a vote, which ultimately passed.

The discharge petition does have some use. It offers means — albeit clumsy — to thwart total oppression by the Rules Committee. Its usefulness would be vastly improved if one minor change were made: the number of votes on a discharge petition should be lowered to 40 percent (174 votes). *A majority should not be necessary because all the discharge petition does is bring otherwise bottled up legislation, reform or fiscal responsibility to a vote.* Once discharged, if the bill is voted down, it would return to committee. It would then take a simple majority to *"Re-Discharge"* it for another vote.

12. All Congressional perks — even down to privileged parking — should be eliminated, providing security is not compromised.

13. Congress has clearly shown that they are totally incapable of policing themselves. All ethical disputes should be resolved in federal court. If they are serving in an honest, forthright manner, they have nothing to fear.

Fiscal Responsibility

1. Eliminate baseline budgeting. It promotes waste, inefficiency, duplication, overlap and corruption. Adopt **Zero-Based Budgeting.** In our current system of baseline budgeting, the basis for each fiscal year's budget is the spending from the year before. At that point, new, wasteful spending is added to *existing* wasteful spending.

A Zero Based Budget would allow the thirteen House committees responsible for appropriation, in concert with the correlating Senate committees, to craft a budget from the bottom-up each year. Each program's cost/benefits would be analyzed and debated on its own merits.

I can hear it now: — echoing through the halls of Congress — "But the federal budget is massive. It will be an incredibly arduous task to construct a budget from the bottom up each year."

Too bad. We pay you well enough. You treat yourselves like Kings and Queens. You have benefits, perks and pensions of equally regal stature. Stop your whining. Sit down and get busy.

On day two of the 104th Congress, the House Ways and Means Committee agreed to "truth-in-budgeting" standards that will calculate spending "cuts" and "increases" from the previous years' spending levels, not from the Current Services Baseline. It also would require a three-fifths majority in the House for tax rate increases. This is a monumental improvement over the existing system, yet falls short of the ideal of constructing an entirely new budget each year, thus eliminating wasteful, arcane and inefficient programs.

2. In *Washington Waste From A to Z*, author Martin Gross suggested an "independent National Inspector General's Office, which would probe — in addition to the present Inspectors General and the GAO — into everybody's business." This would be a Cabinet level post whose only job would be to eliminate budgetary waste and overlap in order to facilitate balanced budgets.

I couldn't agree more. The future of our country rests on immediate and diligent fiscal responsibility.

Elements Of Zero-Based Budgeting

◆ No program should be off budget. And no program — such as entitlements — should be immune from legitimate scrutiny. (See Chart 11-1)

◆ Enact a Balanced Budget Amendment with NO LOOPHOLES other than in time of war or threat to national security. A two-thirds majority of both Houses would be required

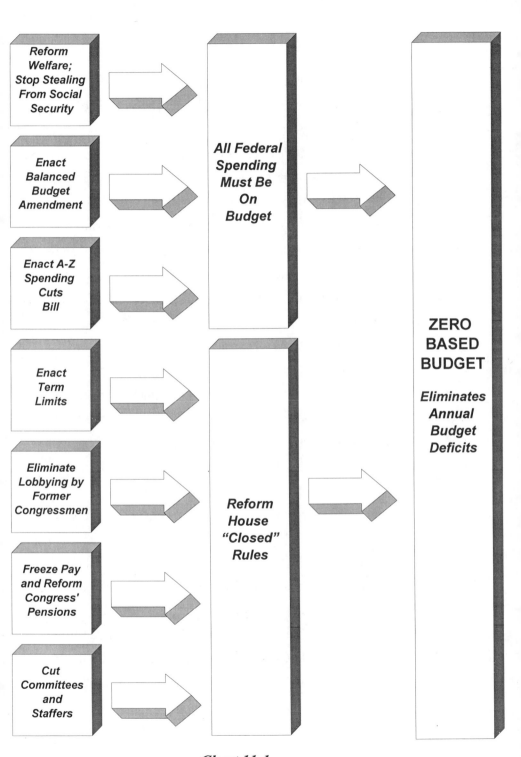

Chart 11-1

to override the Balanced Budget Amendment.

◆ Enact the A-Z Spending Cuts Plan. The A-Z Spending Cuts Plan was originally sponsored by Rob Andrews (D-New Jersey) and Bill Zeliff (R-New Hampshire). It calls for a week long special session of Congress, with a minimum of 56 hours of floor debate — no program would be off limits, and all votes would be recorded. This would allow tax payors to find out once and for all where their Representatives stand on the Mohair Subsidy, or the Helium Subsidy or Screw Worm Research Grants. This format should take place at least twice per session until the budget is balanced.

◆ Freeze Congressional pay and drastically reduce pension benefits. Citizens are elected to Congress to serve their constituency and their country. Offering such lucrative salaries and rich pension benefits after only a few years' service benefits no one but themselves. As I mentioned before, once Congress submits a balanced budget, both in theory *and in practice*, maybe we'll talk about a pay raise. Furthermore, by lowering the financial rewards of Congressional service, maybe we'll elect members that have more noble intentions.

◆ Congress should cut its sessions in half. This will allow Representatives to spend more time in their districts reacquainting themselves with the people they're supposed to serve.

◆ Index Capital Gains to inflation, phased in over three years. After that, eliminate Capital Gains tax entirely. We do not punish our children for achievement. Neither should the government punish us for the same.

♦ Unfunded Mandates would be strictly prohibited (the old line: *"We can't be overdrawn, we still have checks left"* was obviously first uttered in Congress). We will no longer allow them to bankrupt the state governments.

♦ Give the President a line-item veto. Forty-three state governors have line-item veto power, and seventy percent of the American public is in favor of granting it to the President. So, why doesn't he have it? Traditionally, because it would jeopardize the spending ability of the members of Congress, who have added pork projects and wasteful, self aggrandizing amendments to otherwise meaningful legislation, knowing that the President must either approve or reject a bill in its entirety.

Case in point: the 1993 Midwest Flood Relief Bill. Maxine Waters (D-California) attached an amendment that gave away $100 bills to "youths" aged 17-30 enrolled in jobs training programs in her district to purchase among other things, "grooming aids."

Another prominent example was the aid bill for California earthquake victims. (*California has an awful lot of electoral votes.*) Over three billion dollars of the $11 billion bill were pork projects that had nothing to do with relief aid. A shiny new Amtrak station in New York and a museum in South Carolina were among the beneficiaries of the package. Even if President Clinton protested the giveaways (which he did not) it would have been politically impossible to veto the bill, holding up aid to thousands of voters (and jeopardizing all those electoral votes).

House Speaker Tom Foley threw a bone to line-item veto power in 1993 with a bogus alternative called "expedited recision."

Here's how it works.

A bill, like the Flood Relief Package, would be sent to the President, which he, of course, would sign. Then, the President could submit a list of *suggested* cuts to Congress that they could simply ignore.

Is this progress?

On a test vote of the legislation, all but two Republicans voted against it, as did a majority in the House. This, of course, did not sit well with Foley who violated House rules by keeping the vote open for more than the 15 minutes allotted in order to impart his unique powers of persuasion. Those of you who witnessed this exercise in "representative" government on C-SPAN saw the vote clock frozen at 13 minutes until Speaker Foley got enough members to vote the "correct" way. The end result was a 212-208 victory. (This was not the first occasion in which time stood still on Capitol Hill. Senate Majority leader George Mitchell held a vote open for 55 minutes in 1992 in order to kill a product liability reform bill.)

The answer is clearly an undiluted presidential line-item veto. Why should perfectly good legislation be flawed by opportunistic legislators run amok at the public trough. A line item veto is a simple, effective solution — and it's good government.

    ◆   Most importantly, enact Dick Armey's (R-Texas) brilliant "Freedom and Fairness Restoration Act" (discussed in detail in Chapter 14). FFA will completely reform taxes, regulation, bureaucratic intrusion and forever change for the better, the way the federal government does business. It will adopt a flat 17% income tax with generous deductions. You would not only pay much lower taxes, but also your tax return would be the size of a post card.

Now that's reform.

Chapter 12
Putting The Pieces Together —
Reforming The Unreformable

*"People are not lazy. They simply have impotent
goals — that is, goals that do not inspire them."*
— Anthony Robbins

*"The fact that a problem happens to be complex,
does not mandate that its solution must be, as well."*
— Mark Anthony

Many Americans have the noble vision of reforming our
government and returning it to its Constitutional roots, only to find
the enormity — the utter complexity of the problem — too
daunting.

I do not.

Many have proposed areas where significant improvement in
efficiency is possible. But they have been either rebuffed or
ignored. The Grace Commission found that one-third of all federal
spending is lost to waste and mismanagement. Its proposals, if
enacted, would have eliminated $422 billion in federal spending
between 1984 and 1987 alone. By the year 2000, *those same
suggestions would have saved the American taxpayer close to two
trillion dollars per year!*

The Grace Commissions' proposals fell on deaf ears. Some feel
it was because the President, his staff and Congress did not care to
listen. But they're only half-right. *The greater problem was that*

within the system *they created, and the environment it bred,* *change* **could not** *take place.*

Balancing the federal budget, and reforming the way we govern — in theory — would be quite simple. Anyone with a modest sense of the enormity of government waste, inefficiency and incestuousness could theorize considerable streamlining.

Accomplishing this *in practice* is another matter entirely.

The difficulty is evident when you come to terms with the entrenched bureaucracy described in the last several chapters, and the way in which it operates — a bureaucracy that has spawned a constantly swelling government dependency class to ensure its omnipotence. Millions of Americans have their hands firmly ensconced in Uncle Sam's hip pocket. Unless, and until, the American people are willing to say "No more. We don't want government hand-outs"; little can be done to reform the system.

The current liberal paradigm is to proffer government reliance and social solutions to what are clearly personal responsibility and moral problems. Only at the point that a contrasting conservative paradigm is widely articulated — and the former, summarily rejected — can the system truly be reformed.

In the previous chapter I enumerated many reforms for the election process, Congress and the budget. But how can we accomplish any of these reforms if the system is so antagonistic to change?

In order to solve any complex equation, it is necessary to reduce the problem to its component parts, and inspect the relationship which exists between each of these components.

We must look first to the weakest link — the part of the equation that is most easily solved. Once that first bit of reform has been implemented, the remaining parts will eventually fall into place like dominoes. Each successive reform will weaken the position of the remaining problem areas, and as such, component pieces that once seemed like immovable objects in relation to the overall structure, can be dealt with more easily as supporting components are neutralized.

Political prognosticators have long maintained that imposing term limits on Congress will be the "magic bullet" that reforms the system.

This is nonsense. Why?

Because term limits alone will not make a significant difference if we fail to reform the system that served to corrupt our elected officials in the first place. Imposing term limits is a waste of time without reforming the current system of Congressional committees, the army of lobbyists and the special interest supremacy bred by a society that believes government is intended to be a bottomless grab bag for their hedonistic pursuits.

We must start at the root, with election reform. (See Flow Chart 12-1).

The beauty of this plan is that reforming one area has the natural effect of weakening the anti-reform resiliency of the adjoining parts. For example, by enacting substantive election reform, the term limit issue becomes easier to implement because by eliminating campaign abuse, it becomes harder for incumbents to win re-election in the first place.

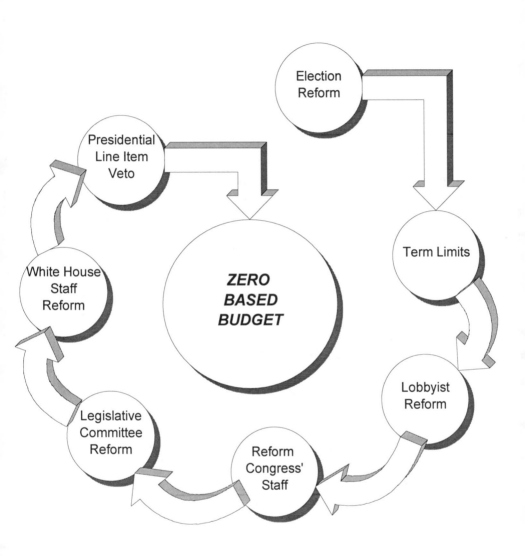

Chart 12-1

In other words, *campaign reform would have the effect of removing some of the old wood, even before mandating removal becomes a reality!*

Term Limits

"The theory is that election to Congress is tantamount to being dispatched to Washington on a looting raid for the enrichment of your state or district, and no other ethic need inhibit the feeding frenzy."
— George Will

"Politicians regularly run for office on the platform that they will provide more and better goods than their opponents. What is not so well known is that the roots of these notions lie in utopianism and socialism."
— Clarence B. Carson

"So long as they are manufactured in the home district, Congressmen have no problem with $500 toilet seats."
— Eric Felten, *The Ruling Class,*
Inside The Imperial Congress, 1993

Imposing term limits is of fundamental importance in reforming government. It has become eminently clear that continual, unabated congressional service will corrupt the most noble of intentions. Legislators are initially sent to Washington, ostensibly, to represent their district. But, the longer they remain there, the more likely they are to shift their influence to the needs of lobbyists, special interests, feeding their inflated egos and building campaign war-chests.

There are, however, those who disagree; like Former House Speaker Tom Foley. In 1992, the voters of Washington state approved term limits by a wide margin. Yet, Mr. Foley took his own constituents to court to block any action. The arrogance is unfathomable and contributed in large part to Foley's 1994 electoral demise. The voters in 13 other states approved of term limits by a two to one overall margin, but in many cases their mandate was rebuffed. In July 1993 Arkansas Circuit Court Judge Chris Piazza tossed out "a term limit initiative approved by 60% of the voters."

"The judge's eight-page opinion 'was written out and ready to be distributed before he had heard the arguments,'"*The Wall Street Journal* noted.

In addition "He [Judge Piazza] ruled that since the amendment did not begin with a three-word clause, 'Be it enacted,' the entire law is invalid." *The Journal* added, "Dick Hatfield, an attorney for the state, says the judge's logic would overturn several parts of the state's constitution, including amendments legalizing horse racing and voting machines."

The imposition of term limits will aid in the next area of reform.

Mark Anthony

Lobbyist Reform

By imposing term limits, the influence of Washington's lobbyist culture is severely weakened.

Why?

Lobbyists do not concentrate their efforts and influence on freshman legislators, for they have relatively little power and do not have the chair of any of the most influential committees. The lobbyists direct their influence to the Mitchells and Foleys, the Byrds and Rostenkowskis and Kennedys and Gephardts; for these are the men who have wielded the real power for years.

By removing the dinosaurs who have built their constituency on pork-barrel spending and cemented their incumbency with the patronage system, lobby reform quickly becomes a reality.

In excess of 6,000 lobbyists are registered with the House Clerk. About 600 of these are members of the Association of Former Members of Congress. That's right, former members of Congress are now helping shape policy at the behest of "special interests." Amazingly, these former legislators have free reign to roam the House floor. This practice should be eliminated immediately.

Many have called for a waiting period before former members of Congress should be allowed to work as a lobbyist. I disagree. They should *never* be allowed to work as lobbyists. These men and woman were elected by the people to represent *them*. By having a system that ensures that elected officials will be richly compensated by outside forces after their public service has terminated, we have added an extra carrot which entices politicians to seek public office to enrich themselves instead of representing their constituency.

Furthermore, no person listed as a "foreign agent" may serve in an advisory capacity for any candidate involved in a local, state or federal election.

Former Congressmen, as well as all senior government officials, will be barred for life from lobbying on behalf of any foreign government or corporation.

No gift — of any kind — large or small, trinkets or trips, may be bestowed on any member of Congress.

Is this harsh? Yes.

Is it *too* harsh? No. Congress has abused this privilege, and now it must be taken away. Period.

Reform Congress Members' Staff, Cut Federal Employees And Legislative Committees

Weaken lobbyists by removing the people they lobby — beautifully efficient isn't it? By curtailing the sway of lobbyists, we get a hold on the faceless committee staffers who doctor conference reports out of sight of the taxpaying public. They stuff a few million here and a billion there, and it's got to stop.

The entire army of federal employees could be easily cut in half. Some may think that this is too extreme. But, I heartily disagree.

It is incomprehensible that anyone could invent a more slothful system of government than currently exists at the federal level.

The twin sisters of waste and inefficiency — "duplication and overlap" — are bleeding the system dry.

Pick a topic: environmental concerns, children's programs, subsidies, inner city grants or education; and you will find them spread out over a multitudinous web of federal agencies and programs.

> *Would anyone argue that the salaries, pensions and fringe benefits of all civilian federal employees be frozen unless and until Congress submits a balanced budget? Would you like to see a "team" mentality ingrained in the hearts of hopelessly inefficient bureaucrats? Would you like to see a mission statement on the wall of every federal office? Imagine the concerted effort of federal employees to be efficient and resourceful if the cookie jar were locked shut until a balanced budget were enacted and adhered to.*

Astonishingly, such suggestions will be viewed as nothing short of anarchy by the beltway crowd. But I ask you, why shouldn't they have to live by the same rules by which the rest of the free market economy must abide? Show me a corporation that runs a perpetual loss, hasn't balanced a budget since the Cubs won the pennant, yet continues to hire and extend ever more lavish benefit packages to its employees. It simply doesn't happen; and therefore, I find it appalling that those who toil in the private sector are continually asked to pick up the tab for those who so blatantly abuse the public trust.

A call for eliminating federal jobs and trimming excessive government benefits should not be construed as mean spirited. The simple fact is, the current situation is completely out of phase. For example: if the average American is told "your friend just got a job with the government," what would the typical reaction be? Most likely it would be envy. The government employee has a level of job security; immediate, heavily subsidized health care; vacation, sick leave and rich pension benefits, that the average American can only dream.

This is morally wrong and grossly unfair.

It is not Government which made America great. Personal property rights, freedom and the rewards of the pursuit of excellence — these are the foundational principles of capitalism, and the fiber that has woven the American dream. When the time comes (as it already has) that employment by the government, which does not produce anything — which hinders and destroys personal freedom and individual responsibility — is far more desirable than the creative vision and rewards offered by the entrepreneurial spirit, a serious problem emerges.

And so it has.

Regardless of the strength of the economy — real or implied — employers large and small are laying off employees; they are cutting or eliminating benefits, and their retirement plans are woefully underfunded. At the same time, regulatory burdens and tax increases are piled on rapidly and egregiously (and now, retroactively). The burdens on business are insufferable — all so that government employees may have the luxuries that the rest of us have been forced to do without.

Mark Anthony

White House Staff Reform

With an annual budget of over $300 million and a staff approaching 1900 people, it's obvious that some serious cutting is in order. Of the staff, over 600 work for the budget office. The bloated White House staff is part and parcel to the overall beltway bureaucracy composed of 5,000 PACs, 300 legislative committees, 6,000 lobbyists, and 4,000 congressional aids. Once PACs, committees, lobbyists and aids have been reformed, the necessity of 1,250 non-budgetary White House employees is eliminated as well.

The White House employees should be cut in half and the budget employees cut by one third, while additional cuts remain a future consideration.

In America, there are many groups attempting to enact positive change in each of these areas. There are groups working toward election reform. There are groups working on term limits; some on lobbyist reform; some on establishing a Presidential line-item veto; and some dedicated to budgetary reform and fiscal responsibility.

But, if true reform will ever be a reality, *a concerted effort needs to be put forth, directed at _one problem area at a time_.* Imagine, if all the aforementioned groups focused their attention on one issue — election reform — and once implemented, moved on to the next, and so one. The combined resources, all trying to enact positive change, would have an unprecedented effect on American government.

Is this vision utopian?

That's a matter of personal opinion. But I believe it to be a much nobler and freer and cogent vision than those whose conception of utopia is in direct contrast — those who view utopia as government deeply embedded into every fiber of human existence.

Chapter 13
Economic Myths Debunked
Or
How Many Economists Are There In A Room Full Of Keynesian Theorists?

"Bureaucrats and legislators in Western governments and most less developed countries have been greatly enamored by Keynesian economics in particular, which gives theoretical support for inflation, high government spending, deficit financing, and the welfare state."
— Dr. Mark Skousen, Ph.D.

"Where will John Maynard Keynes be when governments collapse under the weight of their own debt? Who will be accountable for the misery brought on by the deficit spending, inflation, and government intervention that he and his cohorts deem so virtuous? Sadly, economic theorists whose basic tenets are easily refuted by anyone with a modicum of common sense, will not be available to answer for the misery they have wrought."
— Mark Anthony

Early in my second year of college, I made the difficult decision to drop out. This came as quite a shock to my parents, as I was a Dean's List student. I told them that I had no practical use for the majority of the biases the institutions impart. This is not an indictment of all college education, but it certainly was true of mine.

My interests were in politics and economics. I had the naive belief that truth, harnessed with good intentions, could make a difference. As Earl Nightingale once said, "Ideas and concepts can change your life." More importantly, I believed that ideas and concepts can change the world.

I still do.

But it became clear to me that many colleges were more interested in molding good little liberals than promoting the freedom to analytically and spiritually grapple with the problems of the universe — in our own minds — without the shackles of preconceived neo-marxism.

Two incidents cemented my decision. The first was a second year history course. It was my third history course, and I was fortunate enough to have the same professor as I had for the first two. He was one of the more exceptional teachers I have encountered. He was tough, dedicated and challenging. He was the head of the History Department, and rightly so. I was the only student who had ever received an "A" in one of his courses — an accomplishment I repeated the second time through. The valedictorian of my high school was also in my second history class, but she struggled to manage a "B." The course came naturally to me, I suppose because somehow I knew that American History would play an integral role in my future. I was a motivated learner with an exceptional teacher. I had an enormous amount of respect for the professor. But shortly after classes began in our third course together, I knew I had a conflict, and I sought to resolve it with him. The year was 1981:

"Doctor," I said, "what relevance does this book have to the course matter," as I held up one of the three books the course required.

"It is designed to give you an appreciation of the role that minorities play in American history," he replied.

"This book is *not* about minority roles in American history; it is about the history of minority cultures. Those are two distinctly different matters."

"Well, Mark, it's part of a new required course for History students," he said.

"Doctor," I replied, "I find the imposition patently offensive. I was always enamored of history. I studied the life of Martin Luther King Jr. because he was a great *American,* not because of his ethnicity. I no more admired and studied him because he was black than I studied the Founding Fathers because they were white. American history should not be taught in this context. Am I to assume that next term, we'll be taught a special course on the history of great Italian men — oh, I forgot, we already are — our books now tell us that Christopher Columbus was a slave trader, butcher and purveyor of disease and misery. My, how things have changed. Ironically, Columbus wasn't such a bad guy according to the elementary school history books I had a few years ago."

I dropped the course shortly thereafter. Retelling the story is indicative of much of what is wrong with education today.

The second example is germane to this chapter's theme. It was my initial economics class; an absurd excursion into Keynesian theory: government subsidies, deficit spending, the virtues of controlled inflation and easy monetary policy, central planning and the welfare state. The course was taught by a large, animated man with the voice, build and profile of Alfred Hitchcock. The textbook was incomprehensible, due to the idiocy of Keynesian principles and the obvious dearth of common sense which it embodies.

I thought it both ironic and insulting that we were expected to believe this nonsense after limping through the deficit spending of the Ford administration, and the "stagflation" (slow economic growth coupled with inflation) of the Carter administration.

Nevertheless, I was highly interested in the study of Economics and emerged from the cesspool of Keynesian theory with an "A."

Or so, I thought.

I was the only student who got an "A" on every test in that Economics class. Yet, the "alleged" professor gave me a "B." I consulted with him about the reason for my grade, and he replied, "Mr. Anthony, if you do not see fit to come to my class, I do not see fit to give you an "A." (I never attended after the second week of class, except to take the tests. I couldn't sit through class after class as my fellow students so foolishly bought Keynesian rhetoric. I severely questioned some of the principles early in the second week, but after that I was summarily ignored.)

I replied with candor befitting the occasion,

> "Keynes was an idiot, and his theories are garbage. The only reason they were widely espoused was to facilitate massive government intervention under the guise of the New Deal. Americans bought into that nonsense, and the intrusion hasn't stopped since. Now, instead of admitting the failure of Keynesian theory, you continue to teach it as if it were true. With all respect, professor, your quantity of

knowledge may dwarf mine, but I would rather have a small amount of factual knowledge than a bushel-barrel full of B.S!"

You might have gathered I wasn't the shy type.

That was the last conversation I ever had with the economics department.

I highly recommend Dr. Mark Skousen's book *Economics On Trial.* As a college student Dr. Skousen was similarly disenchanted (though probably not as arrogant). He eventually earned a Ph.D. from George Washington University in 1977 and worked for the government for a number of years. He then went into the private sector and became a successful entrepreneur (an accomplishment that should be prerequisite to teaching economics). He has started many businesses and publishes an investment newsletter. He is also an adjunct Professor of Economics at Rollins College, in Winter Park, Florida; very near to my home. The purpose of his book is to refute the manner in which economics is taught in an estimated eighty percent of America's universities.

There are several books which I believe should be mandatory reading for every high school and college student, and *Economics On Trial* is high on that list. This of course, would be anathema to the men and women who establish the curricula of many of our educational institutions, which strikes me as curious. Why not expose students to both sides of an issue, rather than simply paint with the broad brush of liberal thought? Why not offer both views, and then allow the students themselves to conclude which are the more salient principles? Unfortunately, you'd wait a considerable amount of time to get an answer to those questions.

Myth #1
The Basics Of Keynesian Theory: Big Government, Deficit Spending And Consumption Over Productivity

Pre-Keynesian thought correctly taught that economics is the process of transforming available resources into usable products; improving the product at each stage of production in order to produce a product that will appeal to the consumer in a free-market. *The wages paid to all employees in a free market are thus determined by the level of improvement that they offer to the product or service that their company produces. This is why the engineer is more highly compensated than the receptionist; and the surgeon more than the orderly.*

All levels of improvement; i.e., job functions, are essential to the final production process, but the importance of each *relative* to the production process determines the level of compensation. Furthermore, the level of compensation of like occupations in different companies is determined by the value added by the employee, due to his or her skill level — and ultimately defined by the marketability and profitability of the resultant product or service. That is why Shaquille O'Neal is more highly compensated than the L.A Clipper's third string center. However, the organization could not continue to pay Mr. O'Neal's salary if the team had a perennial losing record and the fans would not pay to see the team, therefore causing the ownership to lose money.

Conversely, Keynes, *General Theory*, published in 1936, put the emphasis on *consumption* rather than *production*. This played directly into the hands of government officials because the American government is the world's largest consumer; yet it produces nothing. Reeling from the depression, the federal government capitalized on the misfortune of the American people and embarked on an unprecedented expansion of its reach and influence, consuming rights and freedoms heretofore unheard of in a democracy built on limited government. They euphemistically referred to their program as the New Deal.

Keynesian theory offered the rationale necessary to impart such drastic reform. The theory indicates that a weak economy is the result of aggregate demand. Skousen wrote,

> "According to Keynes, a nation's prosperity is essentially determined by total final spending in the economy — by consumers, investors, and government. This notion of aggregate final demand was in sharp contrast to the classical view that productivity, technological advancement, and savings were the keys to economic progress. Classical economists believed that the aggregate consumer demand was relatively unimportant as an economic catalyst and that a country's standard of living was determined by its productive power. Consumer spending would largely take care of itself."

This is why our shift from international manufacturing giant to service economy foreshadows a decline in America's economic dominance.

The consumption theory of economic growth has been repudiated by every socialist economy — and at the same time, substantiates the value of productive power in determining the standard of living. The former Soviet Union certainly did not have a consumption problem. The sheer size of the country and the enormity of the population ensured a constant demand for goods and services. But without productive capacity, they could not produce a soft drink like "Coke"; they could not produce blue jeans like Levi Strauss; they could not produce a myriad of other conveniences the quality and quantity of which capitalist societies take for granted.

Why?

Because the lack of profit motive in socialist societies prohibits the savings, private capital investment and development that is required to attain such productive ability. Bureaucrats ignored these facts and instead sought to consume power while they had the chance. In 1937, the Agriculture Marketing Agreement Act gave the USDA the power to appoint farmers to marketing boards for the purpose of controlling what is produced, how much of it is produced and at what price it can be sold. The resultant central government planning has spawned a system that wastes over half of all lemons grown at a loss of resources of $72 million a year; prohibits nectarines smaller than 2 5/16 in diameter and peaches less than 2 3/8 in diameter from being sold; and regulates other fruits and vegetables in a similar socialistic manner.

273

To wit: an amount of raisins grown in Arizona equal to only one percent of the California raisin harvest is hauled to California for eventual distribution. Wrote James Bovard, the "USDA warned in a solemn notice in the Federal Register on November 6, 1992, that 'all non-California raisins received by [California raisin] handlers...[must] be identified, stored separately...and *kept under surveillance* until such raisins [are] disposed of by the handlers.' In an era when the Federal Bureau of Investigation fails to prevent terrorists from bombing New York's World Trade Center, USDA is demanding intensive surveillance of out-of-state raisins."

Although this example illustrates the laughable absurdity of government intervention, it is indicative of the gravity of the problem.   If the federal government believes it is necessary to resort to surveillance of raisins, how much do you think they respect *your* personal property rights?

Maybe Green Peace will launch a "Free the Raisins" movement.

Myth #2
The Importance Of Government's Role In Economic Prosperity: Beware Of Uncle Sam's Economic Statistics

"The biggest problem with acknowledging GDP is that it accepts without question government expenditures as a positive contribution to a nation's output...The government can make GDP rise artificially simply by expanding the money supply or running a deficit, and willy-nilly purchasing goods and services. Government-directed "product" may be valueless or grossly

misused [like a $400 hammer]...but the expenditure itself makes it appear that the nation experienced real growth."
— Dr. Mark Skousen

As Skousen points out, Gross National Product (now Gross Domestic Product) is a byproduct of the Keynesian formula

$$Y = C + I + G$$

where

Y = Gross national product (GNP)

C = Total consumer expenditures

I = Gross investment expenditures by businesses

G = Government expenditures[72]

Adds Skousen, "GNP takes into account only the production of goods and services sold to final users. It excludes all economic activity associated with the production of intermediate goods, wholesale goods and other unfinished products (including inventories) that have yet to reach the final consumption stage."

For example, a leather tannery takes raw cowhide and processes it so that it can be sold to a shoe manufacturer to be assembled into shoes. The economic activity responsible for taking the raw resource (the cow hide) and turning into assemblable material is called circulating capital — and it is *not* counted in GNP.

Why is this so important?

Because this flawed theory tips the scales of economic importance in the favor of *consumption* at the cost of *production.* Since the government is the penultimate consumer, the GNP numbers elicit the facade that government expenditures are far more important to America's economic well-being than capital investment. For example, in 1982, using GNP calculations, government spending was responsible for 65 percent of our national output. However, Dr. Skousen has formulated an alternative statistic called *Gross National Output* (GNO) that takes into consideration the importance of intermediate inputs and private investment which are left out of GNP figures. The results are startling: under GNO, government expenditures fall to only 20 percent of national output while circulating capital and private investment account for a whopping 54.07 percent of all economic activity.

Of course, the federal government will never use such figures because it would bring to light the true steam which drives the economic engine: savings, capital investment and productivity. To do so would compel the government to remove the shackles that inhibit true economic growth — the *availability* of capital. And how would that be done? Eliminate the tax on Capital Gains, and eliminate the federal deficit, thereby removing the enormous drain on available capital that is caused by deficit spending. Says Skousen, Gross National Product "overemphasizes the role of consumption and government spending in the economy at the expense of business." A recent example was the defeat of President Clinton's "Emergency Economic Stimulus Package."

Failure to enact the massive pile of pork caused Chief White House Economic Advisor Laura Tyson to shave a full point off the following year's projected economic growth rates. Her reduction in growth is due to a Keynesian theory called "the balanced budget multiplier." Says Skousen:

> **"Perhaps there is no better example of distortion in Keynesian economics than the balanced budget multiplier. According to this theory, a tax cut has less impact on GNP than does creating a new government spending program of an equal amount."**[73]

Read that again.

The government has used flawed economic theory for decades in order to legitimize its growth. The notion that massive government spending on dubious projects — akin to burning money — is at the heart of our very economic survival, must be abandoned immediately.

Myth #3
'Tis Better To Spend Than To Save

It sounds contradictory doesn't it? How can an economy be healthy if no money is saved and invested? But it's true. Keynesian theory views savings as a vice. Keynesian Economists believe that saving money will cause a decline in consumption, and as such, serve as a deterrent to economic growth. Incredibly, Keynes believed that a lack of consumption was the cause of the great depression, and *he actually took to the radio to urge citizens to embark on spending sprees to help stimulate the economy.* Simple common sense refutes such idiocy. Keynes' theory of "The

Paradox of Thrift" holds water only if savers hoard their money by sticking it in a mattress or burying it in a hole — and even then the detriment is only short term.

Two key points falsify Keynes' theory. Consider for a moment the act of saving. What does one usually do when saving money? He or she places the funds in a bank, or in a money market account if the goal is short term saving. For the long term, the money may be placed in a mutual fund, a certificate of deposit, or bonds among other things. Even if the funds are simply deposited in the local bank, the money doesn't sit idly in a vault. The bank lends the money to other entities who in turn invest in consumer products like cars, homes or appliances. The bank may also lend the funds to a small business to allow an entrepreneur to get started, or lend to an existing business to finance expansion. In any event, the money is always invested somewhere.

But what about money invested in mutual funds or other paper financial instruments? How is that money invested? It's quite simple actually. As Skousen points out, people do not save for the sake of saving. They save for the purpose of *future consumption.* When the free market presents a product or service with a price of $100, that product will sit on the shelf until some consumer desires that product more than he desires the $100 in his pocket. At that point, the consumer will exchange the $100 with the manufacturer who, in contrast, values the $100 more than it values the good or service.

These investments are productive uses of capital. The free market does not throw money at products or invest in capital improvements for any length of time if they are not profitable.

Undesirable goods and services are eventually weeded out of the market and the dollars invested in more worthwhile capital goods, services or consumer products. This is in sharp contrast to what the government refers to as "investments." When a politician lauds a government "investment," it is usually in reference to make-work jobs in which the value received is minor in comparison to the money spent. The bureaucracy necessary to administer the program only adds waste, abuse and inefficiency to the equation.

Furthermore, most non-military government spending is nothing more than transferring wealth from one citizen or group of citizens to another, such as rebuilding "infrastructure"; roads, bridges and the like. Infrastructure has become a buzzword of neo-marxist central planners who believe true prosperity is only achieved by income equality.

Flow-Chart 13-1 illustrates the inefficiency of an economy generated from the "government down."

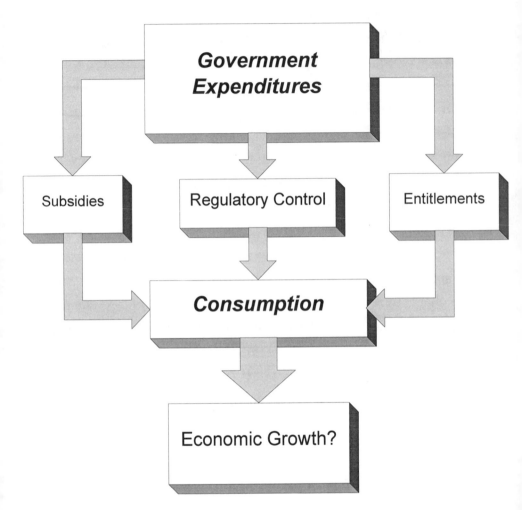

Through massive deficit spending and wasteful central planning, th[e]
federal government drains trillions of dollars of available capital fro[m]
the economy which could have been more efficiently utilized by the
private sector for savings, investment, capital formation and
productivity.

Chart 13-1

Vanishing Republic

Dr. Skousen summed up what he termed *"The Fallacy of the Paradox of Thrift"*:

> "The biggest drawback to the Keynesian anti-savings doctrine is that it runs completely counter to historical evidence. It is in direct conflict with the theory of economic growth, which clearly shows that higher rates of savings go hand in hand with higher rates of productivity and economic growth. Studies by [Nobel Prize winning economist] Franco Modigliani, for example show a strong correlation between a country's savings rate and its compounded annual growth (in per capita disposable income)...Increased savings may mean a temporary cutback in retail sales, but the increase also means that additional funds are now available for investment projects, research and development, capital expenditures, and new processes. Banks, insurance companies, and other financial institutions will have new funds available to lend to entrepreneurs or to form a joint venture on new projects...
>
> "...In sum, an increase in savings means new inventions; new production techniques; the institution of cost-cutting measures; the replacement of worn-out or outdated equipment and buildings; and, in short, an increased standard of living. Thus we see why savings are an essential ingredient in the theory of economic growth and why the alternative theory of savings and capital formation is completely compatible with historical experience in Japan, Germany, and other countries that have adopted this vision of sacrificing for future consumption."

The foundational principle in any attempt at fiscal responsibility is contained in the elements of thrift. For the sake of enriching our lives, and those around us, we often invest — meaning sacrifice the

281

pleasure of current consumption — in order to facilitate future, more desirable consumption. And if the goal of a nation is to truly allow its citizens to enjoy life, liberty and the pursuit of happiness, then savings and private investment is elemental. But in this case, I am not talking about consumption of consumer goods. I am talking about consumption of government hand-outs. Americans must learn to say "No" to current government consumption such as entitlements, subsidies and financially unsound federally insured loans. In doing so, the incredible drain of resources that government spending exacts on the pool of available capital will be alleviated. What future consumption will a national "investment" in thrift offer? It will offer capital availability, increased productivity, a flurry of new businesses, an expansion of existing businesses, and it will create jobs — high quality jobs which will generate the incredible economic growth that will fuel still more investment. (See Chart 13-2) The same people who have been forced out of work by federally caused capital drains and the regulatory pariahs that inhibit economic growth, will now be able to find a job — and the resultant decline in entitlement spending will facilitate an ever declining government drain on the capital pool.

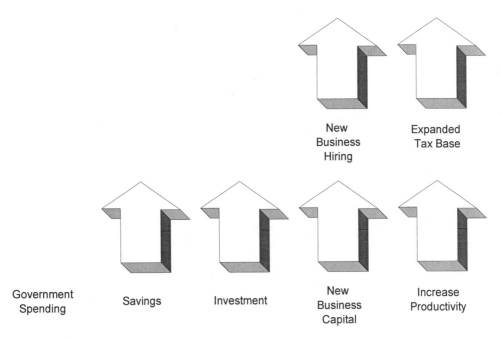

New
Business
Hiring

Expanded
Tax Base

Government
Spending

Savings

Investment

New
Business
Capital

Increase
Productivity

Entitlement
Spending

Sacrificing current government consumption will eliminate the federal drain of available capital, which will lead to increased savings, investment, new business capital and expansion of existing business productivity. The last two items will lead to new job creation and expansion of employment at existing businesses.

Chart 13-2

Clearly, financial security depends on less government, not more. The danger of excessive government consumption of available capital was clearly stated by Thomas Jefferson:

> *"After leaving to labor the smallest portion of earnings on which it can subsist, Government shall consume the whole residue of what it was instituted to guard."*

Myth #4
The Effect Of The Federal Debt On Interest Rates

Keynesian economists and government officials have always contended that deficit spending has no adverse effect on interest rates. Keynesians hold that belief for obvious reasons; to do otherwise would be detrimental to the ability to run continual budget deficits.

The reality, however, couldn't be any simpler. Interest rates are nothing more than the cost of money; and money as all other goods, is subject to supply and demand. The market for United States Treasury debt is the world's largest financial market. But, the global economy does not have an unlimited fountain of capital. The greater the needs of the government, the more it siphons off the available pool. The resultant capital drain crowds out the needs of private industry and offers the remaining funds at considerably greater expense. Chart 13-3 illustrates the amount of savings available for new capital formation relative to the amount absorbed by the budget deficit.

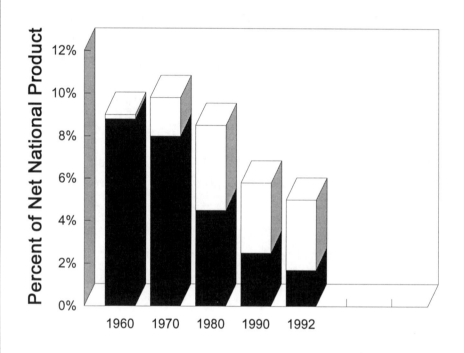

Effect Of Federal Budget Deficit On National Savings

Percent of Net National Product

- 12%
- 10%
- 8%
- 6%
- 4%
- 2%
- 0%

1960 1970 1980 1990 1992

■ Savings Available for New Capital Form
□ Savings Absorbed by the Budget Deficit

Chart 13-3

Source: Economic Report of the President, Feb. 1992

Here's more proof. The national debt was just over $250 billion in the 1950's. At the same time, the long bond was only 2.4% and home mortgages were a little over four percent. The availability of inexpensive money had a phenomenal effect on the private sector. New homes sprung up as fast in the 1950's as foreclosure signs do today.

In 1960 the debt approached $300 billion, and the long bond rose to nearly five percent. By the end of the 1970's the debt was knocking on the door of uncharted territory — one trillion dollars — and the long bond exceeded 10%, and in some cases as high as 12%.

Imagine if the annual deficit were eliminated, and the remaining national debt was amortized over 20 or 30 years, just like a mortgage? Can you envision the economic boom that would result as interest rates plummeted to 1950's levels? How many new businesses would form? How many existing businesses would expand? How many citizens now tied to entitlement programs would be able share in the American dream? Consumers could refinance their obligations at incredibly low rates, and be free of the bondage of 18 and 20 percent consumer debt. (See Chart 13-4)

Let me take a moment to dispel the debt/interest rate myth, pertaining to President Clinton's economic program. Several economists have taken the opportunity to use the bond market's positive reaction to the Clinton plan in order to refute the relationship. As we have already discussed, when the President released his original budget in February of 1993, he called for massive tax increases in order to address the deficit. The Office of Management and Budget, which is part of the White House staff,

Higher
Quality Jobs

Job Growth

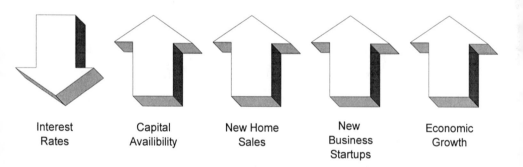

Interest	Capital	New Home	New	Economic
Rates	Availibility	Sales	Business	Growth
			Startups	

Effect of the Elimination of
Annual Budget Deficits

Chart 13-4

widely disseminated their findings that the Clinton budget would cut the deficit $500 billion.

On August 5, 1993, the first Clinton budget squeaked by, but Alan Greenspan finally came to terms with the reality that some of us already knew, and it wasn't long before interest rates rose. This happened even though the OMB and the Congressional Budget Office indicated the deficit would drop below $200 billion in 1994.

Here's what really happened. The bond market reacted favorably to the alleged Clinton paradigm of deficit reduction, and interest rates came down (the stock market obviously knew something the bond market didn't, as the Dow Jones Industrial average dropped some 80 points the day after Mr. Clinton announced his tax increase in a televised address in February of '93). Stock investors knew the reality; not a single program was going to be cut; and, as a matter of fact, over $900 billion would be added to the deficit during the Clinton presidency. Clearly — to those honest enough to realize it — the deficit didn't drop due to real budget cuts because there weren't any. Interest rates dropped because the bond market thought the Clinton gang was serious about deficit reduction (pardon me, until I stop laughing).

The reduction in the deficit was attributable to one thing, and one thing only — *the temporary drop in interest rates.* If any economist would like to refute this fact, show me where $500 billion in *real* budget cuts were made, *not* reductions in the projected increase; i.e., baseline budget cuts.

Myth #5
What Really Happened In The Eighties...
And What Is Happening Now

> *"Socialize the individual's surplus and you*
> *socialize his spirit and creativeness; you*
> *cannot paint the Mona Lisa by assigning*
> *one dab of paint to a thousand painters."*
> — William F. Buckley Jr.

The 1993 Clinton budget plan purloined an estimated additional $35 billion from individual taxpayers in its first year, which knocked at least a half percentage-point off growth in 1994. Regardless of who will pay the brunt of the tax increases (one-third of all retroactive tax increases were paid by "wealthy" taxpayers) the fact remains that those same people — the top 5% of all wage earners — represent nearly 25% of all consumer spending. In July 1994 Fred R. Bleakley, reporter for The Wall Street Journal noted, "U.S. Trust Co. found in a recent survey of affluent Americans that 46% said they would postpone major purchases such as a car or home because of higher tax bills." Not surprisingly, sales of Cadillacs were off 17% from a year earlier — quite curious in light of an "economic recovery."

So now, you have a tax increase that is only supposed to hit the top 2% of wage earners, affecting a guy who works in an automobile assembly plant, which affects a guy working at an automobile tire plant, which affects a guy who manufactures the raw material for the tire plant, which affects the truck drivers who deliver the raw materials, the tires, and the automobiles; which affects the mechanics and salespeople and office workers who are employed at the automobile dealerships...all because of an innocent "contribution" from someone who "profited the most from the eighties." Who woulda' thunk it — the same

Mark Anthony

liberal pundits who derided supply side economics are now faced with the dubious task of defending "Trickle Down Pain." What kind of sense does this make?

President Clinton (and his less than forthright spin doctors) has taken a particular fondness for economic revisionism. The President contented that the 1980's were marked by "slow growth and underinvestment, the rich got richer, and the poor got poorer." He claimed the rich "benefited the most from the 80's" which he termed "the worst economy in the last 50 years." Clinton stated, "the incomes of our forgotten working families had been stagnant for nearly 20 years." Nothing could be further from the truth. We don't need additional tax increases — what we need are few more history teachers.

Following the stagflation that characterized the Carter years (in fairness, he didn't exactly inherent an idyllic economy from Ford) the Reagan paradigm was to rebuild the military, get government out of people's lives, cut tax rates and allow people to keep more of what they earn in order to promote economic activity. Reagan felt that if he lowered tax rates and shifted away from the Keynesian principles of Ford and Carter, private investment would breed economic activity, and in the end, the government would take in *even higher* tax revenues.

He was right.

In the 1980's, America experienced a 92 month economic expansion — the greatest peacetime boom in American history. During that time, 19 million new jobs were created. Furthermore, there were substantial gains in every economic category; the

bottom quintile of the population increased real income by 10% —
as did the top quintile.

On July 8, 1993, an editorial written by President Reagan
appeared in *The Wall Street Journal.* The Former President wrote:

> "...Economic growth is created by people who produce
> things. The more that's produced to meet increasing
> demand, the more new jobs and services are created in turn.
> Other than short-term make-work projects, the
> government does not create jobs; the private sector does.
> How? By investing in new plants and equipment, and by
> researching and developing new products. And how does
> the private sector do all that? By having enough corporate
> profits to reinvest and enough incentives to make such
> expenditures desirable."

The relationship between tax rates and government revenue has
been proven countless times:

Lower Tax Rates = Higher Tax Revenues
and
Higher Tax Rates = Lower Tax Revenues

Speaking before the Economic Club of New York in 1962,
President John F. Kennedy said:

> "Our tax system siphons out of the private economy too
> large a share of personal and business purchasing power.
> Surely the lesson of the last decade is budget deficits are
> not caused by wild-eyed spenders but by slow economic
> growth and periodic recessions. In short, it is a

paradoxical truth that tax rates are too high today and tax revenues are too low and the soundest way to raise the revenues in the long run is to [lower] the rates now."

Statistics bear this out. **In 1988 the top tax rate of 38.5% was lowered to 28%, yet the top one percent of income earners still sent 25% more revenue to Washington.** **During the Reagan years, tax rates were lowered and revenues increased by a whopping 76%.** **The share of taxes paid by the top 1% rose from 17.6% in 1981 to 24.6% in 1991.**

Unfortunately, spending increased by 80% between 1980 and 1990.

The Bush presidency offered the worst of both worlds: massive tax increases combined with runaway government spending. In 1990 the Bush administration offered the second largest tax increase in American history at the altar of deficit reduction; then turned around and created huge new bureaucracies, a flurry of new regulations (and commensurate punishments) and to add insult to injury — *still outspent revenues by nearly 40 percent!*

In 1993 the Clinton administration added steam to what was already a runaway train; with even more government and less personal freedom fed by the largest tax increase in world history — a tax increase which didn't even contain funding for what would have been the mother of *all* entitlements — the Clinton Health Care plan.

Myth #6
Punishing The Achievers

"If ignorance paid dividends, most...could make a fortune out of what they don't know about economics."
— Luther Hodges, Former Secretary of Commerce

"Democrats are endlessly conspiring to find new ways to extract more money from the rich, by means guaranteed to do the opposite."[74]
— Stephen Moore

There has been considerable rhetoric and misinformation regarding exactly who are the poor sots who've crossed President Clinton's line in the sand and dared to earn over $200,000 per year. Lest you think this will only affect the country club set and their ability to wear Armani and drive German automobiles, you are sadly mistaken. The biggest casualty will be the driving force behind the American economy — small business — particularly Subchapter S Corporations and Sole Proprietorships, as 42.4% of all American businesses now file under the personal tax code. The effects will be felt in hiring practices much sooner than you think. How many times over the last few years have you opened your daily newspaper to find yet another *Fortune 500* company cutting tens of thousands of jobs?

> *If the economic environment is so incredibly perilous for the sharks, how do you think it will affect the minnows? And what affect will handicapping small business have on the rest of us?*

The importance of a thriving small business sector to economic health in general is unmistakable. From 1982 to 1988, the total number of Americans who had jobs rose in net terms by 9.2 million. During that same period, government data show that small, new businesses created nearly 14.2 million jobs, with another 4.5 million new jobs being created by companies with fewer than 100 employees.[75] If government steals from these people it breaks the entrepreneurial spirit that drives our economy; thereby forcing a new generation of Americans into government dependence.

President Clinton piously declared, "The middle class is asked to make a modest contribution to paying down the deficit and growing the economy." With all due respect, Mr. President, let's clarify a few items:

> *A)* The middle class had nothing to do with creating the deficit, yet they are repeatedly asked to "contribute" to "paying it down." I would suggest we reduce government's appetite instead of increasing the taxpayers' "contribution."
>
> *B)* Massive tax increases will not in *any* way "grow" the economy.

You see, *you subsidize things that you **want** to occur; you tax things that you **do not** want to occur.* Keynesian economic policy inhibits private sector growth, while increasing the necessity of government assistance.

W. Kurt Hauser, a noted investment advisor stated it perfectly, "The one point that economists of every persuasion, from socialist to capitalist, agree on is that tax decreases stimulate economic activity and tax increases impede economic activity. Tax increases during periods of weak economic activity can be particularly damaging. [Remember, President Clinton told us our economy was in the worst shape in 50 years.] A retroactive tax increase in 1932, also intended to reduce the deficit, plunged the nation from recession to depression."

As the unemployment lines swell (keep in mind, unemployment statistics are far rosier than the actual scenario because private sector job loss is significantly offset by the always increasing government job pool) one point will become eminently clear:

SOAKING THE RICH HURTS EVERYBODY ELSE FAR MORE THAN IT HURTS THE RICH —

WHEN WAS THE LAST TIME A POOR PERSON GAVE YOU A JOB.

◆ In 1991 five percent of all income earners in the U.S. paid 44% of all income taxes.

◆ The top 2.8% paid 36% of all taxes.

But, before envy overpowers reason, consider the following:

◆ **The top 2% of all income earners in the country produce 22% of all economic activity.**

295

Mark Anthony

Are we as a nation expected to take some silent joy in watching the wealthy bleed? Apparently the morality we are teaching are children is this: stealing is wrong...unless the person you're stealing from is really rich. Well, I've got news for you: stealing from the rich is still stealing. The simple fact remains:

You cannot strip the wealth and rewards from the entrepreneurial job creators without stripping the private sector of its ability to create jobs.

Why, then, do liberals continue to do it?   Simply because they believe that the federal government is better equipped to provide jobs than the private sector.

The dirty little secret beltway liberals don't want you to know is this: If we freeze spending increases on all programs but Social Security, we could balance the budget in less than ten years. These are the government's own numbers. They come from the *Economic Report of the President, January 1993,* the Council of Economic Advisors and the OMB. The trick, says Hauser, is "limit growth on such programs as Medicare and Medicaid to the percentage increase in the beneficiary population, plus inflation." You've got to ask yourself: Why would Congress increase these programs at a higher rate than inflation, anyway? Clearly, chaining people to government assistance is *not* compassionate.   It cannot be said enough: *You subsidize things that you want to occur.*

But was it only the top two percent of Americans who were asked to "contribute" more in 1993?   Alan Reynolds, director of economic research at the Hudson Institute in Indianapolis, wrote:

"This is much worse than misleading. It leaves out millions of unmarried professionals and managers. The 36% tax applies to all taxable income above $115,000 for singles, $127,500 for household heads and $70,000 for married people who file separately. There are 5.6 million families with expanded incomes between $100,000 and $200,000...Not one of these taxpayers is counted among the 1.4 million families earning over $200,000. Retired people hit hard by higher income tax rates on Social Security benefits are not counted either."

To garner support for the tax increases that would fund the expansion of social programs, the Clinton administration launched into what even perennial Clinton apologist CBS News called "Class Warfare." Apparently the strategy of the Clinton team is "divide and conquer." From Bill Clinton to Leon Panetta to Laura Tyson, head of the president's Council of Economic Advisors, the dictum was 80% of the 1993 tax increases would be paid by those making over $200,000 per year — or *millionaires* in Clintonspeak.

Below is the actual impact of the 1993 Clinton budget on upper income taxpayers. The numbers are courtesy of the Democratic Study Group.

Income	Average 1992 Federal Taxes	Change Under 1993 Bill	Group Share of Tax Increase
$200,000 +	$135,359	+$23,521	81.3%

Let's take a look at where the money will be spent. On April 8, 1993, the Office of Management and Budget released the 1994 federal budget.   On page two of the 1,500 page document was a table entitled "Budget Totals Reflecting the President's Proposals." Their own numbers indicated that spending would increase by $323 billion over the next five years.

The following data are the actual numbers from the OMB report.

Clinton's Budget Totals
In Billions of dollars, rounded

	1993	1994	1995	1996	1997	1998
Outlays	$1,468	1,515	1,574	1,625	1,690	1,781
Receipts	$1,146	1,251	1,328	1,413	1,476	1,531
Deficit	$322	264	246	212	214	250
Defense Outlays	$277	264	258	252	234	239

Source: Office of Management and Budget

Said Tom Bethell of *The American Spectator*, "spending totals increase from $1,468 billion to $1,781 billion in five years, despite real reductions in military spending. Only in federal budgeting is an increase of more than $300 billion called a 'cut.'"

The Congressional Budget Office reported that an incredible 97.3% of Clinton's spending increases are the result of expanded domestic spending. For fiscal year 1995 domestic spending will rise $11 billion, plus an additional $4.9 billion in health expenditures and user fees — a 7.3% increase — two-and-a-half times the rate of inflation.

Myth #7
The Cost Of Social Programs

Wrote John Mueller, a principal of LBMC Inc, an Arlington, Virginia, forecasting firm:

> "Both theory and evidence clearly show that the main reason for the sharp rise in unemployment in the current EC countries over the past two decades has been the massive expansion of the region's social benefits and the minimum wage. President Clinton's proposals would accelerate the same process in the U.S...Social benefits put an above-market floor under wages, because at some point it is more attractive to collect benefits than to work. So businesses substitute capitol for labor, and workers substitute benefits for after-tax wages...benefits conditioned on not working cause more unemployment than benefits available whether or not one works. But any benefits — even education and training schemes or 'workfare' — that are not tied to *current* employment must contribute to higher unemployment than would otherwise occur."

Testifying before the House Education and Labor Committee on March 5, 1987, Phyllis Schlafly said, "Many other countries have made the mistake of mandating costly [employment] benefits, and they have mandated their citizens right out of jobs."

Mark Anthony

At an April 14, 1993, news conference, President Clinton advocated expanded unemployment benefits and universal health care coverage. Then, the President said, "All the European countries have higher unemployment rates than we do but also stronger support systems for the unemployed."

Said Mueller,

> "That's the point: All the European countries have higher unemployment rates *because* they have 'stronger support systems for the unemployed'...Until the early 1970s, unemployment in the current EC countries averaged less than 3% — lower than in the U.S. After the tremendous increase in benefits (and minimum wages), it is now about 10%...In the EC since 1965, there has been a 96% correlation between current unemployment and transfer payments one year earlier...West Germany is an excellent example of the link between social benefits and unemployment. Transfer payments were expanded from 12% of gross domestic product in 1964 to 17.7% in 1982, and unemployment rose from 0.3% in 1965 to 7.7% in 1983. But, under 'fiscal consolidation,' transfer payments were steadily cut back to 14.9% of GDP in 1991, and West German unemployment was down to 4.8% in 1992...the process is already well under way. From 1965 to 1992, U.S. transfer payments nearly tripled to more than 14% of GDP. **And unemployment has risen on average by more than half a percentage point for each one-percentage-point rise in transfer payments as a percentage of GDP.**" (My emphasis)

300

Research from the National Center for Policy Analysis indicates 1.4 million fewer jobs will be created, and total wages in the economy will be $483 billion lower over the next five years. Couldn't we have learned from the European Community? "In Europe, where payroll taxes are often 50 percent or more and labor markets are extensively regulated, there have been no net new private sector jobs created in 20 years. In the countries that comprise the European Common Market, the unemployment rate has tripled since the 1960s" noted economist Paul Craig Roberts.

Myth #8
The Future Of Our Beleaguered Inner Cities Is Dependent Upon Raising Taxes

Imagine, liberal inner city policies hurt those people the most that they so desperately wish to help. As a matter of fact, liberal policies hurt most the weakest, the poorest and the neediest among us. What does soaking the rich have to do with our impoverished inner cities?

Charles W. Kadlec, Managing Director of J & W Seligman & Co., a New York investment manager, cites the true impact of tax policy on inner cities.

> "Twenty-five percent of the households in the Northeast and 23% in the West are in the top quintile of earnings, compared with only 17% of households in the South...An income of $140,000 may provide a lifestyle of the rich in many parts of the country, but in the major urban centers of

the Northeast and West, it's just enough to put a family squarely in the middle class...the price of food, shelter and the goods and services of everyday life are marked up to defray the extra cost of higher state and local sales, property and income taxes. Imposing a higher federal tax rate on the incomes needed to cover taxes adds an additional cost, or penalty, to doing business in the cities. Employers and employees can avoid this penalty by moving to lower-cost suburbs or the new cities of the South. For those who are left behind, the consequences of the higher tax rates on the "rich" would be devastating. A shrinking job market would limit opportunities for upward mobility and put downward pressure on wages. The migration of businesses and people also would depress real-estate values. The combination of the loss of jobs and a decline in the value of real estate would start a downward spiral in city tax revenues, aggravating the fiscal crises of America's major cities at the very time that the need for welfare and other community services would be rising sharply.

Between 1970 and 1980, total tax collections in New York in inflation-adjusted dollars increased by only 8.6% — less than 1% a year — as one tax increase after another was barely enough to offset a 14.5% decline in real-estate tax revenues. By contrast, *between 1980 and 1990, New York's inflation-adjusted tax revenues increased 43.7%, including a 30% increase in real estate tax revenues* (My emphasis), as the city's growing economy generated revenues from an expanding, healthy tax base. Any tax increase now on its employees would boost demands for wage increases, undermining each company's competitive position and thereby accentuating the desirability of reducing costs by laying off workers or moving out of the cities."

During the 1960's the populations of the six largest American cities (New York, Chicago, Los Angeles, Philadelphia, Detroit and Baltimore) increased by 23,000. However, in the 1970's, runaway inflation and significant increases in the capital gains tax rate took a severe toll, as the population in these cities declined by 1.7 million. During the 1980's — the "decade of greed" — the downward trend reversed itself. President Reagan's tax rate reductions (coupled with the Proposition 13 tax cuts in California) caused population in these cities to grow by 219,000; all the while, inner city mayors and media liberals were claiming that Ronald Reagan was evil incarnate.

A Tale Of Three States

What would happen if a free spending, highly taxed state drastically slashed state income tax rates? Pete Du Pont, Governor of Delaware from 1977 to 1985, knows. He wrote:

> "[B]etween 1979 and 1988, Delaware's top income-tax rate was reduced to 7.7% from 19.8% — a 60% cut in rates. Since the program began, personal income-tax revenue has doubled, and employment has increased 36%. At the same time, the lowest 11% of taxpayers were removed from the tax rolls...welfare caseloads fell by 40% in the decade following the first tax cut; the state's bond rating rose six times; and the unemployment rate fell to two percentage points below the national average, having begun two percentage points above it...Delaware's private sector has grown 67% faster than that of the average state and its

personal income advanced 22% more rapidly than the U.S. average. In 1992, Delaware's poverty rate was the lowest of all 50 states. Delaware has enjoyed a surplus cash position for 15 consecutive years."

New Jersey Governor Jim Florio was more fond of the Keynesian school. Casting aside his campaign rhetoric of "no need" for tax increases, he rammed a $2.8 billion tax increase through the New Jersey legislature. Florio's budget then ballooned by more than 25% — more than three times the rate of inflation — again illustrating that budget deficits are a *spending* problem not a *revenue* problem. Nationally, 3.2 million jobs were created between 1989 and 1993; a meager three percent growth rate; yet, Florio could only dream of such "growth." During the same period, New Jersey gave back 277,000 jobs, a 7.5 percent rate of loss. New Jersey grew at a woeful .3% annual rate between 1990 and 1993, representing a $22 billion loss over historic Garden State growth rates.

In New York, under Governor Mario Cuomo, the paradigm seemed to be "tax 'em 'til they leave." Sadly, the plan worked. Under Cuomo, New York's income tax was 7.875% — 54% above the national average. Add to that a corporate tax rate of over 10% (a hair under Connecticut, the king of corporate taxes) and an effective capital gains rate of 36.5%, and you have the makings of some truly dubious statistics.

Under Governor Cuomo New York had:

◆ 15% of the nation's debt (with only 7.2% of the population)

◆ 18.5% of all Medicaid expenses (with only eight percent of all Medicaid recipients)

◆ 34% of all welfare recipients (1.1 million in New York City alone)

◆ *An amazing 40% of all job loss nationally since 1989*

Said Herbert London, a Republican candidate for governor in 1990 and 1994, "Those numbers suggest why private capital is being crowded out of existence by the expansive public sector and why many people are leaving the state. These statistics also indicate why New York lags significantly behind the rest of the nation in job production. From 1983 to 1993, the private-sector job force increased by 4% in New York and close to 25% nationwide."

Myth #9
The Clinton Economic Recovery

"The talk of capping the domestic discretionary budget is yet another deception. Clinton boasts of cutting or eliminating 115 programs, but these cuts amount to only .05 percent of the $1.5 trillion budget...Actually, domestic discretionary budget authority will rise by $10.1 billion in 1995. Including user fees, the FY 1995 increase in budget authorization in this area comes to 7 percent, or more than twice the rate of inflation.

In fact, from a 1988 bottom of 3.6 percent, the domestic discretionary spending share of GDP will increase to 4.2 percent or more by 1995."[76]
— Lawrence Kudlow,
Chief Economist, Bear, Stearns

"There is no relationship between the level of taxes a nation pays and its economic performance."
— Laura Tyson,
President Clinton's chief economic advisor

I think we need to check what they're putting in the White House coffee. If that's true, Ms. Tyson, then why not raise the tax rate to 90%, eliminate all deductions and pay off the $4.7 trillion national debt? The answer is simple — to do so would destroy the American economy and cause a global economic collapse. Are we to assume that there would be no difference in economic performance if Americans paid 20 percent tax rates as opposed to 90 percent taxes rates? If this woman is the President's *chief* economic advisor, I'd hate to meet the people who didn't make the cut.

The question remains: If the economy is so good, why is inflation-adjusted-income *decreasing?*

Although the scope and purpose of this book is not solely to debate Clinton administration policy, it is germane when the government passes on the largest tax increase in world history and then takes credit for an economic recovery. At the point that Americans blindly bare continual tax increases and accept politicians' promises that they will do us no harm, we have completely abdicated our freedom.

306

Vanishing Republic

Massive retroactive tax increases caused Clinton economic advisors to revise downward 1994 growth forecasts from 3.1% (already reduced from the original 3.3% predictions) to two percent. And this is considered growth? This is akin to Yugo engineers taking credit for advancing automotive art.

Daniel J. Mitchell of the Heritage Foundation put the numbers in perspective in February of 1994, (as well as debunking the constant Clinton gloating of deficit reduction)

> "According to the CBO, the deficit begins to climb rapidly after 1996. By the year 2003, the budget deficit more than doubles, climbing to a record $324 billion... The major reason deficits are expected to explode is the unconstrained growth of domestic spending. According to the CBO, total government spending will increase by $328 billion in five years under President Clinton's budget...*domestic spending will grow 91% faster than needed to keep pace with inflation.*" (My emphasis)

It's laughable that the Clinton economic team would take credit for what amounts to the usual recovery which occurs when pent up capital is released after a recessionary period. And even at that, this "recovery" pales in comparison to other recovery cycles. Lawrence Kudlow, chief economist at Bear, Stearns wrote,

> "On a fourth-quarter-to-fourth-quarter basis, the 1993 economy grew by only 2.9 percent, less than the 3.6 percent in 1992...real growth has averaged a sub-par 2.7 percent compared to a 4.4 percent average growth rate of the prior six recovery cycles...Thus far the recovery has generated 2.3 million new jobs...however the recovery

cycle beginning in late 1982 had generated 7.9 million new jobs at a comparable point in time, and the 1975 recovery 7.2 million."

Mitchell concurs,

"Annual economic growth since World War II — including recession years — has averaged more than 3%...The economy's performance today is particularly discouraging, since economic growth following a recession is normally well above the historical average, averaging more than 5% a year...indeed, an analysis of economic growth rates 11 quarters into a recovery [Feb., 1994] shows that growth has been barely half the level experienced during past expansions."

The Joint Economic Committee of Congress, a GOP organization, found "most disturbing, two-thirds of the first quarter [1994] growth...consisted of inventory build up." In comparison, the 1.9 million jobs created in 1993 were "only three-fourths the average of nearly 2.6 million new jobs per year created" during the Reagan economic recovery. But what kinds of jobs are generated when government crowds out private capital and commits larceny upon the savings of America's job creators? The JEC answered, "An extraordinarily high one-in-three new jobs in the private sector last year [1993] was in eating and drinking establishments and the temporary help industry where both wages and working hours are below national norms."[77] "This is in contrast to the better paying high-tech, high-skilled jobs that dominated the job creation picture of the 1980s when managerial and professional positions grew twice as fast as growth in total employment."[78]

What makes the Clinton "recovery" divergent from those past is a massive retroactive tax increase passed into law eight months into it. The result was immediately felt, wrote noted economist and syndicated columnist Paul Craig Roberts,

> "With the prospective tax increase retroactive to [only] March of this year, [1993] the administration reduced its real economic growth forecast for 1993 to 2.5% from 3.1%. Since his tax package is pending, Mr. Clinton has withheld the budgetary impact of this reduction from congress. However, the impact is easy to calculate. Using the administration's budget rules, the 0.6 percentage-point reduction in real economic growth widens the budget deficit by $65 billion over the 1993-98 period. If this slowdown continues throughout the period, the cumulative increase in the deficit will be $208 billion."

Where Were The Real Budget Cuts Made?

As domestic spending skyrocketed, defense spending was cut to the bone. The Clinton budget team pushed to trim defense spending by $33 billion between 1993 and 1995. By 1997, defense spending would fall to 3.3% of the economy; its lowest level since 1940. At the same time military readiness has been compromised as increasingly more non-defense items are added to the defense budget. Mark Yost of *The Wall Street Journal* editorial staff cited some particularly egregious examples.

"Slated for fiscal 1995 is $1.9 billion for the Defense Environmental Restoration Program; $508 million for the Base Realignment and Closure Environmental Act; $2.2 billion for environmental compliance at military bases (to a large extent, taking defense operations budget funds to pay fines to other federal agencies); $106 million for conservation; $392 million for pollution prevention, and $299 million for Environmental technology...$60 million for Junior ROTC expansion...$71 million for the National Guard Youth Opportunity Pilot Program. These last two are particularly galling considering troop levels are slated to be cut to near 1930s levels and many ROTC graduates are being told they don't have to fulfill their service obligations...$20 million for AIDS research; $25 million for Historically Black Colleges & Universities...Gone is $580 million of future research funds for the C-17 cargo transport plane...$490 million in research funds for ballistic missile defense; gone is $100 million for advanced versions of the F/A-18, the Navy's frontline fighter/attack plane."[79]

The Clinton administration also hoped to transfer peacekeeping costs from the State Department to the Defense Department; those funds would have come directly out of the operational budget. Said Rep. Jon Kyl (R- Arizona), "They tried to portray it as a simple transfer, but without funding it, that money for peacekeeping would have come out of some unit's operations budget."[80]

Particularly galling is the Environmental Protection Agency's disregard for the role of the Defense Department. While the North Koreans are building who knows how many nuclear devices and delivery systems, the EPA is fining military installations.

Environmental cleanup at military bases was estimated at $14 to $18 billion. Those estimates have been revised upward to $30 billion, *or more.* No one is denying the value of reasonable cleanup expenditures, but it is clearly a compromise of military readiness — and ultimately national security — to extract these funds from the operations budget.

"In Alaska, Fort Richardson in Anchorage and Fort Wainwright in Fairbanks were fined a combined $1.9 million. The violations? '...alleged noncompliance of EPA regulatory requirements which to a large extent involved record keeping, materials labeling and storage procedures,' said Col. George Vakalis, commander, U.S. Army Garrison, Alaska. In other words, open paint cans." Testifying before a Senate subcommittee in March 1994 General Dennis J. Reimer of the U.S. Forces Command "testified that the cost of environmental programs for his command have risen 214% since 1990. These increases aren't funded separately; they come directly out of his Operations and Maintenance budget, which is supposed to go for training and upkeep. According to Gen. Reimer: 'We spend more on environmental programs than we do on training the 1st Cavalry Division'"[81]

If North Korea invades South Korea, we can throw recycling bins at them.

Our troops deserve *much* better than this.

Chapter 14
Economic Freedom —
Elimination Of Capital Gains Tax
And
Enactment Of Flat Tax

"Government has an important role in helping develop a country's economic foundation.   But the critical test is whether government is genuinely working to liberate individuals by creating incentives to work, save, invest, and succeed."
— Ronald Reagan, October 30, 1981

"An economy hampered by restrictive tax rates will never produce enough revenue to balance our budget, just as it will never produce enough jobs or enough profits."
— John F. Kennedy, December 14, 1962

"A successful economy depends on the proliferation of the rich, on creating a large class of risk-taking men who are willing to shun the easy channels of a comfortable life in order to create new enterprise, win huge profits, and invest them again."
— George Gilder

*"Wealth is, for most people, the only honest and likely path to liberty.   With money comes power over the world. Men are freed from drudgery, women from exploitation. Businesses can be started, homes built, communities formed, religions practiced, education pursued.
But liberals aren't very interested in such real and material freedoms. They have a more innocent — not to say toddlerlike — idea of freedom. Liberals want the*

312

*freedom to put anything into their mouths, to say bad
words and to expose their private parts in art museums."*
— P.J O'Rourke

Hong Kong is not confronted with the fiscal crises that have befallen large American cities. Maybe that's because of their radically different fiscal policy. Until recently, 46% of Hong Kong's residents paid no taxes. In 1994, Financial Secretary Sir Hamish Mcleod assessed recent tax revenues and *removed* an additional 420,000 taxpayers. Currently 58 percent of the citizens pay *ZERO TAXES.*

And what about the *evil* rich: with a top marginal tax rate of only 15 percent, they contribute *70 percent* of all tax revenue. The result of low tax rates and economic growth in this large city is a projected $34 billion surplus by 1997.[82] There is no cottage industry of tax accountants attempting to interpret 9,000 pages of tax codes (in 1914, the original statute had 14 pages);[83] no encrypted truths that allow a well trained Internal Revenue auditor to find fault in 99.9 percent of all tax returns.[84]

Why Do We Need A Capital Gains Tax, Anyway?

"The anti-savings mentality has led to a deleterious economic policy of the West — taxing savings and investment at high rates while encouraging consumer debt by making interest payments tax deductible...Meanwhile, Far-Eastern countries and some European nations have adopted an anti-Keynesian, pro-savings

attitude and have experienced, not coincidentally, much higher growth rates."
> — Dr. Mark Skousen, *Economics On Trial*

"In 1993, the performance of the U.S. stock market was 32nd on an index of 35 countries. Americans invested $40 billion more abroad last year than foreigners invested here — thus reversing a $500 billion net surplus of capital flowing into the United States in the 1980s."[85]
> — Stephen Moore

"The liberal interest groups all share a desire to tax and spend other people's money in the elitist presumption that the political class knows best."
> — Dick Armey, (R-Texas)

Why is it necessary to punish thrift? Why is it so dangerous to life and limb; to save and invest — that the government feels the need to punish it? The blatant idiocy of such government intervention is clearly illustrated when real-life analogies are applied.

> *Imagine the allowance you give your child. Imagine telling him, "If you take your allowance and spend it — spend it on anything: comic books, video games, candy bars; whatever — you may spend the entire amount any way you see fit. However, if you put it in the bank and let it collect interest for the next ten years so that you can go to a good college, then you'll have to give me 28 percent of the amount of interest you've earned."*

314

Historically, the government has rewarded consumption by providing tax incentives, yet at the same time punished saving and investment. Credit card debt was tax deductible, until the 1986 Tax Reform Act phased out the deduction over a number of years.

These tax deductions were simply replaced with the ability to deduct interest on home equity loans. "According to the American Bankers Association, home equity debt increased by 120 percent between 1985 and 1991. Home equity 'lines of credit' were up 475 percent...American banks...hold nearly $500 billion in home equity loans and credit lines."[86]How many of these loans would have been unnecessary if the government didn't punish saving and investment?

This policy, again reverts back to Keynesian theory. Said Dr. Skousen, "For decades, members of the economics community have fallen under the Keynesian spell, emphasizing the importance of demand over supply, and that consumption is more important than saving. For them, the key to prosperity is found in going deeply into debt."[87]

The economic truth is exactly the opposite, writes Skousen:

> "If we include all expenditures in the intermediate stages, then we have a real measurement of total spending in the economy. I call this new statistic [Gross Domestic Output]. I estimate that GDO — total economic activity — is nearly 50 percent higher than GDP! Using this larger statistic, we find that consumer spending actually represents only about *one-third* of the economy, while gross business investment accounts for over half of the

economy! Thus, we come to the opposite conclusion:
Investment is far more important than consumption.
The U.S. economy, like all economies, is investment
driven, not consumer driven.

Economic history proves this to be the case. Japan,
Germany, and many developing nations have proven that
higher investment, not higher consumption, is the key to
economic growth."[88]

Should we be surprised that today's politicians view investment
as evil when one examines the economic textbooks by which most
college students are brainwashed? Paul Samuelson, probably the
most prolific writer of economic textbooks, wrote the following
with William D. Nordhaus in *Economics* (1989).

**"The Soviet economy is proof that, contrary to what
many skeptics had earlier believed, a socialist
command economy can function and even thrive."[89]**

In the same textbook Samuelson and Nordhaus wrote,

**"The most efficient economy in the world may produce
a distribution of wages and property that would offend
even the staunchest defender of free markets."[90]**

Applying that same logic, I suppose those less swift among us
should be patently offended by Carl Lewis' ability to run fast. Or
those not musically inclined should be offended by Van Cliburn's
ability to play piano.

In their 1988 version, they bestowed this profundity:

> **"Many doctors, artists, celebrities, and business executives, who enjoy their jobs and the sense of power or accomplishment that they bring, will work as hard for $150,000 as for $200,000."**[91]

In a chapter entitled, *"The Economics of Karl Marx,"* William Baumol and Alan Blinder (yes, the same Alan Blinder that President Clinton appointed to the Board of Governors of The Federal Reserve) wrote,

> **"The writings of Marx are stamped by brilliance and originality...they contain many sparkling and powerful passages. Many of Marx's ideas are still highly illuminating, even to non-Marxists...In short, he contributed enormously to current thought within the discipline of economics as well as in politics throughout the world."**[92]

Also, credit Baumol and Blinder with this razor-sharp insight:

> **"While savings may pave the road to riches for the individual, if the nation as a whole decides to save more, the result may be a recession and poverty for all."**[93]

In *Economics* (1990) Campbell R. McConnell and Stanley L. Bruce produced this gem (these are the same men who wrote the economics textbook that I had my aforementioned college experience):

> **"It is difficult to conceive of governmental bankruptcy when government has the power to create new money by running the printing presses!"[94]**

Tell that to post World War II Germany, where a wheel-barrel full of currency would purchase a lovely new loaf of bread.

McConnell and Bruce also wrote:

> **"Society cannot have its cake and eat it too."[95]**

Not after society pays its tax bill.

Contrary to the suppositions of these — and I use the term loosely — economists, reams of factual data indicate that an explosion of economic growth would result from the elimination of the capital gains tax. Let's take a look at the most widely held liberal arguments against lowering or eliminating capital gains taxation.

Theory #1
The Government Would Suffer Large Revenue Losses If The Capital Gains Tax Were Lowered Or Eliminated

How anyone can make this argument in light of the overwhelming amount of data that clearly refutes it, is quite astounding. There is an estimated $7 trillion in "old" investments sitting idle (just since the capital gains increase in 1986) because of the "lock-in-effect." People with considerable gains in financial instruments like stocks and mutual funds, and hard assets like homes, are reluctant to sell their investment because of the penalty imposed by the capital gains tax. It is important to note that this imposition does not simply affect the bank accounts of those holding these "old" investments. "The high capital gains tax blocks the flow of money from old investments to *new* ones."[96] The effect is new firms with promising products or services are starving for venture capital.

Stephen Moore wrote:

"The most pernicious impact of the 1986 capital gains tax rate increase, however, has nothing to do with depriving the government of revenues. It is that entrepreneurial activity has been stifled. Today small businesses are not being formed and expanded, jobs are not being created, and investment is not growing at the pace that it was in the 1980's. Capital gains are the reward that investors receive for engaging in vital risk-taking activities — e.g., starting a new enterprise. Since almost three-quarters of new ventures go belly-up within five years, entrepreneurs and investors are essentially balancing the inherent risk of large losses from a new business against the opportunity of a high payoff. Raising the capital-gains tax substantially reduces the attractiveness of the pay-off in return for risking one's money...the availability of seed capital for small start-up firms exploded in the 1980s — until the 1986 Tax Reform Act; since then it has nose-dived. In 1986 real venture capital finances for promising young firms was $4.2 billion; this funding level fell to an anemic $1.4 billion in 1991. Even a rebound in 1992 only brought the level to

$2.5 billion. This is called a credit crunch — and it is in large part a byproduct of muddle-headed, anti-investment tax-policy.

"Between 1986 and 1991 the number of firms receiving venture-capital financing dropped off a cliff — from 1,512 to 792. There was an improvement to 1,100 firms receiving financing in 1992, but this was still lower than in any year in the 1980s.

"The Venture Capital Association concludes what seems patently obvious to all but our elected representatives in Washington: 'Informal investors, who commit some $50 billion per year to small growth companies, have reduced their venture investments because the current tax code does not provide them with incentives to earn capital gains income.'"[97]

No major nation taxes capital gains at the rate of the United States.

The decrease in new investment is a big revenue loser for Uncle Sam. In 1986 capital gains were increased 40 percent from 20 percent to 28 percent. At the time of the increase, the Congressional Budget Office forecast $300 billion in capital sales in 1992. The actual amount was only $70 billion. The CBO was off by a "mere" $230 billion. The resultant loss in tax revenue cost the government $65 billion.

The great flaw in all government economic projections is that they are based on static analyses. That is, the government assumes it can adjust tax rates up or down with no bearing on the behavior of the tax payer. This is ludicrous. When taxes are increased, it is fallacious to assume that consumers will continue to spend; and businesses will continue to invest at the same pace.   By the same token, when taxes are lowered, the government's static analyses apparently assume that taxpayers take the windfall and stick it in their mattress or bury it in their back yard.

Is it any wonder these same people can't balance a budget?

Although the overwhelming majority of economists agree that lower tax rates increase growth and revenues, and tax increases limit the same, this truth is obviously lost on government economists.   To honestly face the dynamics of the tax code would allow you the freedom to spend more of your money as *you* see fit — rather than how they see fit.   *"The data since 1986 fit a consistent historical pattern: Higher capital gains tax rates mean fewer capital gains to tax."*[98] (See Chart 14-2)

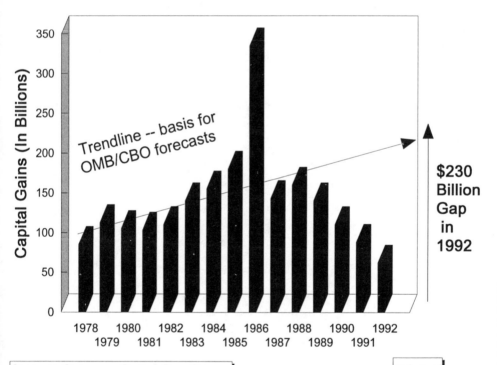

CAPITAL GAINS REALIZATIONS

IN TAX RETURN DATA

Capital Gains (In Billions)

Trendline -- basis for OMB/CBO forecasts

$230 Billion Gap in 1992

350
300
250
200
150
100
50
0

1978 1980 1982 1984 1986 1988 1990 1992
1979 1981 1983 1985 1987 1989 1991

Sources: Commerce Dept. & Bear Stearns

■ Actual

Capital gains were reduced from 48 percent to 28 percent in 1978, and tax receipts increased each year — even though the country was mired in a recession. In 1982 the rate was lowered to 20 percent; and the result: "Federal collections nearly quadrupled over the next four years,"[99] as Chart 14-3 indicates.

Year	Taxes paid on capital gains income (in mil)	Year	Taxes paid on capital gains income (in mil)
1977	$ 8,104	1984	$21,800
1978	9,104	1985	26,500
1979	11,669	1986	49,700
1980	12,459	1987	32,900
1981	12,684	1988	38,900
1982	12,900	1989	36,020
1983	18,500		

Source: U.S. Department of the Treasury

Chart 14-2

Malcolm S. Forbes Jr. summed up the irrefutable benefits of lowering capital gains.

> "A lower levy would stimulate enterprises. It would free capital to go to the most promising opportunities. Government would end up gaining. Look at history. In 1978 the rate was cut from a maximum of 48% to 28%. The Treasury Department warned that such a steep

reduction would cost the government $2 billion. Instead, revenues in 1979 went from $9.1 billion to $11.7 billion and climbed higher each subsequent year. In the early 1980s the levy was downsized again to 20%. Between 1981 and 1986, federal collections of this tax zoomed from around $13 billion to over $49 billion. But in 1987 the capital gains tax was sharply boosted. Result: Receipts fell 34%. The same pattern is true on the state level. After 1986, local collections from this exaction fell far short of expectations."[100]

Gary and Aldona Robbins of TaxAction Analysis, the tax policy arm of the respected Institute for Policy Innovation, found "a capgains cut would add 3 percent to the gross domestic product, create 721,000 new jobs and spur a wave of asset sales and new investment that would bring in $150 billion in additional tax revenue."[101]

Theory #2
Reducing Capital Gains Is A "Giveaway" To The Rich

Former Senate Majority Leader George Mitchell, one of the most partisan men in Washington, blocked efforts to reduce capital gains early in the Bush presidency. Mitchell, with the rest of the liberal legislators in tow, recited the same dogma of capital gains leniency being a "tax give-away to the rich."

Wait a minute. Clearly, the practice of taxing capital gains is "double-taxation." Americans are first taxed on their income and again taxed on any gains realized from the instruments in which they invest.

Is Senator Mitchell telling us that it is a "giveaway" if the government only taxes income ONE TIME? Why not just take it all?

Are we to further assume that the rich are the only people who own a home, or a business, or have money invested in stocks or mutual funds? Evidence points to the contrary.

"IRS data show that more than half of all taxpayers who report long-term capital gains earn $50,000 a year or less and three-fourths make $75,000 a year or less — hardly income numbers of the filthy rich."[102]

Real capital gains in 1993 were only half of what they were in 1985. In addition, capital gains in 1990 and 1991 were at the lowest rate since 1978. Conversely, "When that tax was at its postwar low between 1982 and 1986, 18.7 million jobs were created, including a record number of high-paying ones; 14 million of these came from new businesses."[103]

Why is this concept so difficult to grasp?

At the time of the capital gains debate during the Bush presidency, the CBO claimed that 60 percent of the proceeds of a reduction in the capital gains tax would find its way into the pockets of those making over $200,000 per year. And just what does the CBO think the "rich" were going to do with the windfall? Surely, they would either reinvest it; purchase a home, a new car, or other consumer goods; or place it in a financial instrument which would ultimately find its way into some firm as venture capital.

You see, this is called *economic growth*; and the private sector is considerably better equipped to see that these funds are invested in worthwhile pursuits than some government bureaucrat. "A study by the Republican staff of the Joint Economic Committee for Rep. Dick Armey, a Republican from Texas, finds that if the capital gains rate had remained at 20 percent and realizations had continued to grow at their 1980-85 pace, revenues would have been almost $60 billion higher from 1986 to 1991 — even at the lower tax rate."[104]

The ultimate benefit of eliminating capital gains taxation is so enormous, as to almost be incalculable; while the detriment of continuing to punish thrift and investment is clear. "Jude Wanniski of Polyconomics makes the eye-popping point that a $1 investment that doubles annually and is sold every year will be worth $1 million after 20 years; but if that dollar is taxed at 35% every year, it will be worth only $22,000 over the same period."[105]

This is not a tax issue. It is a matter of wealth redistribution. It is nothing more than the elitist divination of imperial governance. It is the practice of punishing the hard work of some citizens in order to bestow the fruits of their labor upon those who produce nothing — all under the guise of compassion.

The Founding Fathers espoused the Judeo-Christian belief in the value of thrift. Now, our government tells us — through its policy of abstracting the profits of thrift — that it is better equipped to "invest" America's wealth than those who sacrificed current consumption for future benefit. The policy of taxing capital gains is both fiscally wrong and morally bankrupt. It is unfathomable to think that a nation is better off by turning over so much of its prosperity to a government that can't balance a budget, has a debt approaching five trillion dollars, and steals money from the Social Security Trust Fund in order to purchase $400 hammers, among other things.

A Flat Tax
H.R. 4585 —
The Freedom And Fairness Restoration Act
Sponsor: Dick Armey (R-Texas)

"Our government is too big, and it spends, taxes and regulates too much. Of all the supposed crises we're facing today, this is the one that really matters...Today, the average family now pays more in taxes than it spends on the basics of food, clothing and shelter combined. All told, nearly 40% of the nation's income is now spent not by the workers who earned it, but by the political class that taxed it from them."
— Dick Armey

"We have traveled far down the slippery slope of imperial government and have succeeded in eroding the Bill of Rights to the point that there soon will be little left. Mr. Armey's bill would do much toward turning back the tide of warrantless searches, disappearing property rights and criminal prosecution where no intent to commit a crime can be shown."
— Albert G. Young, Publisher
The Common Sense Press

327

"The economy would explode with growth. Taxes are not merely a means of raising revenues but are also a price. By lowering the price on work, profits and innovation, we'll get more of them. Each time we have lowered the tax on each extra dollar earned, the economy and government revenues have gone up."
— Malcolm S. Forbes Jr.

This book is about enacting positive change in America, by positively reforming American Government and improving several key cultural areas. Of all the topics contained herein, this may be the most important because it deals with so many "crises" threatening American freedom. Not only confiscatory taxation, but also the loss of private property rights, exploding governmental regulations, and clandestine intrusions into the inner sanctum of personal freedom. "Payroll-Tax Deposit Rules top the list of regulations branded as 'the most significant burdens to small and midsize businesses,' says a survey of owners of these businesses by an Arthur Anderson unit in Chicago. Next came OSHA regulations, followed by environmental rules."[106]Interestingly, the Founding Fathers gave no Constitutional authority to any of these practices. If there exists a "magic bullet" of government reform, it is Dick Armey's Freedom and Fairness Restoration Act.

Armey's proposal was the most effortlessly written segment of this work because the bill is so brilliant in its simplicity, honorable in its intent, and noble in its purpose. A summary of the Freedom and Fairness Restoration Act can be obtained compliments of the office of Representative Armey.

From the introduction to the summary of H.R. 4585:

"This is the true crisis facing America in the 1990s. The Freedom and Fairness Restoration Act will begin a roll back. It launches a frontal assault on Big Government, radically changing virtually everything the government does...The U.S. public sector is now larger than the entire economy of any country in the world save Japan and the United States itself...Taking into account the total cost of government — taxes as well as regulation — an American works from January 1st through July 10th not to support himself and his family, but to support the government.

If being an American means freedom from the unfair demands of distant rulers — if it means being able to use one's own efforts to build a better future for one's children — then this state of affairs is very wrong. The growth of government is a grave danger to the American Dream.

Americans must now make a fundamental choice: Should the government become ever larger as our freedom diminishes — or should we take dramatic action now to halt the growth of government and restore the promise of greater freedom to our citizens? It is a comprehensive assault of Big Government, designed to halt its growth...by radically reordering the three major activities of the government — taxing, spending, and regulating."

Generous Allowances

Rep. Armey's proposal would tax income at a flat 17%. There would be no special tax breaks and no loopholes. The liberal cry of regressivity is blatantly devoid of substance or logic. First of all, I have rarely heard a whimper of discontent from liberals regarding the most regressive tax of all, the 15.3% Social Security

Tax that is levied on the first dollar earned. The Freedom and Fairness Restoration Act eliminates the marriage penalty and offers a generous allowance of $13,100 for an individual, $17,200 for a single head of household, and $26,200 for a married couple. In addition a $5,300 deduction would be allowed for each child, which is roughly twice the current deduction.

> *Therefore, a married couple filing jointly, with three children and an annual income of $42,100 would pay no federal income tax.*

How can anyone claim this to be regressive?

Elimination of "Double-Taxation"

Saving and investment would no longer be punished by double-taxation. FFA repeals the estate tax (made retroactive in the 1993 budget) as well as taxes on dividends and the Clinton tax increases on Social Security recipients. This bill taxes all income earners equally. It removes the disincentive to sacrifice and achieve. How do we justify our current system "charging a higher rate of taxation to someone who elects to drive his taxi 70 hours per week than to someone who works 40 hours per week?"[107]

Wrote Congressman Armey,

> **"Fairness is in fact the flat tax's great virtue. It's based on the idea of fairness we learned in grade school:** *Everyone should be treated the same.* **Rather than have**

fallible politicians decide — for their own reasons — which groups should surrender more or less of their earnings to the government, the flat tax sets a single objective standard. No matter how much money you make, what kind of business you're in, whether or not you have a lobbyist in Washington, you will be taxed at the same percentage as everyone else."[108]

Businesses would be treated equally fair, taxing the difference between revenue and expenses at the same 17 percent. The billions of man hours that are currently spent preparing taxes would be eliminated, and the resulting windfall would either be spent on consumer products, saved or invested.

Mortgage interest would no longer be deductible, but home sales and new construction would still explode. Interest rates would drop measurably because of an abundance of available capital, as the shackles of capital gains taxation are removed. Businesses would invest in new plants and equipment, new businesses would form because of the availability of venture capital; job growth would explode and income would rise, while an overwhelming increase in the demand for housing would increase existing property values.

Spending Caps And Program Sunsets

The Armey plan would also impose unbreachable spending caps and sunset virtually all existing federal programs. Federal spending (including entitlements) would be frozen for one year; and thereafter, the growth of said programs would be limited to the rate of inflation. *In the first two years, the caps would save an estimated $600 billion.*[109]

Program sunsets are part and parcel to Zero-Based Budgeting discussed earlier. Congress would be forced to debate all programs on merit each fiscal year.

Armey wrote,

> **"Today, congressional committees routinely write new spending bills authorizing 'such sums as may be necessary.' Under this plan, 'such sums' will come straight from existing programs. The days of the congressional blank check will be over...we have programs enacted in the 1930s that have never been reviewed.**[110]
>
> **"This provision would genuinely reinvent government by forcing Congress to review virtually every federal program. Sunsetting forces Congress to periodically review the effectiveness of programs, set new priorities, and reduce unnecessary spending."**[111]

Breaking The Regulatory Stranglehold

Overwhelming government regulations are the hidden tax on commerce and freedom. The impact is estimated at $580 billion per year! "But, no one knows for sure because the government doesn't add up the costs or even consider prudent alternatives. When bureaucrats and members of Congress impose regulations on

Americans, they quite literally have no idea what they are doing."[112]

Armey's plan would:

> **"Force the president to produce a regulatory budget, exposing for the first time the hidden cost of regulations. Congress would be required to do a cost-benefit analysis and risk assessment on any bill with new regulatory authority. For the first time this hidden taxation would be brought to light.[113]**
>
> **"Within one year of passage of the bill, OMB would be required to determine the costs of federal regulations to the American economy. OMB would also be required to calculate the cost of federal regulations to state and local government. If OMB determines the cost of regulations will exceed the previous year's level, it would be required to submit to Congress proposed changes in existing legislation or regulations which would keep regulatory costs in line with the previous year."[114]**

This is something I espoused long ago. Similarly, Rep. John Mica (R-Florida) has proposed legislation that would require the Environmental Protection Agency to perform cost/benefit analyses, but the bill has yet to make it to the floor. (At the same time the EPA is lobbying for Cabinet level status.) It is particularly galling that they want more power, yet refuse to perform due diligence.

Of what are these agencies afraid?

Most importantly, The Freedom and Fairness Restoration Act would eliminate the predatory policies of innumerable government agencies.

> "Many private property owners have had their land
> essentially seized from them through regulatory takings
> that prohibit most uses for the land."[115]
>
> "[T]he plan specifically rolls back the most egregious
> effect of regulation — the spreading erosion of property
> rights. Any time government regulators write a rule
> that reduces the value of a person's property by a
> significant amount the government must compensate
> him — just as it would if it confiscated his land to
> build a public park or highway."[116]

Finally, The Freedom and Fairness Restoration Act would
eliminate the withholding tax.

> "The plan takes aim at the crucial deceptive device that
> has made Big Government possible: Income tax
> withholding. If taxpayers over the years had paid their
> taxes the same way they make rent or car payments,
> the government never could have grown as large as it
> has. [Under FFA, taxpayers would simply write a
> monthly check.] Only by taking people's money before
> they ever see it has the government been able to raise
> taxes to their current level without igniting a rebellion.
> My plan would end withholding and put a permanent
> check on the confiscatory appetites of the political
> class."[117]

Dick Armey is nothing short of an American hero. He has
exhibited courage and vision by proposing legislation that would
single-handedly give American government back to the American
people. However, his plan will be a long, arduous battle. Albert

Young, publisher of *The Common Sense Press,* wrote, "Rep. Armey's 'Freedom and Fairness Restoration Act' succeeds in threatening every power group in the country. No mean feat. My prediction is that it will be met first by silence (probably will never get out of committee), next (if that doesn't work) by ridicule, and finally (if it's still going) by an all-out attack...Big Labor, of course, depends on government for its survival, and big business frequently gets government help to limit competition. Many lawyers, lobbyists, and accountants would be put out of business altogether. These are formidable forces. Nevertheless, it is a battle worth fighting."[118]

The inherent battle is that Rep. Armey proposes sweeping reforms that are not espoused by the liberal establishment — in fact they would effectively *destroy* the liberal establishment. No longer would they be able to spend your money as they see fit. No longer would they be able to seize your property at will, or sacrifice your business at the altar of environmental extremism.

> *It is for these reasons that the congressional reforms outlined in the previous chapter must be implemented before there is any chance of enacting the reforms outlined here. As you read further, the complete picture will come into focus, as all the different reforms I have elucidated come together. For that reason, I'll be returning to the Capital Gains Elimination/Flat Tax issue when we address welfare reform, as the two issues are related in a very important way that is fundamental to the overall message of this book.*

Mark Anthony

If there is one issue that the American people should rally around, it is The Freedom and Fairness Restoration Act. FFA gives back so many freedoms in so many areas. We could keep more of what we earn. Saving and investment would explode. Economic growth would abound. Federal bureaucracies would be forced to prove their worth, or be disbanded. Why should bureaucrats have such job security when their very existence is based on limiting and categorizing the rights of American citizens? Special interests and lobbyists would lose their stranglehold on the legislators who swore to represent *your* interests. Our legislators would be held accountable to the same realities and limitations that their constituents are beholden to: namely, that it is impossible to indefinitely spend more than one takes in; and immoral to confiscate that which is not yours.

This is the defining issue that will demonstrate once and for all if we have government *by the people* — *or to the people.* Wouldn't it be wonderful to watch the lobbyists and special interests attempt to justify their opposition? If any legislator would disagree with The Freedom and Fairness Restoration Act, how transparent their motives would be. It would become eminently clear which politicians wish to serve, and which are solely interested in gratifying their egos and padding their pocketbooks. Every voter could clearly see on which side his or her legislator stands.

In shining the glowing light of truth, it would become simpler to vote out those who continue to advance big government, regulatory assault and creeping erosion of our most basic rights. The American public (and the 1996 election) deserves a defining

336

issue like this. After all, it is our money the government is wasting — our freedom and private property rights they are stealing. We must demand accountability; otherwise, I would ask those irresponsible legislators to explain to my children and grandchildren why *they* must pay for such reckless and imprudent governance.

> *"We who live in free market societies believe that growth, prosperity and ultimately human fulfillment, are created from the bottom up, not the government down. Only when the human spirit is allowed to invent and create, only when individuals are given a personal stake in deciding economic policies and benefiting from their success — only then can societies remain economically alive, dynamic, progressive, and free. Trust the people. This is the one irrefutable lesson of the entire postwar period contradicting the notion that rigid government controls are essential to economic development."*
> — Ronald Reagan, September 29, 1981

If you would like more information regarding The Freedom and Fairness Restoration, please ask your Congressman, or contact Rep. Armey's office at:

The Honorable Dick Armey
301 Cannon House Office Building
Washington, D.C. 20515-4328
(202) 225-7772

Chapter 15
Civil Rights Reform Must Precede Capital Gains Reform

"We want to get our clients' money as far away from Bill and Hillary as we can. The President is a negative for the U.S. market. I'm embarrassed that I voted for him and contributed money to his campaign."
— Barton Biggs, Chief Investment Officer, Morgan Stanley

"What more is necessary to make us a happy and a prosperous people?...a wise and frugal government, which shall restrain men from injuring one another, shall leave them otherwise free to regulate their own pursuits of industry and improvement, and shall not take from the mouth of labor the bread it has earned. This is the sum of good government, and this is necessary to close the circle of our felicities."
— Thomas Jefferson

The Clinton paradigm is only a small part of the problem. Don't be deceived into thinking that a one term Clinton presidency will be the turning point to a new American freedom.

Far from it.

Mr. Clinton and his staff are simply the current delivery system of flawed governance that began with President Roosevelt and the New Deal; and magnified by decades of virtually uninterrupted one party rule in Congress.

Economist and Nobel Laureate, Milton Friedman, estimated "the cost to the private sector of complying with [government] regulations is at least $430 billion annually — 9 percent of our gross domestic product!"[119] Other estimates place this figure closer to $600 billion.[120]

To unleash the $6 to $7 trillion dollars "locked-in" by the capital gains tax into the current regulatory and civil rights environment would be economic suicide. A flood of new capital cannot flourish in such an environment and would surely go abroad; as is happening already, verified by Barton Biggs' comment.

It becomes quite clear that civil rights and regulatory reforms are deeply intertwined with fiscal policy. The scope of the problem is truly daunting, and an insult to the basic tenets of American life on which our country was founded: Natural law, Limited Constitutional government, private property rights, freedom of speech and freedom to contract.

In an earlier chapter I used a typical small businessman as a metaphor to juxtapose with government in order to illustrate the absurdity of the federal bureaucracy. That analogy is particularly helpful in illustrating the enormous barriers to economic growth caused by government expansionism. Imagine the trials which confront our weary small business people...

The Freedom To Contract And Hire

"All but the hopeless reactionary will agree that to conserve our primary resources of manpower, government must have some

control over maximum hours, minimum wages, the evil of child labor, and the exploitation of unorganized labor."[121]
— Franklin D. Roosevelt, 1937

"As the twentieth century has progressed, governments are increasingly preempting individuals' opportunities to build their own lives through their own agreements. In area after area, government officials have asserted a prerogative to make decisions for individuals, to forcibly impose those decisions on people, and to punish people who made agreements outside of government control — outside of the narrow channels in which government officials permit private citizens to contract...The Fair Labor Standards Act contains no definition of 'fair labor'; instead, the act permits politicians to endlessly manipulate labor markets for their own advantage. The Fair Labor Standards Act is basically a blank check to allow political manipulation of the labor markets to reward some people by throwing other people out of the labor market. Once politicians achieved the power to define 'fair' labor, they also claimed the power to ban people from laboring."
— James Bovard, *Lost Rights*

With FDR's words, as well as the enactment of The 1938 Fair Labor Standards Act (FLSA) the government gave itself the right to decide who may work, what is the minimum they must be paid, how much they must be compensated for overtime, and the ability to destroy jobs at will by indiscriminately raising the minimum wage. There is almost universal consensus among economists that enforcing a minimum wage costs jobs. In 1983 the General Accounting Office found "virtual total agreement...that employment is lower than it would have been if no minimum wage existed...Teenage workers have greater job losses, relative to their share of the population or the employed work force, than adults."[122]

In 1988, roughly 60% of all minimum wage workers were age 16-24; and 70% of them worked part-time.

Liberals couch their argument in compassion. "These are poor working class Americans whose families need the additional income," but evidence shows that mandated wage increases only hurt. Minimum wage laws place price supports on the cost of labor by forcing employers to pay wages above that which an employee's skill level would normally command, thereby effectively raising the bottom rung of the economic ladder beyond the reach of many.

Unfortunately, these displaced workers are not simply teenagers and students. Early in the Clinton Presidency, Labor Secretary Robert B. Reich proposed raising the minimum wage to $5 an hour and indexing it forever to inflation. But even Mr. Reich isn't completely devoid of economic acumen. He wrote President Clinton a memo indicating "most minimum wage workers are not poor. And the potential effects of a minimum wage increase on employment should of course be weighed." *A Wall Street Journal* editorial noted, "In 1988, according to the Fortune Encyclopedia of Economics, only 8% of workers who received the wage minimum maintained families, and not all of those were poor. But by pricing such workers out of the labor market, Mr. Reich might very well make them poor." Carlos Bonilla of the Employment Policies Institute claimed that 422,000 jobs would be lost if the minimum wage were raised to $5 an hour. Yet again in January 1995, only two days after the Republican majority opened the 104th Congress, President Clinton drug out that old liberal chestnut and called for a one dollar increase in the minimum wage. Class warfare is alive and well in 1995.

Young teenagers are denied jobs because of government's piousness. Between 1990 and 1992 jobs held by teenagers declined by over a million. Burger King was slapped with labor violations at 755 American franchises. Its main offense: allowing teens under the age of 16 to work beyond 7:00 P.M.

What gives the government the right to tell these kids they can't work even if they want to? Is this not an invasion of the teenagers' right to contract?

By mandating whom a business owner may hire, and how much they must pay him or her, the government has effectively given some employees a job, or a negligible raise, while condemning others to *no wage at all.*

Mr. Reich made it clear early on that his department was more intent in reviving oppressive labor practices, than allowing individual workers and small businesses to freely go about their business. For all his Harvard educated knowledge, Reich's philosophy, no matter how eloquently he wishes to state it, is quite simple:

Employer...*bad,*
Worker...*good,*
Union...*really good.*

The obvious philosophy of federal labor jockeys is *divide and conquer.* In an August 3, 1993, article, *Financial World* noted one of "Clinton's first executive orders reversed Republican labor policies that had been despised by the AFL-CIO...Clinton canceled a Bush executive order that put limits on the ability of unions to use member dues for political activities." In a labor environment where employees have little choice whether to join the local union, their mandatory dues represent little more than extortion based on the dearth of input they receive for their contribution. The Clinton/Reich directive exacerbates the problem by *relieving union leaders from having to account for how union dues are dispersed.* If there is a purpose to this executive order other than to pander to big labor unions, I've yet to find it. Mr. Clinton and Mr. Reich were also responsible for lifting the ban on the air-traffic controllers union instituted by "evil" President Reagan. A move which was totally symbolic as the FAA was under a hiring freeze at the time.

Mr. Reich quickly formed a 10 member commission to resurrect the outdated, but politically correct, labor policies of the New Deal. Reich, ostensibly took this action to "level the playing field." Unfortunately, when liberal elitists seek to level the playing field, they always seem to tilt it to a 90 degree angle in favor of their politically correct, yet counterproductive, policies.

The Wall Street Journal editorialized, "not a single member [of Reich's commission] represents the nine-tenths of private workers and management that aren't unionized. Jack Faris of the National Federation of Independent Businesses, which boasts 603,000 members, might be prevailed upon to speak for the sort of companies that created all the new jobs in the past 15 years. He's been informed that *Mr. Reich can't see him — ever."* (My emphasis)

343

Certain actions speak volumes about intent, about moral center, core beliefs and the role the bureaucracy wishes to enforce on the serfdom toiling in its domain. Early one morning Comrade Reich phoned the CEO of Bridgestone/Firestone Inc., and informed him he was about to levy his company with a bevy of safety violations. Shortly after the call, Reich made his presence known, with local police and Secret Service escorts in tow. He personally delivered an alleged 107 safety violations, along with a $7.5 million fine to the company's Dayton Tire Co. plant in Oklahoma City. "Declaring the plant in 'imminent' danger to workers, he dispatched lawyers to the federal courthouse [in Oklahoma City] to get an emergency order forcing Dayton Tire to comply with safety rules or risk being held in contempt of court. Mr. Reich's dramatic moves were intended to show the Clinton administration's determination to reinvigorate the government's far reaching regulatory apparatus."[123]

Said Reich,

*"American workers are not going to be sacrificed
at the altar of profits."*[124]
(That's why they *have* a job, Mr. Labor Secretary —
the pursuit of profits.)

An unfortunate accident precipitated Reich's visit to the Dayton Tire plant. Bob Julian, who had 25 years of experience, was fatally injured when he reached into a jammed tire making machine. Another man lost his arm in a similar incident. Although these are horrible incidents, industrial accidents cannot be magically eliminated by government decree. The labor department took advantage of a tragic situation by levying fines that were sure to eliminate the jobs of the very workers they allegedly wanted to protect. Reported *The Wall Street Journal,*

> "'There is growing disillusionment,' says Deborah Bright, a New York consultant who has counseled a slew of companies and their employees during the layoffs of recent years. 'People are swirling around in this maze, uncertain about their own job security. They're paying higher taxes. Then they see the government coming in with all these new regulations and fines. Where is the logic? Where is the sense? They don't see a benefit themselves?'"[125]

Said one employee, "he came here with his guns cocked and just didn't know what the hell he was doing." Secretary Reich certainly did know what he was doing. He was in clear defiance of the inspectors who visited the plant prior to his decision to levy the fine. Three of the four inspectors found *no* imminent danger. The other inspector "reached the opposite conclusion only days before Mr. Reich's visit." Nor did Federal District Judge Timothy Leonard find any imminent danger, as he denied the government's preliminary injunction against the tire manufacturer.[126]

Reich's ivory-tower, central planning, elitist mentality is in sharp contrast to working-class Americans who are concerned about whether they will have jobs next year, and whether they will be able to afford new school clothes for their children next month. These are people who give something back to society every day. They produce things, whether it be a good or service. Each day when they clock-out, they have left the wood pile just a little larger than they found it that morning.

What does Mr. Reich add?

What does *any* bureaucrat add?

They only force the worker to add more wood to the pile, just to keep from going backward; *and then one day they show up at the factory...and suddenly there is no more wood to chop.* Reported *The Wall Street Journal*, "Rick Chesser a local farmer who grows wheat and alfalfa on Dayton Tire land said, 'Too much power, it sounds like to me'...'It's kind of frightening, isn't it?'"[127]

Union Expansionism

There is a much more surreptitious aspect to minimum wage hikes: to make union membership more attractive, which is the reason for the link between higher minimum wage laws and large labor unions. "Organized labor favors a high minimum wage because that reduces management's resistance to union recruiting. Where cheap alternative sources of labor are eliminated, high-priced union labor no longer looks so bad to company managers," editorialized *The New York Times*.[128]

Public safety workers, such as firefighters and police, are often overworked and underpaid, and bargaining in good faith helps them achieve more equitable wages. But other than that, Union power in the United States has little to do with workers' rights. It has everything to do with allowing the government to set up a system which selectively bestows uncommon rights on favored groups. In many cases, unions and their tactics are simply an extension of government intrusion into citizens' personal rights. In 1914 Congress passed the Sherman Antitrust Act which made it virtually impossible to litigate against unions for restraint of trade. In 1932 the Norris-Laguardia Act disallowed federal courts from using injunctions to end strike-related violence. But the most insidious action of all was the National Labor Relations Act of 1935 (The Wagner Act). The act forced employers to bargain with unions and facilitate forcing employees to pay union dues. The following passage is taken from this Act:

> **"Experience has proven that protection by law of the right of employees to organize and bargain collectively... promotes the flow of commerce by removing certain recognized sources of industrial strife and unrest."**

Juxtapose that with the Preamble to the Constitution of The United States:

> **"We hold these truths to be self-evident, that all men are created equal; that they are endowed by their creator with certain inalienable rights; that among these are life, liberty, and the pursuit of happiness."**

Somehow the phrase "collective bargaining" is absent from the Constitution. I have nothing against the concept of unions or collective bargaining, in theory. The problem lies with government approved union coercion; which as history has shown, is inseparable from most union activity. In many cases, collectively

347

bargained labor costs are far above what the market will bear. In New York City the janitors union has garnered an annual wage in excess of $50,000, yet janitors are only required to mop the floors twice a year. Delivery drivers for the New York *Daily News* were often paid in excess of $100,000. Artificially high wages are viciously protected by the employees who collect them, and why not — to be paid what the market will truly bear would at least cut their pay in half. Such inequities are guaranteed to breed violence and inefficiency. If collectivism worked, then Communist Russia would have had the world's highest standard of living. The *Daily News* strike offered some of the most violent union backlash in recent memory. Newsstands were burned down, firebombs were thrown, replacement drivers were beaten with baseball bats, and advertisers were harassed, threatened and beaten. At the same time, Mario Cuomo, New York's boldhearted former governor heralded "the courage and sacrifice of the union movement."

Such actions are also routinely condoned by The National Labor Regulatory Board, (NLRB) which has a hideous record of siding with unions regardless of how much violence and carnage they have wrought (or implied). Steve Antosh wrote, "In the *Georgia Kraft* case, the Board found no violation where union members cursed a nonstriker in his home in the presence of his family, and stated they 'would take care of him' when they returned to the plant. The Board characterized these statements as 'ambiguous.' In the *A. Duie Pyle* case, a union threat to burn down a worker's home was ruled by the Board to be noncoercive because it was not a threat of personal violence and was not accompanied by positive action to implement the threat."[129] In 1979, the NLRB again sanctioned such actions, announcing "Although an employee may have engaged in misconduct [by issuing threats or inflicting violent acts], he or she may not be deprived of reinstatement rights absent a showing that the conduct was so violent...as to render an employee unfit for future service."[130]In other words, if you are accosted by an angry union member with a baseball bat, broken bones would be a punishable offense, but cuts and bruises would not. So much for equal protection under the law.

During the Greyhound strike of 1990, sniper fire rained on passenger buses in over fifty separate incidents, less than half of all scheduled routes could be completed and ridership dropped to one-third the norm. Replacement bus drivers had to contend with Molotov cocktails, bricks and bottles among other dangerous distractions. Amidst rampant union violence, the NLRB ordered Greyhound to fire "any and all replacements in order to provide work for strikers" and "provide immediate and full reinstatement." The NLRB placed the onus directly on Greyhound management, accusing them of "an unfair labor practices strike" and ordered them to pay $143 million in compensation. Eventually, the NLRB negotiated a cease-and-desist order and a consent decree with the union, which never accepted responsibility for the violence. Even after the consent decree, union violence continued which the NLRB ignored. Just three months after the strike began, Greyhound was forced into bankruptcy. Greyhound CEO Fred Curry was patently offended by the actions of the union and the *inaction* of the NLRB. He was quoted in USA Today, "I've dealt with supply-demand risks all my life, but I've never lost money as a result of criminal activity, and I deeply resent it. It's been open warfare."[131]

"The NLRB's definition of 'bargaining in good faith' apparently carries an unlimited obligation for company officials to continue bargaining with representatives of a group that are violently trying to destroy the company...A key point of the government prosecution of Greyhound during a 1991 administrative law trial was that the company illegally fired workers after the workers abandoned their buses and walked off their jobs. Specifically, NLRB lawyers argued at length that Greyhound had committed an illegal 'unfair labor practice' by firing two strikers who were convicted and sentenced to jail for shooting at a Greyhound bus carrying passengers. The NLRB argued that the workers had been engaged in union activities during the strike and shooting and thus that their activities were protected under federal labor law and that Greyhound owed them back pay — including the time they were in jail."[132]

Most egregious of all is the blatant intrusion on free speech imposed by NLRB mandates. Federal law prohibits employers and employees from meeting outside the heavily biased union guidelines as outlined by Congress and the NLRB. In doing so, interactive discussions between management and labor regarding working conditions, or safety, or employee benefits are a violation of The National labor Relations Act. This is a pathetic intrusion of the First Amendment by the very people who spout the gospel of *workers* rights. It should be noted that these workers are *Americans* first. They have rights and freedoms; the limitation of which is not the province of bureaucrats. Alexander Hamilton

350

wrote in *The Federalist Papers:* "A power over a man's subsistence amounts to a power over his will." How can eliminating such basic inalienable rights, endowed by our creator, be so effortlessly taken away by our government?

> *"People almost never petition Congress to restrict their own freedom of contract; rather, one group petitions politicians to restrict everyone else's freedom for their own benefit...As no man is entitled to a share of his neighbor's income, no man is entitled to have his neighbor's freedom restricted so as to get more of his neighbor's income."*
> — James Bovard, *Lost Rights*

*Un*equal Employment Opportunity

"A society that puts equality — in the sense of economic equality of outcome — ahead of freedom will end up with neither equality nor freedom. The use of force to achieve equality will destroy freedom, and the force, introduced for no good purposes, will end up in the hands of people who use it to promote their own interests."[133]
— Milton Friedman

"We...here at EEOC believe in numbers...our most valid standard is in numbers...The only accomplishment is when we look at all those numbers and see a vast improvement in the picture."[134]
— Clifford Alexander, EEOC chairman, 1968

"An increasingly serious [business] cost is the inherent dishonesty and unfairness in branding as discriminators employers whose only sin is hiring the best employees they can find."[135]
— Stuart Taylor

The Equal Employment Opportunity Commission was born of the 1964 Civil Rights Act, a progeny of Great Society utopianism. Because there existed some people who discriminated by race, the government saw an opening, and capitalized; and another bureaucratic Leviathan was spawned. The initial intent of the Civil Rights Act was certainly noble, and without the creation of the abomination that the EEOC has become, it no doubt would have been a service to society. This may sound crass, but the evidence is clear. The two bedrock principles of the Civil Rights Act are:

A) that racial quotas are specifically prohibited, and

B) a clear intent to discriminate must be present before an employer is found guilty.

However, the EEOC wasted little time in subjugating the very law that created it. Hugh Davis Graham wrote:

> "The EEOC's own first Administrative History clearly stated, 'Under the traditional meaning' which was the 'common definition of Title VII' an act of discrimination 'must be one of intent in the state of mind of the actor'... By the end of the Johnson Administration the EEOC, by its own self-description, was disregarding Title VII's intent requirement."[136]

The landmark case of *Griggs v. Duke Power Co.* opened the flood-gates to civil rights activism. As usual, the trampling of the Constitution was abetted with the capitulation of liberal rulings by Supreme Court Justices, which completely defy reason or common sense, and certainly have no basis in natural law.

Duke Power Co. had a policy of not promoting employees without a high school education or the ability to pass a written test. The guidelines sound fair enough; and at the very least have reasons grounded in the general safety and well-being of the employees. Furthermore, *Duke Power Co. had a program that paid the education costs so that unqualified employees could receive the requisite schooling free of charge.* Even if such a benefit had not existed, Duke would have been well within the guidelines by disallowing the promotions. The Civil Rights Act of 1964 specifically states that employers may discriminate based on "business necessity" or Bona Fide Occupational Qualifications (BFOQ). Is it unreasonable to preclude an employee of a power company from promotion because he or she does not have basic skills? Regardless, Chief Justice Warren Burger ruled against Duke: "[Title VII] proscribes not only overt discrimination but also practices that are fair in form, but discriminatory in operation...good intent...does not redeem employment procedures or testing mechanisms that operate as 'built-in headwinds' for minority groups and are unrelated to measuring job capability."

Herman Belz noted, "Since 1966, the underlying purpose of the EEOC test guidelines was to place enough obstacles in the way of employee selection so that employers would choose to hire by race rather than objective criteria of merit."[137]But when one takes an

353

objective look at the definitions and practices of the EEOC, the nature and severity of its reverse discrimination is rather putrid. The EEOC slanders and belittles the very people it is ostensibly attempting to defend, and does so with such blatant severity that anyone else would be banished under the guise of political correctness; should they make such comments. Case in point: the concept of *Race Norming.* Race normed tests, like the General Aptitude Test Battery, have been fixed by the U.S. Labor Department so that different ethnic groups with different test scores would magically get "equal" test scores. Wrote University of Delaware professors Jan Blits and Linda Gottfredson:

> "Race-norming frequently doubles or triples scores for blacks, especially for higher skilled jobs. For example, if a black, a Hispanic and a white or Asian all received raw scores of 300 on a test for machinist, cabinet maker and similarly skilled work, the black would be referred to an employer with a converted score of 79, the Hispanic with a converted score of 62, and the white or Asian with a converted score of 39 — and the employer would not be told the race of any of the applicants."[138]

This is patently offensive and enormously insulting. If you or I, or anyone outside the festering sore that has become the beltway bureaucracy, made the proclamation that blacks are not as smart as Hispanics; who are not as smart as whites; who are not as smart as Asians — we would be publicly flogged. But the EEOC assumes such truths, and they are somehow the arbiters of equity and fairness. These pathetic regulatory fiends have written their own rules in order to rig the outcome. They have surreptitiously given themselves the power to determine who wins and who loses, all the while cloaking their deception in utopian good intentions. Even a fool could see that their actions are a self-aggrandizing abomination of the citizens' racial fears; all the while belittling the minority groups they claim to help.

Shelby Steele, a black professor at San Jose State University, wrote, "Under affirmative action, the quality that earns us preferential treatment is an implied inferiority...The effect of preferential treatment — the lowering of normal standards to increase black representation — puts blacks at war with an expanded realm of debilitating doubt, so that the doubt itself becomes an unrecognized preoccupation that undermines their ability to perform, especially in integrated situations."

The EEOC's Uniform Guidelines on Employee Selection Procedures contain these pearls of wisdom:

> *Adverse Impact:* "a substantially different rate of selection in hiring, promotion, or other employment decisions which works to the disadvantage of members of a race, sex, or ethnic group."

> *Unfairness of Selection Procedure:* "a condition in which members of one race, sex, or ethnic group characteristically obtain lower scores on a selection procedure than members of another group, and the differences are not reflected in differences in measures of job performance."

> *Disparate Treatment:* "where members of a race, sex, or ethnic group have been denied the same employment,

promotion, membership, or other employment
opportunities as have been available to other
employees or applicants."

And there you have it: the penultimate bureaucratic net. The
EEOC has specifically written the guidelines in such a way that
they can mosey into virtually any business in America and find the
employer guilty of discriminatory hiring practices if an applicant
were rejected because he or she isn't smart enough, or skilled
enough, or fast enough or strong enough. Nothing matters to the
EEOC except the numbers. This is outrageously insulting to
anyone who takes the entrepreneurial risk of opening a business.
No longer may the entrepreneur hire the most qualified, the most
skilled, the best potential employee — he or she must hire one
applicant from column A, one from column B and one from
column C — in order to meet the "fairness" guidelines of the
EEOC.

What about the individual with superior capabilities who was
turned away, so that someone with inferior skills — but more
politically correct pigment — could by hired? How fair is this
scenario?

Peter Brimelow and Leslie Spencer wrote, "Today, industrial
psychologist John Hunter estimates that total U.S. output would be
about $150 billion higher if every employer in the country were
free to test and select on merit. That's about 2.5% of GNP."[139]

Justice Antonin Scalia, in a 1987 civil rights case, wrote in his
dissent:

"The Court today completes the process of converting this from a guarantee that race or sex will not be the basis for employment determinations, to a guarantee that it often will...we effectively replace the goal of a discrimination free society with the quite incompatible goal of proportionate representation by race and by sex in the workplace...it effectively requires employers, public as well as private, to engage in intentional discrimination on the basis of race or sex."[140]

Legal fees in discrimination lawsuits average $80,000, not to mention penalties extracted by the EEOC. A 1988 report by the General Accounting Office found that of the 60,000 complaints filed with the EEOC the year before, only three percent of the cases had justifiable cause to proceed. Yet, in over four times as many instances the employer paid a settlement, even though there was no determination of wrongdoing by the EEOC.[141]

In 1989, the EEOC sued a Florida trucking company for failing to hire an upstanding young man who just happened to serve jail time on felony charges. In light of the circumstances — the company suffered heavy losses due to theft, at an average of $100,000 a pop, 85% of which were traced back to employee misconduct — the company's action seemed reasonable. When one factors in the applicant in question had done time for larceny, the trucking company's decision not to hire him was a no-brainer. The EEOC reasoned that the trucking company's hiring practices were discriminatory on the basis that Hispanics have higher felony conviction rates than whites. In light of such behavior, how can these people *ever* accuse *anyone else* of discrimination?

357

Judge Jose Gonzalez Jr. was not particularly pleased with the EEOC's obvious racial slur. He said, "to say that an applicant's honest character is irrelevant to an employer's hiring decision is ludicrous. In fact, it is doubtful that any one personality trait is more important to an employer than the honesty of the prospective employee...To hold otherwise is to stigmatize minorities by saying, in effect, your group is not as honest as other groups."

The EEOC actively pursues what it deems discriminatory hiring practices, and more often than not, they find what they're looking for. In many cases the EEOC, in effect, took action against companies for *not* discriminating. How else would you explain the noted case against Daniel Lamp Company in 1991? The small company in southwest Chicago employed 26 people at the time; all of whom were either black or Hispanic. Lucille Johnson, a black woman was declined a job and brought her case to the EEOC, which concluded that Daniel Lamp was guilty of unfair hiring practices because it did not have 8.45 black employees. In the well documented case, Morley Safer of CBS's "60 Minutes" asked Jim Lafferty, director of legislative affairs for the EEOC, if a company "has three black employees and doesn't hire a fourth for whatever reason, and that fourth accuses him of discrimination, do you prosecute?" "Yes we do," affirmed Lafferty.

In its lawsuit, the EEOC demanded that Daniel Lamp "correct unlawful employment practices on the basis of race and to make whole Lucille Johnson, and all other Black potential applicants for employment aggrieved by the unlawful employment practices." Further, the EEOC "demanded that Daniel Lamp not only pay her back wages of some $340, but also that it spend $10,000 in advertisements to detect other blacks who might have answered want-ads, and to pay them another $123,000. The EEOC then actively pursued anyone who had applied to Daniel Lamp to inform them of a potential claim.

What recourse does a business have when fighting a government agency with unlimited resources (your tax dollars)? The company has little choice; it can simply go out of business, ruining lives and costing jobs; or it can pay the fines compelled by the EEOC — in which case lives are still irreparably harmed. In the Daniel Lamp case, the owners finally agreed to pay $8,000 a month for three years into a settlement fund. Another Chicago firm, World's Finest Chocolate, paid two million dollars in settlement. Their offense: "Their method of recruitment was primarily by word-of-mouth through their existing workforce, which at the time, was primarily white, thereby excluding blacks from knowing about the jobs."[142]

To allow a government agency to walk into a business, examine its hiring records and conclude that the company is evil and racist because it doesn't have an ethnic mix suitable to the sensibilities of the bureaucracy is dangerous indeed. To give that group the power to determine fairness, without a vested interest in the outcome, is to give them the power to destroy without consequence. When one's continued substinence is predicated on finding bigotry, inequality and injustice where it does not exist, the society as a whole will pay a dear price. Such indiscriminate authority to threaten, intimidate and destroy is a violation of natural law, which descends from the unalienable rights bestowed by our Creator. To set up a system of demi-gods empowered by their doting sycophants will surely breed a society where the weak ride herd over the strong, and the immoral feast at the table of the virtuous — while the virtuous are condemned to toil in the fields in order to support those who choose to produce nothing.

Disabled For Dollars

"The definition of 'disability' casts so wide a net that it includes even allergies and learning problems. And because disabilities are self-identified by the employee under the ADA, that means that the accommodations required of the employer are also defined by the employee. Once an employee identifies himself or herself as having a 'disability' there are virtually no limits to what accommodations can be demanded."[143]
— Lawyer, Julie C. Janofsky

"An individual's need for an accommodation cannot enter into the employer's or other covered entity's decisions regarding hiring, discharge, promotion, or other similar employment decisions, unless the accommodation would impose an undue hardship on the employer."
— EEOC, Regulations to Implement the
Equal Employment Provisions of the
Americans with Disabilities Act

"The Justice Department has sadly neglected its duty to define the law. Instead of making firm decisions, the government appears to prefer seeing small businesses dragged into court."[144]
— National Federation of Independent Business

Please don't be offended by the title of this section. There are millions of Americans with legitimate disabilities. They are not to whom I'm referring.

Typically, Congress couches social programs and liberal legislation in terms of compassion and equity, which on the surface makes the programs difficult to oppose, except by the most courageous representatives. This is done entirely on purpose, as closed rules have become the hallmark of Former House Speaker Foley's tenure. By employing last minute rewrites of conference committee versions of legislation, it has become normal to call for a vote before members of Congress have any idea on what it is they're voting. As a result, media portray as evil anyone on the wrong side of such feel-good legislation like the Americans with Disabilities Act.

President Bush proclaimed, "The ADA works because it calls upon the best in the American people...The passage of the ADA, the world's first declaration of equality for people with disabilities, made this country the international leader on human rights." But "Equal Opportunity" under the ADA is the act of government forcing a company to pay tens of thousands of dollars to "enable" a handicapped person to work — while costing other employees the ability to be hired.

The flaw in this scenario is that people have *rights*, while government has *powers*. As citizens, you and I have certain rights. Those rights are limited to the extent that they begin to impugn the rights of others. On such occasions it is the government's responsibility to take away or limit the rights of those who transgress. But now the government has given itself cause to dole out special rights like candy, and too often the rights of others are seriously abridged in order to compensate.

Reasonable people could agree that when you walk into a restaurant, you should be able to assume that those handling the food you are about to place into your mouth are free of contagious diseases. But common sense and public health have been compromised by the arbiters of fairness. James Coleman, attorney for the National Council of Chain Restaurants, fumed, "What we were told in no uncertain terms was — 'We [Washington bureaucrats] are going to use the restaurant industry as a vehicle for forcing a change in public attitude with respect to AIDS. If it costs you money, too bad.'"[145] The EEOC decreed, "Determining whether an individual poses a significant risk [of transmitting a disease] of substantial harm to others must be made on a case by case basis." In effect, it is the employer's responsibility to prove that an employee poses a significant risk, rather than the infected employee to prove that he or she does not.

The EEOC wrote,

> "The HHS [Health and Human Services] is to prepare a list
> of infectious and communicable diseases that are
> transmitted through the handling of food. If an individual
> with a disability has one of the listed diseases and works in
> or applies for a position in food handling, the employer
> must determine whether there is a reasonable
> accommodation that will eliminate the risk of transmitting
> the disease through the handling of food. If there is an
> accommodation that will not pose an undue hardship, and
> that will prevent the transmission of the diseases through
> the handling of food, the employer must provide the

accommodation to the individual. The employer, under these circumstances, would not be permitted to discriminate against the individual because of the need to provide the reasonable accommodation and would be required to maintain the individual in the food handling job."

Just how much "accommodation" is an employer required to make? EEOC assistant legal counsel, Chris Bell, noted, "Whether or not a personal assistant would be required for toileting and eating is going to have to be determined on a case by case basis. We didn't rule it out...It may be in some circumstances that it will be required." We'll just wait until someone sues. Then we'll watch a small businessperson dragged into court. He or she will be forced to spend tens of thousands of dollars — then maybe we'll know if employers will have to allocate human resources to provide toilet assistance.

The greatest risk to public health is the irrationality which allows HIV-positive employees to work in the health care occupations where transmission of the disease is a definite threat. In 1992 a New York hospital had its Medicare and Medicaid funding eliminated because the hospital disallowed an infected pharmacist from preparing intravenous solutions. The hospital offered to transfer the pharmacist to another job while maintaining equal pay. The Journal of the American Hospital Association explained the inherent risk: "Pharmacists often stick themselves accidentally and must break glass vials in order to prepare IV solutions. In a worst-case scenario...pharmacists could stick themselves with a fine-gauge needle and be unaware of it. That needle would then be inserted in a bag with solutions, contaminate the solution, and then infect a patient." The hospital, faced with an enormous loss of government revenue, had no alternative than to pay $330,000 for "emotional damage" suffered by the pharmacist.

Research analysis by the Centers for Disease Control estimated that 128 patients contracted AIDS from medical professionals in 1991. Nonetheless, health care workers are not required to disclose personal medical information regarding infectious diseases that may be transmitted to their patients. Does a doctor or care giver have a greater right to personal privacy than the imminent risks posed to the health of thousands of unknowing individuals under his or her care?

The inherent flaw of liberalism is that it refuses to rationally examine the results of its actions.

> *"Medical and rehabilitation professionals seek to minimize the number of Americans who are truly disabled and to make the handicaps as minimally disabled as possible. But Congress, with the ADA, has acted as if disabilities should be a pork barrel, distributed to as many people as possible. Congress has turned disabilities into prized legal assets to be cultivated and to be flourished in courtrooms to receive financial windfalls. The ADA creates a powerful incentive to maximize the number of Americans who claim to be disabled, since the claim of disability amounts to instant empowerment in the eyes of the law, converting disabilities from a physical liability into a political asset."*
> — James Bovard, *Lost Rights*

Well said.

The solution is beautiful in simplicity and obvious in reason. The EEOC has outlived its usefulness. The leaders, lawyers and advisors of the organization should be replaced with men and women who will conduct their office by the strict guidelines set forth by the Civil Rights Act of 1964, and as such, all racial quotas would be strictly prohibited. Also, in accordance with the original language, spirit and intent of the law, it must be expressly proven in all discrimination cases that intent was present. In 1964 Senate Majority Leader Hubert Humphrey proclaimed "The express requirement of intent is designed to make it wholly clear that inadvertent or accidental discriminations will not violate the title or result in entry or court orders. It means simply that the respondent must have intended to discriminate."

Congressional members must be required to read legislation before voting. This in itself will force shorter, more concise legislation; eliminating "Omnibus" bills loaded with clandestine special interest provisions. How can we expect accountability from Congress if they don't know to what it is they're being held accountable. Furthermore, extensive open debate on the House floor is imperative. What is the purpose of having such wonderfully informative public service tools like C-SPAN if legislation is rewritten in a form unrecognizable to the American public — as well as to the representatives who vote on it. "Closed-rule" is an insult to the entire constituency. It places extravagant power in the hands of a select few, invariably producing flawed, pork-laden monstrosities which are then surreptitiously rammed through at incredible expense to taxpayers

— not to mention the abrasive effect on property rights and general freedoms.

Dwindling pools of new capital, reckless legislation, predatory regulative enforcement, retroactive tax increases, double-taxation of capital gains, the imminent threat of pernicious litigation — who in their right mind would start a business in this environment? As we observe in disgust the government's systematic destruction of the private sector, recall what I mentioned in the introduction: the strong devour the weak. The larger the bureaucracy; the weaker the private sector — the more omnipotent the government becomes. I no longer feel it is cynical to believe this shift in influence is being done entirely on purpose.

Chapter 16
Welfare Reform

"The government of the United States, under Lyndon Johnson, proposes to concern itself over the quality of American life. And this is something very new in the political theory of free nations. The quality of life has heretofore depended on the quality of the human beings who gave tone to that life, and they were its priests and its poets, not its bureaucrats."
— William F. Buckley Jr., *National Review*, August 7, 1965

"There is one unmistakable lesson in American history: a community that allows a large number of young men to grow up in broken families, dominated by women, never acquiring any stable relationship to male authority, never acquiring any set of rational expectations about the future — that community asks for and gets chaos. Crime, violence, unrest, disorder — most particularly the furious, unrestrained lashing out at the whole social structure — that is not only to be expected; it is very near to inevitable. And it is richly deserved."
— Daniel Patrick Moynihan, 1965

"Welfare's purpose should be to eliminate, as far as possible, the need for its own existence."
— Ronald Wilson Reagan, *Los Angeles Times*, January 7, 1970

"Our chief want in life is somebody who will make us do what we can."
— Ralph Waldo Emerson

367

Does the welfare system need to be reformed? No.

Does it need to be eliminated? Yes.

Should we just end welfare?   Short and simple — cut off all benefits? No.

The only course of action more cruel than calculatingly addicting generation after generation of Americans to the welfare state would be to eliminate their benefits without offering them an honest opportunity to support themselves.

Therefore, my welfare reform proposal attacks the problem on a unique front. *Before we demand personal responsibility we need to promote an economic environment that provides an enormous amount of jobs (not make-work jobs) in a relatively brief time period.* (Refer to Chart 16-1)

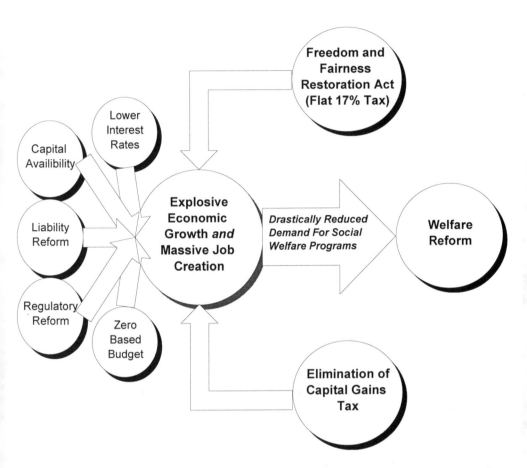

Welfare Reform as currently proposed government regulations is a useless and impracticable endeavor because the welfare state itself is caused by government intervention. True Welfare Reform requires no additional government programs and no additional tax dollars.

True Welfare Reform begins by creating an economic environment that will offer current welfare dependents an opportunity to become productive members of society. This is requisite on implementing the government reforms detailed in this book; a *Flat Tax,* removal of *Capital Gains Taxation, Regulatory and Liability Reform,* and *Zero-Based Budgeting.* The latter will provide *Lower Interest Rates and Capital Availability.*

Chart 16-1

Mark Anthony

The following suggestions would serve as a good start in curbing the welfare state.

1. People do not want welfare; they want an opportunity. It's time that liberals get their heads out of the sand and face the fact that government does not — it cannot — create jobs; investors do. The only way to create jobs is to allow investors to have profits and venture capital to invest. The way to generate profits and capital availability is to enact the *Freedom and Fairness Restoration Act* and eliminate the *Capital Gains tax. The Freedom and Fairness Restoration Act* will allow Americans to keep more of what they earn. It will mandate *Regulatory Reform* and drastically reduce government spending (especially if a *Zero-Based Budget* is enacted in tandem). Lowering government spending will eliminate the government's deficit financing needs which drain *Capital Availability.* More *Available Capital* translates into lower interest rates. *Regulatory Reform* and *Liability Reform* mean a better environment for existing businesses to thrive.

The result will be *Explosive Economic Growth* and *Massive Job Creation,* which will have the effect of *Drastically Reduced Demand For Social Welfare Programs.*

2. Once we have created an economic environment that *could* transform the dependency class into productive, working citizens, we need a system to teach them a viable skill. However, I have a sharply contrasting view of job training than Robert Reich and the rest of his Rhodes Scholar theorists. Government administered job training is wasteful, inefficient and unproductive.

Job training should be turned over to those more qualified; to those with an incentive and vested interest in the continued success of the trainee. It should be turned over to private business.

I recommend a one year apprenticeship period for basic clerical positions and two years for more skilled, technology intensive occupations. Generous tax incentives would be offered to the hiring firms, as well as a portion of the trainees' benefits subsidized. The benefit subsidies would be phased out over time.

3. Author Martin Gross proposed consolidating the welfare bureaucracy into one department: the Department of Welfare. Even though such a department would have sharply reduced responsibility as the welfare rolls shrink, consolidation would certainly streamline the delivery system.

4. America cannot continue to subsidize illegitimacy. Welfare mothers will not receive additional benefits for having additional children out of wedlock.

5. If a beneficiary has not completed high school or its equivalent or if he or she has a criminal record of any crime worse than misdemeanor, that beneficiary's welfare benefits will only be paid at a 70% level. Benefits would be raised to 85% upon completion of a high school education (the education would be paid for out of existing welfare funds). If the beneficiary has completed a high school education before entering the welfare rolls, but has a criminal record, he or she would need to complete five hundred hours of community service in order to be raised to the 85% level. Full benefits would only be payable if the beneficiary were married and the other parent resided in the same domicile. Of course, the beneficiary's income would increase

higher still if he or she entered the private sector job training program.

6. The rate of the increase in benefits for those who choose not to work would be indexed to inflation — only if they maintain a minimum of eighty hours of community service per month. We will no longer pay welfare benefits to someone who does nothing. If an able-bodied welfare recipient will not get an education, *or* enter a private sector job training program *or* complete regular, ongoing community service, that person will not receive any increase in benefits, period.

7. Food stamp abuse would be strictly monitored. Two billion dollars lost annually to waste, fraud and abuse will not stand. A compliance team of 5,000 federal employees will "police" the system. There will be zero-tolerance. I will not continue to have my tax dollars used to buy drugs, alcohol or prostitutes. Food stamps will use a cashless, credit-card type system that could easily be integrated into the existing debit machines in many grocery stores. If a food stamp recipient attempts to barter or otherwise abuse goods purchased through the system, he or she will be permanently purged from the system. Retailers who defraud the system will lose access to the program for their establishment and serve a 6 month prison term.

Immigration

Many have endorsed erecting physical barriers around our country. That is nonsense. The symbolism of such an action is not worth whatever effectiveness it may bring.

1. Increase the border patrol from 4,000 to 20,000 strong. Able-bodied male and females currently on the welfare roles could be trained in National Guard-type skills and used in a constructive manner to assist in border compliance efforts. It is efficient and sensible to use the human resources wasted by one social problem in order to help solve another. Furthermore, it would provide a skill, employment and self-esteem to thousands of young people. Equip the more highly trained professional border patrol with four-wheel drive vehicles, surveillance apparatus and night vision technology.

2. Eliminate the incentive to enter the country illegally. Cease social services, welfare, education and non-emergency medical care for illegal aliens. Anyone attempting to gain illegal access to benefits would be deported.

3. Implement tamper-proof, counterfeit-proof identification cards and Social Security Cards. Why shouldn't we enforce these abuses as aggressively as we do those who counterfeit the currency?

4. Foster cooperation between the Immigration and Naturalization Service and the Social Security Administration. The Internal Revenue Service rewards those who report citizens who cheat on their taxes. Why not do the same with immigration.

5. Cut grants of political asylum to 20 percent of the existing level.

In Conclusion

"Trust in the Lord with all your heart, and do not lean on your own understanding. In all your ways acknowledge Him, and He will make your paths straight."
Proverbs 3:5-6

The year was 1890. Joseph Andreuzzi left his wife and boarded a ship in his hometown of Paterno, Italy. He was going to the new world...*America*...the land of opportunity.

Landing at Ellis Island, Joseph made his way south where he found his first job in the new land as a laborer in the coal mines of Pennsylvania. For the next three years he saved every penny. In 1893 he took half of his savings and sent it to Italy. With the money, Joseph's wife Rose purchased *her* ticket to the new world.

As she landed in America, the circle was half-way complete.

Reunited with Joseph, they took the other half of their savings and invested the money in a local watering hole that became the home-away-from-home for his fellow coal miners. Over the years the pub became a small restaurant. The small restaurant became a larger establishment as each of their ten children dutifully lent a hand. Joseph and Rose became a pillar of the community.

The circle was now complete.

They had set sail for the new world. They had burned the ship behind them — *giving themselves no choice but to succeed* — and succeed they *would* in the land of opportunity.

Joseph Andreuzzi did not leave his wife, his friends and his homeland because America offered the best welfare system in the world. He did not set sail for the new world because of the social safety net the American government offered.

He set sail to pursue the American Dream.

For, America offered all that his mind could conceive...all that his heart would believe.

Joseph Andreuzzi is my Grandfather.

Civilization often finds itself at a crossroads. And the path not taken has implications that affect the children of many generations to come. We are faced with a complex problem, a seemingly daunting task. The foes are formidable; their resolve mighty. In times, such as this, our sanity is in peril if we do not lean on a Higher power.

I write this as a 31 year old American of Italian descent. Joseph and Rose came to this country many years ago so that they may build a better life for their descendants. But I, born on American soil, do not have the assurance the same will be true for *my* descendants.

I love The United States Of America. I spent eight years attending one of the finest Catholic elementary schools in the country. We started every day with *The Pledge of Allegiance* and *The Lord's Prayer*. I learned the history of our Founding Fathers. I learned the Judeo-Christian beliefs that helped build our nation. I learned about honor, and respect and love of my fellow man. I learned that America is a land of unlimited opportunity, where one has no bounds on his accomplishments or his dreams.

One of my fondest memories was in seventh grade. It was 1976. America's Bicentennial was upon us. The entire school stood outside at the foot of the flag.   In the warm morning sun — with God smiling down upon us — we sang the most beautiful rendition of *The Battle Hymn of The Republic* and *God Bless America* that 500 hundred young, jubilant, thankful voices ever had.   I'll never forget the inner feeling that consumed me.   I had never felt that way before.   There couldn't have been a child alive, more proud to be an American, than I was at that moment.

I want *my* children to know that feeling.

1   Clarence Carson, *Basic American Government,* (Wadley, Alabama: American Textbook Committee, 1994).

2   IBID., p. 451.

3   IBID., p. 383.

4   IBID., p.p. 398-99.

5   IBID., p. 389.

6   IBID., p. 393.

7   James Bovard, *Lost Rights, The Destruction of American Liberty,* (New York: St. Martin's Press, 1994), p. 153,154.

8   Gilbert C. Fite and Jime E. Reese, *An Economic History of the United States,* (Boston: Houghton Mifflin, 1965, 2nd ed.), p. 665.

9   Bovard., op. cit., p. 154.

10   IBID., p. 155.

11   Clarence Carson, op. cit., p. 398, quoting Arthur M. Schlesinger, Jr., *The Politics of Upheaval,* (Boston: Houghton Mifflin, 1960) p. 447.

12   Clarence Carson, op. cit., p. 400.

13   Clarence Cason, op. cit.

14   Clyde Wilson, "Restoring the Republic," *Chronicles: A Magazine of American Culture* (June, 1992), p. 17.

15   Russell Kirk, *A Lecture on Natural Law,* Policy Review, Summer 1994, p. 78.

16   Clarence Carson, op. cit., p. 153.

17   Pat Robertson, *The New World Order*, (Dallas: Word Publishing, 1991) p. 219.

18   Clarence Carson, op. cit., p. 53.

19   Russell Kirk, op. cit., p. 77.

20   Clarence Carson, op. cit., p. 44.

21   IBID., p. 173.

22   Russell Kirk, op. cit., p. 78.

23   Clarence Carson, op. cit., p. 175.

24   Pat Robertson, p. 241-42.

25   James Bovard, op. cit., p. 1-4, 6.

26   Clarence Carson, op. cit., p. 150.

27 IBID.

28 James Bovard, op. cit., p. 16.

29 IBID., p. 17.

30 Jonathan Tolman, *The Dry Facts About Wetlands*, Wall Street Journal, August 25, 1993.

31 IBID.

32 Bovard, op. cit., p. 34.

33 IBID., p. 35.

34 IBID.

35 IBID., p. 33.

36 IBID., p. 19.

37 IBID.

38 IBID., p. 27.

39 IBID., p. 27-28.

40 IBID., p. 21.

41 Wayne LaPierre, *Guns, Crime and Freedom,* (Washington, D.C.: Regnery Publishing, 1994), p. 129.

42 IBID., p. 133. Data from: James Q. Wilson, *What Works? revisited: new findings on criminal rehabilitation,* The Public Interest, 61:3, 11-13 (Fall, 1980).

43 IBID., p. 139. Data from: *Washington Post,* November 19, 1979, page A4; and Charles A. Murray & Louis A. Cox, *Beyond Probation: Juvenile Corrections and the Chronic Delinquent,* (Beverly Hills: Sage Publications, 1979).

44 IBID., p. 139. Data from: Professor Michael K. Block, University of Arizona, based on *Crime in the United States, FBI Uniform Crime Reports,* 1960-92, and *Correctional Populations in the United States,* Bureau of Justice Statistics, Washington, D.C., 1992.

45 IBID., p. 140. Data from: Block, *Crime in the United States.*

46 IBID., p. 140-41. Data from: Michael K. Block and Steven J. Twist, *Lessons from the Eighties: Incarceration*

Works, Commonsense, National Policy Forum, Washington D.C., 1994, p. 78.

[47] IBID., p. xv

[48] IBID., p. 169-70.

[49] Jeff Snyder, *A Nation of Cowards,* Public Interest, Fall 1993.

[50] Benjamin Franklin, Motto of the Pennsylvania Historical Society, 1959.

[51] Paul Craig Roberts, *How to Grow the Deficit,* The American Spectator, May 1993.

[52] Walter E. Williams, *The Role of Government In A Free Society,* Vision & Values, Grove City College Alumni Association Publication, Grove City, PA., August 1994.

[53] David Hale, *Small Business, Tax Plan's Victim*, Wall Street Journal, July 9, 1993.

[54] Kevin Phillips, *Arrogant Capital Washington, Wall Street, And The Frustration Of American Politics*, (Toronto: Little, Brown & Company), 1994, p.xiii.

[55] IBID., p. 31.

[56] Kevin Phillips, op. cit., p. 98, 39.

[57] IBID., p. 47.

[58] Martin L. Gross, *A Call For Revolution,* (New York-Ballantine Books) 1993, p. 198.

[59] IBID., 195-96.

[60] Phillips, op. cit., p. 83, from a report by McKinsey and Company.

[61] David Mason, *The Dog That Didn't Bark, Who Put the Muzzle on Congressional Reform?* Policy Review Number 70, Fall 1994, p.64.

[62] IBID., p. 64.

[63] Eric Felten, *The Ruling Class, Inside The Imperial Congress,* (Washington, D.C., Regnery-Gateway) 1993, p. 96-95. Felton quoted *Hill Rat,* by John Jackley, (Washington, D.C. Regnery-Gateway), 1992, p. 12.

[64] Quoted in Felten, p. 93.

65   IBID.

66   IBID.

67   David Mason., op. cit., p. 62.

68   IBID., p. 63.

69   IBID.

70   Rep. Pete Hoekstra, *Breaking The Congressional Lockgrip, The Case for a National Referendum,* Policy Review , Number 69, Summer 1994, p. 83.

71   IBID., p. 84.

72   Dr. Mark Skousen, *Economics On Trial,* p. 39, Irwin Professional Publishing, 1991.

73   IBID.

74   Stephen Moore, *Capital Crime*, National Review, August 9, 1993.

75   Geoffrey Smith, *Of Geese and Golden Eggs (changes in capital gains taxes),* Financial World, September 3, 1991.

76   Lawrence Kudlow, *Budgetprop,* The American Spectator, March 1994.

77   Joint Economic Commission Report, 1994.

78   Donald Lambro, United Features Syndicate, Inc., May 16, 1994.

79   Mark Yost, *Beef Up Defense — Cut The Pork,* Wall Street Journal, July 1, 1994.

80   IBID.

81   Wall Street Journal Editorial, *The Army's Latest Foe,* May 24, 1994.

82   William F. Buckley Jr., *Raise tax revenues by lowering tax rates,* The Conservative Chronicle, 3/15/94

83   Thomas DiBacco, *Simpler in the Beginning,* Washington Times 4/15/92.

84   James Dale Davidson, *The Squeeze,* (Simon and Schuster, 1980) p. 36.

85   Stephen Moore, *High capital gains tax induced U.S. economic funk,* Washington Times, June 6, 1994.

86   Larry Burkett, *The Coming Economic Earthquake,* Moody Press, 1991, 1994.

87   Dr. Mark Skousen, op. cit.

88   IBID.

89   IBID.

90   IBID.

91   IBID.

92   IBID.

93   IBID.

94   IBID.

95   IBID.

96   Malcolm S. Forbes Jr., *Let's hope President Clinton learns the right lessons,* Forbes, June 21, 1993.

97   Stephen Moore, *Capital Crime,* National Review, August 9, 1993.

98   Stephen Moore, op. cit.

99   Malcolm S. Forbes Jr., *Back to basics: lower rates = more revenues,* Forbes, February 3, 1992, (subsequent table is from same article).

100   Malcolm S. Forbes Jr., *Bogus Argument,* Forbes, August 20, 1990.

101   Donald Lambro, *Capital gains tax cut would spur economy,* Conservative Chronicle, May 30, 1994.

102   IBID.

103   Malcolm S. Forbes Jr., *All-American tax cuts,* Forbes, March 29, 1993.

104   Stephen Moore, *High capital gains tax induced U.S. economic funk,* Washington Times May 6, 1994.

105   Malcolm S. Forbes Jr., *How to get the Dow to 37,000,* Forbes, May 5, 1990.

106   Tom Herman, *Tax Report*, Wall Street Journal, August 7, 1994.

107   William F. Buckley Jr., *Armey tax plan picking up steam,* Conservative Chronicle, July 28, 1994.

[108] Dick Armey *Review Merits of Flat Tax*, The Wall Street Journal, June 16, 1994.

[109] Buckley, op. cit.

[110] Armey, op. cit.

[111] *Freedom and Fairness Restoration Act, A Comprehensive Plan to Shrink the Government and Grow the Economy*, summary of H.R. 4585, from the office of Rep. Dick Armey.

[112] Armey, op. cit.

[113] IBID.

[114] H.R. 4585 summary.

[115] IBID.

[116] Armey, op. cit.

[117] IBID.

[118] Albert G. Young, in a letter to the editor of The Wall Street Journal, June 23, 1994.

[119] Report of the National Performance Review — Vice President Al Gore, *Creating a Government That Works Better and Costs Less,* p. 32., 1994.

[120] Dick Armey, op. cit.

[121] Clifford F. Theis, *"The First Minimum Wage Laws, "* Cato Journal, Winter 1991, p. 727.

[122] U.S. General Accounting Office, *"Minimum Wage Policy Questions Persist, "* 1983.

[123] Asra Q. Nomani, *Labor Secretary's Bid To Push Plant Safety Runs Into Skepticism*, The Wall Street Journal, August 19, 1994.

[124] IBID.

[125] IBID.

[126] IBID.

[127] IBID.

[128] Editorial, *The Minimally Useful Minimum Wage*, New York Times, March 21, 1977.

[129] Bovard, op. cit., p. 105-6.

[130] IBID.

131 James Cox, *Greyhound's Last Stop? Strike-forced Chapter 11 Is a Bitter Pill,"* USA Today, May 6, 1990.

132 Bovard, op. cit., from an interview with Rosemary Collier, September 9, 1993, (New York: St. Martin's Press, 1994), p. 110.

133 Milton Friedman and Rose Friedman, *Free to Choose,* (New York: Harcourt Brace Jovanovich, 1980), p. 139.

134 Herman Belz, Equality Transformed (New Brunswick, NJ: Transaction Books, 1991), p.28.

135 Bovard, op. cit., p. 169.

136 Hugh Davis Graham, *The Civil Rights Era,* (New York: Oxford University Press, 1990), p. 243.

137 Belz, op. cit., p. 132.

138 Bovard, op. cit., p. 175.

139 Peter Brimelow and Leslie Spence, *When Quotas Replace Merit, Everybody Suffers,* Forbes, February 15, 1993, p.80.

140 Bovard, op. cit., p. 168.

141 U.S. General Accounting Office, *Equal Employment Opportunity: EEOC and State Agencies Did Not Fully Investigate Discrimination Charges,* October 1988, p. 31.

142 Bovard, op. cit., p. 173.

143 IBID., p. 184.

144 Press Release *Disability Rules Too Vague, Small-Business Group Charges,* National Federation of Independent Business, 2/28/91.

145 Joan Oleck, *AIDS in the Kitchen,* Restaurant Business 7/20/92, p. 51.